THE UNIVERSITY AS AN

INSTITUTION TODAY

THE UNIVERSITY AS AN INSTITUTION TODAY

TOPICS FOR REFLECTION

Alfonso Borrero Cabal

International Development Research Centre
Ottawa

UNESCO Publishing
Paris

Published jointly by

the International Development Research Centre
PO Box 8500, Ottawa, ON, Canada K1G 3H9

and

the United Nations Educational, Scientific and Cultural Organization
7 Place de Fontenoy, 75732 Paris 07-SP, France

© IDRC / UNESCO 1993

Borrero Cabal, A.

The university as an institution today : topics for reflection. Ottawa,
ON, IDRC; Paris, UNESCO, 1993. xxiv + 239 p.: ill.

/Higher education institutions/, /educational theory/, /historical
analysis/, /aims of education/, /educational reforms/, /educational
administration/, /institutional framework/, /cultural development/ —
/universities/, /equal opportunity/, /literature surveys/, /research
policy/, /OECD/, /UNESCO/, /IDRC/, /university degrees/, /evaluation/,
/future/, references.

UDC: 378.001.1

A microfiche edition is available.

ISBN 0-88936-685-3 (IDRC)
ISBN 92-3-102939-8 (UNESCO)

Printed in Canada

CONTENTS

◆

PART I. INTRODUCTION

PART II. THE UNIVERSITY: WELL ADMINISTERED AND WELL ORGANIZED

PART III. TO ADMINISTRATE IS TO SERVE

FOREWORD

◆

In the 1980s, higher education became an extremely important element in the organization of modern society. There is now growing awareness in both the industrialized and developing worlds of the vital role played by higher education. As socioeconomic development becomes more knowledge intensive and relies increasingly on professional and managerial staff with advanced training, higher education acquires a key role in any development program and in the general organization of modern society. The missions of higher education are constantly extended to cover areas and functions aimed at both the progress of society and, more specifically, the development of the whole system of education. At the same time, the new dimensions of economic and technological competition at the regional and global levels have led to new demands on higher education in the areas of research and service.

This awareness has occurred in a time of serious global crisis at the tertiary level. Several Eastern European countries, for example, after changing their economic and political systems, have decided to adapt higher education to new needs. Some universities in industrialized countries face the problem of declining student populations, and most of them have experienced a period of zero increase, if not a reduction, in budgetary allocations. In many developing countries, systems of postsecondary education have grown enormously, particularly in the number of students and professors. At the same time, there has been an explosion in foreign debt, with the consequent aggravation of social problems. In the 1980s, investment in social programs, including education, has been cut considerably in Africa, Asia and the Pacific, and Latin America and the Caribbean. This has had grave repercussions on postsecondary education.

The equation has become complex. As investment has been

cut, the student population, particularly in the developing world, has shown continuous growth, rendering postsecondary education the most dynamic sector in the education system. From 1975 to 1986, the number of students in postsecondary education worldwide increased by 18.4 million: 4.5 million in the industrialized world and 13.9 million in the developing world. According to statistics from Unesco (the United Nations Educational, Scientific and Cultural Organisation), students in higher education represented 28.2 million in 1970, 47.5 million in 1980, 58.4 million in 1988, and likely 61 million in 1990. In 20 years, their number worldwide has more than doubled. There is no doubt that the second half of this century will remain in history as a time of great expansion in higher education throughout the world.

This explosion was stronger in the developing world. Between 1970 and 1988, the number of students has increased eightfold in sub-Saharan Africa, sixfold in Eastern Asia and the Pacific, also sixfold in the Arab States, by four and half in times in Latin America and the Caribbean, and twofold in Southern Asia. In the industrialized world, the level of increase was more modest, averaging 56%, a reasonable rate given the fact that enrolment in institutions of higher education had reached an elevated level many decades earlier.

Worldwide in 1988, 13.5% of 18- to 23-year-olds were attending higher education courses. However, in the industrialized world, the level was 36.8%; in the developing world, 8.3%. In other words, a young adult in an industrialized country is four times as likely to follow studies at the tertiary level as is a young adult in a developing country. In sub-Saharan Africa, the difference increases to 17 times.

It is clear, however, that the quantitative expansion is not the only important trend observed in higher education during the last decades. The need to maintain or improve academic quality and to examine the relevance, effectiveness, and efficiency of the system have also been serious issues. Certain indicators — such as the high level of repeating classes in some countries (including in the developed world), the extension of time spent at universities by young people, the drop-out rates, the high cost of services, and the inability of graduates to enter or adapt themselves to the workforce — demonstrate the seriousness of these issues. In the last decade, many countries from all continents have thoroughly evaluated their higher education systems and, as a result, either implemented reform or shown interest in reform.

We have witnessed a strong diversification of higher education, in terms of intellectual structures, programs, duration of study, and qualifications obtained. Other general trends concern the increasing internationalization of higher education. According to Unesco, in the 62 countries responsible for an estimated 95% of foreign students in the world in 1990, the number of students abroad increased from 916 thousand in 1980 to almost 1.2 million in 1990 (29%). Most foreign students come from developing countries (757 thousand in 1990).

What are, under these circumstances, the most important current trends and prospects in higher education? When Unesco was preparing its current Medium-Term Plan, covering the years from 1990 to 1995, a series of consultations was held to identify the main issues for higher education in all regions of the world. Two themes were identified everywhere:

◆ **Relevance** — including the role of higher education within societies, democratization, the need for diversification, links with the world of work, and the responsibilities of higher education in relation to the whole system of education.

◆ **Quality** — including reforms and innovations, distance education, interdisciplinarity and continuing education, planning and management of resources, organization of programs, and qualifications of teachers.

These two sets of issues — relevance and quality — have been completed by a series of suggestions and proposals concerning mobility and strengthening international cooperation. These findings are not new. What is new is that more and more people and governments are aware of their importance.

Within the framework of these reflections, several studies were undertaken by Unesco on the evolution of the idea of the university. Several regional meetings and one special consultation of nongovernmental organizations (NGOs) were organized to better identify the needs of the countries and to analyze how the social actors, such as the academic community, the associations, the governments, and the institutions themselves, felt about these matters. In addition, a forum was organized in 1991, sponsored by Unesco and the University of Pittsburgh, on research on higher education with particular emphasis on the developing world. This series of reflections produced an impressive set of publications and special documents (see Bibliography), including *Trends and Issues Facing Higher Education in Asia and the Pacific* (Unesco 1992a), a special issue of the journal *Higher Education in Europe* (see Gellert 1991), and a special issue of *New Papers on Higher Education* (Unesco 1991c).

Unesco's strategy in this exercise was to give rise to a debate that could serve to not only identify and clarify problems but also involve the academic community as policymakers in the search for solutions. To prepare a book on higher education is not difficult; to motivate people to participate in the development of higher education is more complex. To reach this objective, the main partners of Unesco were the United Nations University (UNU) and the main NGOs that specialize in higher education.

After the regional consultations, it was thought that a synthesis document would be necessary. It was seen not as a limited compilation of regional findings, but as an integrated and coherent explanation of the main issues and challenges facing higher education at the global level. The output was expected to be a reference document raising world challenges in higher education, convincing policymakers and decision-makers of the importance of the issues, and giving the academic community guidance in the organization and functioning of institutions of higher education.

In the Unesco regional consultations, the following observations came up repeatedly:

- The university system is isolated from society.

- The rapid quantitative expansion has negatively affected the quality of courses and programs.

- Scarce resources have been concentrated on a small number of fields.

- The university has lost its monopoly on the creation of knowledge.

- Many scientists from developing countries emigrate to the industrialized world in search of better conditions for both work and research.

One highlighted aspect was that universities do not exist for themselves. External forces have a tremendous impact in the life of universities. It is impossible, for example, to study the financial situation of universities in developing countries without analyzing the consequences they suffer from debt and structural adjustment policies. Universities are not isolated from societies; in fact, many of their problems are a reflection of our changing world. Pursuing their mission of training young people to respond to the needs of society — taking into account the rapid development of knowledge and skills — requires continuous reflection on structures and programs and the ability to adapt to new needs.

The links between society and the university are therefore strong. So, before defining the new missions of our universities, it is essential to define the kind of society humanity wants to build and the kind of international order we want to support.

Economic development cannot follow rigid structures and only one model for all countries and regions. This is clearly evident in the failure of cooperation strategies based on the transmission of models, as has been done in Africa with old colonial systems. The Unesco consultations found that more and more people have become aware of this fact. In all regions, the adoption of foreign concepts and values and the neglect of regional and national cultures and philosophies have had negative repercussions on societal systems. Foreign assistance, therefore, is not needed to solve problems, but to create endogenous capacity.

Endogenous and sustainable development has been conceived by the United Nations (UN) on the basis of IDS — the International Strategy for Development — approved some time ago by the UN General Assembly. IDS considers that economic development should be based on two foundations: diminution of poverty and development of human resources. With regard to the latter, the universities have become key actors in the strategy for development as never before, as their role has been vital in the advanced training of qualified personnel.

The need to search for solutions to global problems is the responsibility not only of governments but also of each and every individual. Today, two issues stand above all others: the environment and peace. The 1992 UN Conference on Environment and Development — the Earth Summit in Rio de Janeiro — showed the direction to follow with respect to the environment. It was accepted that environmental issues are integral to human development; the major result of the Earth Summit is that environment and development are now recognized as two sides of the same coin. Thus, Agenda 21 — the Summit's blueprint for action in all major areas of environment and development — combines the full range of the "environment agenda," which emerged from the Stockholm Conference, with the "development agenda," or at least major parts of it.

The second element — peace — is well defined in a document by the Secretary General of the United Nations, Boutros Boutros-Ghali, presented in 1992 to the Economic and Social Council (ECOSOC): *The Agenda for Peace.* The analysis set out in the section entitled "Post-Conflict Peace Building" closely coincides with the basic principles of the "culture of peace" that Unesco is seeking to promote throughout its programs.

The main challenges facing institutions of higher education

today are to democratize access and maintain a high level of quality in the services provided to society. Some analysts, looking at institutions that have been unable to adapt, have concluded that increased enrolments have resulted in state budgets being unable to meet university expenses. This has generated social inequity, making the wealthiest people the most privileged.

This is true in some parts of the world and in some institutions; however, the analysis risks going too far if it concludes that developing countries should not invest in higher education. This is unacceptable. Without a good system of higher education, developing countries will not overcome the barriers for improving quality of life; they will become forever dependent on the industrialized world. With the end of the Cold War, the main problem in the world is "underdevelopment." We cannot expect to solve this massive problem without development policies in which the strengthening of universities for training and research is central.

The educational system constitutes a whole: if a part of the system does not operate properly, the whole system breaks down. Higher education is responsible for training managers, experts, and researchers needed for sustainable and equitable development. Withholding or slashing resources at this level can represent a dead end for many countries on the road to real independence. It is also impossible to reinforce primary and secondary education without a good system of training at the higher level. Teachers in primary and secondary schools need to be trained, training that mainly occurs in institutions of higher education. In several countries, universities are also the only institutions able to provide educational research, which is essential for policymakers to make valid decisions.

In October 1991, Unesco decided to launch the UNITWIN (university twinning) Programme associated with a Unesco Chairs' Scheme to strengthen interuniversity cooperation and academic mobility. These two associated initiatives are intended to enhance the capability for advanced training and research and to contribute to the development of know-how for the rapid transfer of knowledge to developing countries. The Unesco Chairs' Scheme involves the creation, in partnership with universities and other international bodies or funding agencies, of professorships that enable visiting scholars to provide core expertise in developing centres of excellence in key disciplines and the fields related to sustainable development.

In 1986, Canada's International Development Research Centre (IDRC) launched a major study devoted to the maintenance and development of the scientific community in Latin America. This study involved comparative analysis across 12 countries of national policies and practices concerning the training and maintenance of researchers. It produced important data, which have been explained and analyzed in the book entitled *Investing in Knowledge: Strengthening the Foundation for Research in Latin America* (Brunner 1991).

This study provided major insight into the role of the university in capacity building and human resource development. It gathered together a number of related research activities and resulted in the creation of a network of researchers devoted to, among other things, institutional development in Latin America. It proved to be an important element in the efforts aimed at supporting human resource development for research and development.

In November 1990, IDRC agreed to support and participate in the Latin America part of Unesco's global exercise. Later, IDRC decided to join Unesco and UNU in the final analysis of the findings generated from the various consultations and in the elaboration of a report related to trends and issues in higher education from a global perspective. IDRC considered that their participation was a contribution to the larger debate on issues related to capacity building. It was also a means to capitalize on the opportunity to integrate IDRC's accumulated knowledge into the assessment of higher education needs and the formulation of sensible future policies.

IDRC decided to finance a study entitled "Global Trends and Issues in Higher Education." It consisted of analyzing and reviewing all the documentation generated throughout the Unesco regional meetings (Africa, Arab States, Asia and the Pacific, Europe, and Latin America and the Caribbean) convened between October 1990 and May 1991. It also included an analysis of similar studies undertaken by UNU and the results of the second NGO–Unesco consultation on higher education held in Paris in April 1991.

At the suggestion of Unesco, IDRC also supported four studies on issues that, according to the regional consultations, needed some additional reflection:

♦ "The continuing education and its impact on higher education," commissioned to Professor Carlos Tunnerman of Nicaragua;

♦ "Cost–benefit considerations in higher education," commissioned to Professor Glen Harris of Canada;

♦ "Alternative models of universities" consisting of a case study related to the concept and experience about "community universities," which have distinctive attribute in contrast to the traditional public or private models, commissioned to Professor Geraldo Magela Teixeira of Brazil; and

♦ "Higher education in the Third Millennium: policy and research agenda," commissioned to Professors Hans Schuetze and Kjell Rubenson of Canada.

It was decided to appoint an expert to prepare the global in-depth study. For Unesco, it was necessary to find someone with ethics beyond reproach and universally recognized expertise in the field of higher education. After several consultations, Unesco, with the agreement of IDRC and UNU, invited Professor Alfonso Borrero Cabal, a Colombian philosopher, theologian, architectural historian, and educator, to prepare the report. At that time (1990), he was also a member of the Council of UNU and a frequent consultant to IDRC. Since 1961, Professor Borrero Cabal has dedicated most of his time to higher education, studying the evolution of the idea of the university and performing various administrative functions at the University Javeriana in Bogota, Colombia, including serving as Rector from 1970 to 1977. Since 1977, Professor Borrero Cabal has been Executive Director of the Colombian Association of Universities, Director of its Permanent Symposium on University, and Director of the journal *Mundo Universitario*.

This book, authored by Father Alfonso Borrero Cabal, S.J., is very comprehensive. As Professor Walter Kamba (Zimbabwe) said:

> Father Borrero's study is a most comprehensive analysis of the university as an institution. Its strength lies in the highly original concept of the university that has been adopted and that allows the author to bring to the fore new aspects, seen from a new angle, when compared with recent or less recent writings on higher education. The other element of strength of the study resides in the use made of the results of the regional consultations on current trends in higher education organized by Unesco over the last two years.

Borrero Cabal's original study was discussed at length at a meeting in Vancouver, Canada, in July of 1992. This meeting was attended by representatives of Unesco (M.A.R. Dias and D. Chitoran), IDRC (Paz Buttedahl), and UNU (Professor Justin Thorens), as well as a small group of international experts including Walter Kamba (International Association of Universities), Wang Yibing (National Centre for Education Development Research, Beijing), and Prof. Esmat Ezzat (Suez Canal University, Egypt). The following experts were also present: Glen Harris (University of Alberta, Canada), Prof. Yara M.F. Santos (Pontificia Universidade Católica de Minas Gerais, Brazil), Steven Rosell (Project on Governing in an Information Society, San Rafael, CA, USA), Hans Schuetze (University of British Columbia, Canada), Kjell Rubenson (University of British Columbia, Canada), Mutindi Ndunda (University of British Columbia, Canada), and Prof. Maria Beatriz R.O. Gonçalves (Pontificia Universidade Católica de Minas Gerais, Brazil). Professor Borrero Cabal was also present.

The final text, presented in this book, takes into account the results of these discussions. It is Father Borrero's document; he was absolutely free to draw his own conclusions, but within a special framework, under a contract, and accounting for all the documentation and findings of the Unesco regional meetings and studies. The text does not intend to present a sequence of data or historical events. It is a compound aimed at creating a basic framework of problems and prospects in higher education. It is a collection of historical facts, theories, comments, positions, problems, and prospects.

History is important and was present in all regional exercises. The evolution of the idea and praxis of the university helps to understand the present and makes the elaboration of prospects easier. Theory is necessary for the clarification of concepts. Many studies' use and abuse of terms without clarifying, for example, what is formal and nonformal education, means that they become more lampoonist than analytical documents. Also, comments, positions, problems, and facts are often mixed without clear separation and are presented without theories. Important words are used without an explanation of concept, giving rise to misunderstanding and sophisms.

Borrero Cabal has made a serious effort in applying methodological rigour to the sequence of chapters and the use of concepts. The study has an original schema, not common in studies on higher education. Administration is the focal point of the analysis. After dealing with the historical evolution of the university idea, he presents the two "implicit senses" contained in the meaning of the verb administrate: "the internal sense of institutional organization and the external or outward-projecting sense of service." The book concludes with an epilogue on planning and the evaluation of achievements attained by the university as a social institution. As pointed out by Professor Carlos Tunnermann Bernheim, the book examines with great conceptual and methodological rigour the fundamental aspects of the university institution: its missions, functions, and objectives; its philosophy as an institution; its structures; its service to culture and professions.

Borrero Cabal avoids polemics and limits himself to the analysis of the institutions of higher education, the outside world being analyzed only as the object of the university's action or mission. Some experts believed that the document should go further and analyze some challenges in the final period of the century and their implications in higher education: the slowing of the economy in several parts of the world; the increasing economic disparities among nations and within nations; problems linked to external debt and structural adjustment; the increase in marginalized populations in situations of critical poverty; the degradation of the environment; the demographic explosion; the enormous increase in knowledge and information and the tendency to transform them into mercantilism. Some felt that the book should stress the fact that the world has changed and the more serious challenge for educational institutions, and special universities, is now the gap between North and South.

This book cannot cover everything, however. The action of institutions of higher education should be seen as part of a whole complex strategy. In the case of Unesco, the framework for action is based on documents like IDS, *The Agenda for Peace*, and Unesco's Third Medium-Term Plan (1990–1995), which mentions that "on the threshold of the twenty-first century, humankind faces three major challenges — development, the protection of the environment and peace." This plan has foreseen activities aimed at enhancing the quality and relevance of higher education to respond more effectively to the rapidly changing needs of society; activities aimed to reinforce the contribution of higher education to the education system as a whole; and a concerted international plan of action for strengthening interuniversity cooperation with particular emphasis on support for higher education in developing countries. That was done through the UNITWIN Programme and associated Unesco Chairs' Scheme, mentioned earlier.

This book will be closely followed by the 1993 World

Education Report, which will be mainly dedicated to higher education and in which conceptual elements will be completed by statistical data and concrete examples. A document with proposals for policymakers and decision-makers will also soon be disseminated worldwide by Unesco.

During the Vancouver meeting, the international panel of experts realized that the schema Borrero Cabal adopted allowed him to deal with practically all important problems that institutions of higher education now face. This book stands by itself and, we hope, will be considered as a reference document for historians, policymakers, decision-makers, international organizations, and the academic world in general.

Unesco, IDRC, and UNU hope that this effort will help all of those who look to give to the institutions of higher education the conditions to be able to face the challenges of the end of this century. Replying positively to the question "University still?," Professor Federico Mayor, the Director General of Unesco, during an international conference in Caracas in April 1991, stated:

> A university is for the training at a high level of citizens capable of acting efficiently and effectively in their various functions and activities, including the most diverse, up-to-date, and specialized; for the lifelong and intensive education of all citizens who so wish; for the updating of knowledge; for preparing teacher trainers; for identifying and addressing great national issues; for contributing to the analysis and solution of the major problems affecting and concerning the whole planet; for cooperating with industry and the service sectors in the progress of the nation; for forging attitudes of understanding and tolerance; for providing governments with the scientifically reliable information required for decision-making on such important areas as the environment, in the context of the progressive "scientification" of political decision-making.
>
> A university is to disseminate and popularize knowledge. Above all, a university is to create, to promote scientific research, innovation, invention. A university is of quality, not one whose degrees are often meaningless. A monitoring university can foresee events. A university is for objective criti-

cism, the search for new paths to a brighter future. A university with new curricula is for a genuine, participating citizenry, for a pedagogy of peace. A university is for reducing unacceptable economic and social asymmetries. A university is for the moderation of the superfluous. In short, a university is for the strengthening of freedom, dignity, and democracy.

A university is fully situated in the world context, with its threats that know no frontier and with its vast possibilities. A university is adapted to the rhythm of contemporary life, to the distinctive features of each region, each country. For this and because of this, the institutional and conceptual transformation of the university represents an essential part of the wider process of change, of the necessary transformation of society as it approaches the new millennium.

Marco Antonio Rodrigues Dias
Director, Division of Higher Education
Unesco

PREFACE

◆

At the end of the second millennium, society and its institutions, nations and governments, civilizations and individuals are all involved in a worldwide inventory to prepare for the arrival of the 21st century. The Unesco–IDRC meeting on global trends and issues in higher education was, therefore, very timely.

This explains the title of this book: *The University as an Institution Today*. The university should be ready to provide a reflective analysis of its current assets and to propose aims for the future. Since the end of World War II, forums, seminars, conferences, panel discussions, and all types of institutional associations have studied the university and suggested courses for its immediate future. However, the effort of the Unesco–IDRC meeting was more dramatic and effective.

This book contains predominantly, but not exclusively, the results of the Unesco–IDRC meeting. As expected, it is also linked to previous documents and bibliographic material on the university and includes topics and themes that are usually dealt with in institutions of higher education.

Whether one takes a quick, superficial view or a more careful look at the many agendas, conferences, and proceedings, it is clear that the same things are talked about but not always with the same diagnoses and plans because of the variety of circumstances in which university work takes place. For the meeting, the universities were grouped according to Unesco's geographic regions.

Consulted references revealed an interest in the university's development from its medieval origins. A theory of the university considers the immediate process of higher education and its future. Finally, university administration, which is now a specific field of academic study, is discussed. The university can be seen as the motor driving the real growth of nations.

The convergence of the themes of history, theory, and administration explains the interwoven plan of this book. After highlighting university history, Part I — the Introduction — deals with administration in terms of the internal institutional organization and the external or outward-projecting idea of service. The following section presents the theory of the university's missions, functions, and roles, because without the goals the university sets itself to determine its functions, it drifts off course. There can then be a decline in the institutional physiognomy shown in the roles that make it stand out as an autonomous entity that exercises its academic liberties responsibly.

Thus, history as a teacher, university theory as a comprehensive vision with comparisons and conclusions, and administration as governer of the internal practices of an organization interweave and alternate in this text. The aim of this book is to impose order on the abundant wealth of documents resulting from the Unesco–IDRC meeting, all of which had different methods of organization and required complementing bibliographies and documents to unite the ideas.

Part II deals with the first meaning of administration: the organization and internal functioning of the university. In it, the structures are discussed, particularly the academic structure needed to organize human resources, such as directors, professors, students, and support personnel. Second, the material resources — physical, technical, financial, and economic — are considered. These are necessary for the university to carry out its teaching, research, and technological functions.

Part III deals with the external sense of administration, that of service to society by building a culture, the professions, the university extension services, and the relations linking the university to the international and national scene. Finally, the idea that the university ought to be an historic, dynamic institution that benefits all people is considered.

The book concludes (Part IV) with an epilogue on planning and evaluation of the achievements of the university as a social institution.

PART I

◆

INTRODUCTION

THE UNIVERSITY'S HISTORIC, GEOGRAPHIC EXPANSION

◆

The modern interest in studying the origin and development of the university as an institution dates from the 19th century. In 1567, Middendorp initiated the historiography of universities in a work reprinted in 1602 and, in 1672, Jean Launoy completed an index of the most "renowned schools." However, starting with four volumes by Meiners, published by the University of Göttingen between 1802 and 1805, covering the history of the formation and development of "higher schools," other works started to appear. The year 1840 can be seen as the beginning of publications on individual universities. In 1885, Denifle's work on the origin of universities and their growth until 1400 appeared, followed by Friedrich Paulsen's history of learned teaching in German universities, establishing the relation between the development of human thought and the history of universities. Paulsen (1906, 1986) begins with the 15th century; Kauffman's history of German universities, published from 1888 to 1896, complements Paulsen's work.

In 1895, Rashdall published three volumes on the universities of Europe in the Middle Ages (Rashdall 1936). Stephen d'Irsay (1933) concisely recounted the history of universities from their scholarly beginnings in the medieval period, mentioning the schools of classical antiquity, until the first decades of this century.

New studies, both succinct and extensive but always well grounded and documented, appeared to update the historic perspective on this institution of higher knowledge. Many studies focused on the lives of students, their characteristics, customs, and number; they also showed interest in teaching and pedagogical methods. Not long ago, the International Commission for the History of Universities began a study of European universities, under the direction of Hohn Flechter. British universities, following in the steps of Lawrence Stone, have inquired into the university's quantitative records since the Renaissance; researchers in France are working on the same task.

These historians and many modern scholars study the conditions behind the birth and rapid expansion of the university movement and point to two of its greatest moments in the medieval period. "At the time of the spontaneous inception of its first universities," Justine Thorens (1992) wrote, "Europe was in a state of intellectual and political turmoil." It was also in religious turmoil. In the 11th century, the "Dispute of the Investitures" created the necessary distance between the secular power of the emperors and the spiritual power of the church, also protecting the academic liberties of the "studium." Prominent in the Dispute were Pope Gregory VII and German Emperor Henry IV. The first breaches in the feudal system became apparent with urbanization and the spectacular development of cities, some of which, especially in Italy, were organized into communes, thus giving rise to a new social class. Similarly, international trade and contacts with other civilizations upset all customs and ways of thinking, resulting in a first Renaissance, that of the 12th century.

Expansion started when, with the end of "ex-consuetudine universities" (d'Irsay 1933, vol. I), the next stage was begun, that of universities established by civil powers, the "ex-privilegio universities." The oldest of these was in Naples, founded in 1224, but there was also a university founded in Palencia, Spain (1210) that disappeared at the end of the 13th century. The second important moment can be seen in the 14th and 15th centuries. This period has been neglected by historians (Verger 1973). The Reformation in the 16th century saw the birth of new universities. Rodin (1988) points out that, "The sciences in Europe are older than the scientific institutions, anyway older than the universities and the scientific research institutes," in other parts of the world the reverse was true. This should be kept in mind when studying the periods of university growth on different continents.

With the discovery of the New World by Christopher

Columbus in 1492, the idea of the university was transferred. The Catholic Church and religious communities agreed to join forces with the Spanish Crown to build institutions of higher education as early as possible: Santo Domingo in 1538 and Mexico and Lima in 1551. The work of Rodríguez Cruz, O.P. (1975) documents the origin of these and successive university foundations during the conquest and the colonial period. These universities were based on the Renaissance pattern of Salamanca and Alcalá de Henares (Brunner 1990).

In North America, the book *New England First Fruits* (cited in Rudolph 1965) states that after building shelters and a house of prayer and organizing their government, the immigrants sought to look after the advancement of knowledge and preserve it for posterity. Harvard was established in that early enthusiasm and was soon followed by the other "colonial colleges": the college founded in Connecticut (1701) and later moved to New Haven that, after 1718, was called after its benefactor, Yale; the College of New Jersey (1746), today known as Princeton; William and Mary (1693), Jefferson's alma mater; King's College (1744), today known as Columbia University in New York; the College of Philadelphia, which dates from 1755 and is now the University of Pennsylvania; the College of Rhode Island (1765), now Brown University; Dartmouth College (1769) in New Hampshire; and the Queen's College of New Jersey (1766), later known as Rutgers. According to Rudolph, all were founded by different denominations of Protestants to train ministers and pastors. The early immigrants wanted to encourage learned men, as in Renaissance Europe. In 1799, the series of "old-time colleges" was started. In 1861, there were 1822 colleges of different denominations, including some that did not last long.

Starting with Samuel Johnson's definition of a university as "a school where all the arts and faculties are taught and studied," Americans wanted to give their institutions an individual flavour. They were aware that, as Abraham Flexner would say in 1930, "a uniform type of university, persistent through the ages, was never transferable from one country to another."

In the United States, the term "university" was attractive even before 1785, when many "state universities" were being built, and before the "university era" that flourished after the Civil War (1861–1865). This growth in universities was stimulated by the Land-Grant Morrill Act, signed by Lincoln in 1862 and named after Vermont Congressman Justin Smith Morrill. Each state and educational facility interpreted the idea of a university differently. In the West, it seemed almost idealistic; it was thought that universities could be founded overnight, requiring only enthusiasm. Toward the middle of the 19th century, Daniel Coit Gilman wrote that the word "university" sounded pretentious. It is feasible to deduce (Pierson 1950) that in the period around the mid-19th century, serious "colleges" began to provide "higher kinds of work" — a kind of higher or broader education — while others did no more than claim, without having won the right to, the name university.

In the long run, the concept of university in the United States was heterogeneous and eclectic. It encompassed collegiate ideas from the English tradition, assimilated what it could from 19th-century German research universities, and, taking some ideas from France as well, developed its own formula. The English tradition molded its culture and made the university the birthright of nobles and aristocrats. However, although the English university tradition did not altogether ignore schooling for the common man, it emphasized principles of democratic urbanity, and encouraged scientific research with useful social applications.

The North American university emphasized and taught the principles of business administration to the point that the notorious respect of the Germans toward professorship was replaced by the collective unit the "department." As Wilhelm von Humboldt (1959 [1810]) wrote:

> If the relation between teacher and student in schools is of one type, a completely different one prevails in the university; there, the former does not exist for the latter; rather, both exist for science. The presence and cooperation of students is an

integral part of research work, which would not be as successful if students did not back up the teacher.

In Canada, the oldest establishment of higher education,
Laval University, was founded in 1852. The Commission of
Inquiry on Canadian University Education (Smith 1991, p. 14),
after affirming that universities in the country were "fundamen-
tally healthy," compared higher education in Canada with that in
the United States:

> Not only is the country [US] of greatest importance to Canada,
> but our post-secondary education systems are much more
> similar to each other than those in other parts of the world.
> Our learned societies often share memberships and our uni-
> versity labour pool is, to a certain extent, commonly utilized.
> There are differences, of course. While the private market
> plays a large role in the financial support of many U.S. private
> universities, usually by means of very high tuition fees, the
> government is the main financial supporter of Canadian uni-
> versities. The result of this is relatively equal funding per
> student across the Canadian university system, with no insti-
> tution being particularly rich or poor. The Commission heard
> no public or private comments to suggest that graduates of any
> particular Canadian university were poorly prepared or were
> unlikely to be accepted into postgraduate studies in competi-
> tion with graduates of other institutions. Such comments are
> often heard in the United States with respect to some of their
> institutions.

> Given that private universities in the United States receive
> twice the funding per student that Canadian universities can
> expect (and the top ones five or six times as much), it is
> unlikely that any Canadian university will have as many strong
> departments and subdepartments as the most prestigious
> American schools. At the same time, there are excellent
> departments in Canadian universities and some of these are
> described as equal to or better than their opposite numbers at
> some U.S. private universities. More important, though
> impossible to prove, the Commission has received the general
> impression that most if not all Canadian universities would,
> on balance, rank with the top half of U.S. universities, taken
> as a whole.

Successive waves of colonization during the 19th century brought different university traditions to Asia (Husén 1987). Other related factors also influenced this expansionist phenomenon. In Japan, once Shogun Kekei had abdicated and the Tokugawa Shogunate had fallen, the modernization of the state began in the Meiji period (1868–1918) and the country was opened to Western science. In 1885, Mori Arinori stated three essential objectives for the educational system: enrich and strengthen the state, provide new ideas to change the old mentality, and preserve traditions (Nagai 1971).

The Japanese looked to France and Germany for models. Since the 17th century, Japan had admired the German research universities; this influenced the Royal Decree of 1885 creating the first Japanese universities: Tokyo (1886) and Kyoto (1897). The universities' goal was "promoting instruction in the arts and sciences and inquiring into the mysteries of knowledge according to the needs of the state" (Nagai 1971). Keio (1890) and Waseda (1905) were the first private universities in Japan.

In 1946, a mission from the United States arrived in Japan to establish a "new educational system." By 1970, there were 473 institutions similar to the junior colleges of the United States and 379 "4-year institutions" or universities (Nagai 1971; Thomas 1985). This was the result of the minister of education's 1964 White Paper.

Tibawi (1979, p. 21) states:

> This is not the place to give a survey of Arab, still less Islamic history. Suffice it for our purposes to say that before his death in A.D. 632 Muhammad left the Arabs as a community and as a state bound together by the bond of religion. Within a century after his death the Arabs had extended their political sway outside Arabia eastward to India and westward to Spain. All the territory of the Persian Empire in Asia and most of the territories of the Byzantine Empire in Asia and Africa, in addition to those of the Visigoths in Spain, were conquered.

> But contrary to popular belief, Islam was not imposed on any of the various peoples within this large empire, nor was the Arabic language forced upon the conquered races. By a slow

process, however, both Islam and Arabic were adopted freely by the majority so that gradually the empire became a multi-racial unit in which Islam was the dominant faith and Arabic the sole vehicle of literary expression.

The debate about the origin of the university in Islam and its influence on the "universitates" of the medieval period continues. In the same way, there were precedents for the medieval concept of the Western, Christian "universitas" in the schools of antiquity, Plato's Academy, the Aristotelian Lyceum, the Museum of Alexandria, and several others. There were also the remote "study centres" in Japan, during the 7th and 8th centuries (Sansom 1985). Ribera y Tarrago (cited in Rashdall 1936, vol. I) suggested "the possibility that the medieval university owed much to conscious imitation from the Arabian system of education," a point of view reaffirmed by Heer (1962, p. 236):

> In the Christian part of Spain this civilization was an object of fear and wonder. During this period the Castilian language took over a number of Arabic words which had to do with government, technology and cultural matters in general. The cultured Hispano-Arab princes of the Taifas had their latter-day successors in Frederick II, the Hohenstaufen Emperor, and the Spanish and Portuguese "philosopher" kings of the twelfth and thirteenth centuries. The atmosphere of these courts was such that culture was equated with argument; public disputations were staged between scholars and theologians of the three religions, Islam, Judaism and Christianity.

From the Islamic point of view on the origin of universities, Tibawi (1979, p. 30) affirms:

> The rival caliphs in Cairo claimed descent from the Prophet, and fortified their claim through a well-planned state education, designed principally for adults and disseminated from a central institution known as "Dar al-Ilm" (literally house of learning). A mosque established on the morrow of the capture of Cairo was soon used as another repository of learning according to the doctrine of the new rulers. This mosque is now well-known as al-Azhar, supposed to be the oldest university in the world.

The recent situation in the 21 member states of the Arab region, according to Osman (1983, p. 10), is that they lack "any racial homogeneity as they represent several racial and ethnic groups including the Caucasian, the Berber and the Negro," with "widely differing socio-political systems and levels of economic development." In terms of education,

> The whole region suffered from neglect...during the many centuries of foreign domination, to the extent that the Arab language, which has always been held in great reverence in all countries of the region, came to be mastered by relatively few. The concern about the restrictive attitude of European colonialism toward education was so widespread that in almost all countries national liberation movements began as voluntary popular associations for the building and management of schools. It was therefore natural that on attaining national independence all countries accorded very high priorities to education.

Concerning higher education, the same author (p. 15) continues:

> By the end of the Second World War there were only 9 institutions of higher education of some significance functioning in the whole region. Four of these were private, foreign-run, small universities and three were purely religious institutions specializing in Islamic and Arabic studies. Their general impact was very limited due to their size, their narrow range of subjects and their general orientation. Attention to higher education began somewhat slowly in the 1950s and gathered momentum in the 1960s and 1970s. The number of fully-fledged universities had by 1979 reached 55, with much larger student and staff populations and a wider range of fields of studies. A number of other post-secondary institutions have also been established covering the majority of the countries. Also whereas only 5 countries had some form of higher education before the war, 14 other countries have, during the last two decades, established their own institutions with several countries spreading their institutions more widely within the country. Only three Arab countries still remain without any higher education institutions of significance.

Nevertheless, Kazem (1991) points out that

For historical and cultural reasons, the Arab people every-where have almost a sort of mythical faith in education. Education has for long obvious association with status and mobility and higher education represents to the masses oppor-tunities and identification with higher status, power, affluence and elitism.

The types of universities in the Arab region are varied. Osman (1983, p. 23) points out:

A major obstacle here is the existence of several types of models of higher education systems and mainly universities which tend to have their own organizational and curricular structures and their own orientation and approach to higher education. The oldest of these models in the history of higher education in the world is the traditional Islamic University, which has been functioning in the region for over 1000 years and specializes in Islamic and Arabic studies. Several of this type of institution still exist in several countries and have recently been joined by some new "Islamic Universities," which differ from other modern universities mainly in name and in emphasis on religious subjects. The bulk of Arab universities and other higher education institutes which are described as "modern" belong to different university models. The oldest and most widespread in the region is the "French model" which exists in all Arab countries which were under French domination, and had strong influences on the Egyptian university system. The second model in importance is the "British model" which characterizes the universities in coun-tries which were under British rule. The "American model" which was until recently restricted to a few private American universities, has assumed more significance in recent years in some of the countries which launched their university systems during the last decade. While it may not yet be accurate to identify an "Egyptian model," as Egyptian universities still exhibit strong French influences, the Egyptian university sys-tem has developed some significant features of its own and has influenced some of the newer universities in the region due to their dependence on Egyptian teaching staff, senior adminis-trators and other personnel.

Even taking into account the roots of higher education that were planted on the African continent by European colonialism — such as those with a British flavour promoted by Asquith, those with more indigenous values encouraged by Sir Eric Ashby, and those cultivated by the French (Sutton 1969; Fordhan 1970; Ashby and Anderson 1972) — university expansion in Africa is very recent (Unesco/BREDA 1992). Taiwo (1991) states:

> Unlike Europe and America, and with a few exceptions such as Sankore in Timbuktu and Al-Azhar in Egypt, the history of higher education in Africa is relatively a recent one. For example, the whole of anglophone West Africa could not boast of more than seven universities (with two in Ghana, two in Liberia, two in Nigeria and one in Sierra Leone) by mid-1962. And in the francophone West African countries the story is no better. There were in fact only two universities (one in the Ivory Coast and one in Senegal) by mid-1962 in the francophone countries of West Africa.

However, as Auala (1991) affirms, "History shows that most African nations have strived to establish at least one national university immediately after independence." According to Ishumi (1990), this is contrary to the "regional approach and regional orientation in higher education of the colonial times," such as at Makerere University College in Uganda which "was actually a regional federal institution designed to cater to East African needs (Uganda, Kenya, Tanganyika, and Zanzibar). Similarly, the university set up in Southern Rhodesia in Central Africa was intended to serve Southern Rhodesia (now Zimbabwe), Northern Rhodesia (now Zambia), and Nyasaland (now Malawi). So also was the University of Botswana, Lesotho, and Swaziland originally designed to cater to these three countries of southern Africa.

The reasons that the different countries had for creating universities in the postcolonial years were, in fact, similar (Ishumi 1990):

> Producing well-educated and functionally competent middle- and high-level manpower to manage the various sectors of the national economy; creating and imprinting a positive

international image for the newly independent state by construction of respectable institutions and expansion of existing ones for an increased pupil and student enrollment; reducing and ultimately eradicating mass illiteracy; and creating within the national community a literate, innovative and creatively self-reliant cadre whose productivity and skills would form an asset in the production and accumulation of national wealth in the years after formal schooling.

These and similar objectives, taken into account as early as 1961 at the Conference of African Ministers of Education in Addis Ababa, are recognized and shared at the primary and secondary levels of education.

The introduction to the *Consultation of Experts on Future Trends and Challenges in Higher Education in Africa* (Unesco 1991a) points out "three phases in the development [of] African higher education, to wit: the phase of university symbol of sovereignty marked by the classical style; the phase of expansion to meet the urgent needs of training the cadres, and the phase of crisis with the draconian reduction of financial means." During these three phases, higher education institutions introduce innovations or reforms into the structures, the programs, the periods of training, long-distance education, and information and communication technologies.

Causes for the crisis phase have been pointed out in *Presentations de la problematique* (Unesco 1991a). They include economic difficulties; uncontrolled, rapid growth in the number of both students and professors; a lack of qualified, experienced professors; a lack of coordination in the creation and activities of universities and other institutions; a lack of "pertinence" concerning development and socioeconomic realities; the frequent absence of a defined policy in the area of higher education and its missions; lack of salary incentive for professors; and lack of motivation among students "due to the uncertainties and apprehensions aroused by somber perspectives of employment."

Priorités de développement economique et social pour les années 90 (issued by the Sixième conference des ministres de l'éducation et des ministres chargés de la planification économique des états membres d'Afrique in Dakar, 8–11 July 1991) examines Africa's socioeconomic development in the 1980s.

> [This decade] encouraged the false impression of security and optimism that was nourished in the decades of African independence in the sixties and the seventies, but it also caused a series of crises that triggered the collapse of the pillars of the economy that had already suffered the combined assaults of world recession, the heavy burden of foreign debt, unfavorable exchange conditions, the energy and food crisis, and natural catastrophes.... The crisis led to a series of reform policies in programs for structural change that never came near to approaching the basic structural causes for the problems of African development. Even worse is the fact that the indicators of human development, such as education, health, nutrition, employment...have significantly worsened during the decade of the eighties.

At the end of the 1980s, real salaries had fallen: "in addition to the shrinkage of jobs in the formal sector, this fall has brought about a massive increase in activities in the informal economic sector." This could have been praiseworthy; however, "given the fact that the informal sector leads to weak productivity...and to subsistence wages, even family budgets have to be modified in order to satisfy the most basic needs...and expenses belonging to education have been eliminated."

Nevertheless, the report of a symposium (OAU 1979), in which prominent Africans and several heads of state participated, contains valid opinions:

> For the first time, we are proposing a basic question: what kind of development does Africa require and how can it be obtained? The hypothesis underlying this question is that we do not want to continue imitating the economic systems of other countries; we have realized that African countries cannot continue in search of political centers and such strategies, giving the impression of wanting to be a pale imitation of America, France, England, or China; the time has come for us to reflect seriously on the emergence of a typically African development strategy that is not looking abroad, or based on a simple copy of other societies, or leading to modernization

based on other cultures. In other words, the time has come for African governments and its peoples to encourage the emergence of a means of development and a way of life that are African, that are based on its rich cultural heritage, its social structure, its economic institutions and its considerable natural wealth; a way of development and a way of life that, despite other societies and other cultures, are not imitative of or alien to the cultural heritage of Africans.

What is needed is a "développement endogène" (Salifou 1983) or "eduquer ou perir" (Ki-Zerbo 1991). To attain this goal, Ishumi (1990, p. 29) says:

It is evident that efforts have been made in the different countries in Africa to strengthen programmes aimed at promoting higher education. Expansion of student enrolment at local tertiary and university institutions, growth and diversification of scholarships at overseas institutions and an expansion in the teaching and research staff at local higher education institutions all point to positive trends not only in the individual arenas but also in a progressive alignment of programmes to the need for production of well-educated, well-trained human resources to face the socio-economic challenges of post-colonial society.

Notwithstanding the achievements in this direction, the discussion of trends in the mobility of students, teachers and researchers does point to a few problems that have been encountered or created in the process. Cases of lagging enrolments, of imbalances in admission particularly in relation to the sciences and the humanities, and cases of mis-allocation and underutilization of manpower so expensively produced have been referred to. Also, destabilizing factors in higher education staffing levels and problems of the research climate have been pointed out. For any effective synchronization of progress, these problems should receive corrective attention.

For instance, the salary structure and reward system in general could be so designed as to attract and retain experts in the fields for which they were trained, to which they would obviously make the greatest contribution possible. Also, there is need to redress the chronic imbalances in admission to university and other tertiary institutions in favour of the sciences and science-based programmes. This is in view of the heavier reliance of society on science and technology for the solution of the myriad development problems and challenges in the future.

Teachers and researchers will require positive encouragement in their work, which involves high-level critical thinking and practical investigation for informed policy options and guidance towards appropriate socio-economic adjustments and progress. Some of the simplest yet critical considerations in this regard are tools of work: teaching material, books, reference materials, laboratory equipment, research funds — many of which have not been made available to higher institutions of learning for the past decade or so. Yet these are expected to be centres of excellence and fountains of development ideas and practice!

Harmonization of higher education programmes will be needed much more now and in future than has so far been possible if African countries have to realize a breakthrough to the 21st century.

In concluding this synopsis of the origin and geographic spread of the university movement, it is important to emphasize the emotional overtones embodied in the word university: the ideal, which is never reached, of higher learning leading to a higher education that results in higher service to society in its different, successive historical moments.

THE DYNAMIC DEVELOPMENT OF THE UNIVERSITY INSTITUTION

◆

This brief overview of the worldwide expansion of the university as an institution — organized according to Unesco's geographical regions — also implies its transcultural historic, dynamic development: political, social, economic, cultural, and scientific. Major changes in these conditions include the scientific and epistemological break in the concept of knowledge current in the

16th century (Kuhn 1962), the changes caused by the Industrial Revolution toward the end of the 18th century, and the development of modern nation states in the 19th century.

Rashdall's (1936, vol. III, p. 458) comments, written at the end of the 19th century, are still pertinent:

> The very idea of the university as an institution is essentially medieval, and it is curious to observe how largely that idea still dominates our modern schemes of education. [It is not necessary] that the teachers of different subjects should teach in the same place and be united in a single institution — still less that an attempt should be made to make the teaching body representative of the whole cycle of human knowledge. It is not necessary that studies should be grouped into particular faculties, and students required to confine themselves more or less exclusively to one. It is not necessary that a definite line of study should be marked out by authority, that a definite period of years should be assigned to a student's course, or that at the end of that period he should be subjected to examination and receive, with more or less formality and ceremony, a title of honor.

Nevertheless, the same author continues:

> All this we owe to the Middle Ages. Similar needs might no doubt in course of time have independently evolved somewhat similar institutions in a somewhat different form. But, in the form in which we have them, teaching corporations, courses of study, examinations, degrees, are a direct inheritance from the Middle Ages....
>
> How much is lost and how much gained by the educational machinery which the Middle Ages have created for us would be a difficult inquiry. That something is lost is evident. Something of the life and spontaneity of old-world culture certainly seems to be gone forever. Universities have often had the effect of prolonging and stereotyping ideas and modes of thought for a century or more after the rest of the world has given them up. It is surprising how slowly an intellectual revolution affects the course of ordinary education. But educational traditions are marvelously tenacious, quite apart from institutional machinery such as that of the universities; and education itself must always be, from the necessities of the case, a tradition. In

all machinery there is some loss, and yet it is only by means of machinery that culture can be permanently kept alive and widely diffused. The machinery by which this process is carried on among ourselves is as distinctly a medieval creation as representative government or trial by jury. And it is a piece of institutional machinery which has outlived almost every other element in the education which it was originally intended to impart.

In modern universities, there is a similar awareness that something has been lost but much has been preserved, in particular the medieval institutional framework (Cantor 1991). German historian Friedrich Heer (1962), in his work on the Middle Ages, mentions this in referring to the university:

> The university, and the intellectualism it nurtured, is a specifically European phenomenon. In the universities were laid the foundations of the scientific culture of our modern world, in them grew up the habit of disciplined thinking, followed by systematic investigation, which made possible the rise of the natural sciences and of the technical civilization necessary to large industrial societies.

The Organisation for Economic Co-operation and Development (OECD 1987) states that, over the centuries,

> The university has put its flexibility to the test. Different forms of economic, social, and political organization have appeared and disappeared. Some of those still subsisting are completely transformed as to their functions, aims, and structure. But universities, even the newest, poorest and smallest in the modern world, still preserve missions, ideas, values, conventions, and customs that, in the life of their professors and students, still recall those of their predecessors in Paris, Oxford and Bologna during the 13th century.

> [The similarities with the past] are not reduced to the wearing of a professorial gown or respect for certain ceremonies; very developed university systems exist in which these symbols are practically invisible. Institutional continuity is not limited to appreciation of the humanities, because nowadays there are universities that are wholly dedicated to technical subject areas in their research and teaching activities. Nor is it limited

to the community in residence; in most universities, the majority of students are beyond the control of the establishments; there are those who return home, either to their parents, or to somewhere else.

Links of another type "relate the present with the past and...give the structure of university life its distinctive character in the bosom of the institutions of higher learning in existence." Although the medieval university believed that the search for truth depended more on the exegesis of texts than on scientific discovery, this can also be used to justify the existence of institutions principally dedicated to the intellectual life. Over the centuries and despite difficulties, this devotion to learning has earned the university social as well as state recognition of its autonomy. The universities' style of internal government is another link with the past (OECD 1987):

> Their form of administration translated the different areas of knowledge that universities make the effort to conserve, increase, and transmit; this frees them from any metaphorical similarity with the principles that govern contemporary bureaucratic organizations: "earnings" "production" "profitability." Collective direction, the weakness of central authority, and the fact that the academic units, the departments, or faculties that make up a university take the initiatives reflect the very essence of the university's intellectual objectives. Together with these manifestations of continuity between the past and the present can be included the fact that the university as an institution has survived wars, political and religious persecutions, poverty and negligence, and the changes of recent years, the most radical since the period of the Enlightenment. The number of universities, professors and students is multiplying, the benefits of the university have extended to a multitude of areas, and its efforts in the service of basic and applied research are available to public and private enterprise.

These reflections on the historic, dynamic process of the university make us consider the continuous, vital movement of an institution that needs to fit into a changing social environment. Although there have been fluctuations in its prestige and some hesitation in the orientation of its missions or fate

(Mallinson 1981), the university must become part of the international scene. Thus, the university's government becomes more
complex and greater attention is given to administration as a
specific study area.

UNIVERSITY ADMINISTRATION AS A SPECIFIC AREA OF STUDY

◆

Today, the number of institutions in university systems and
different postsecondary systems worldwide is huge. Seidel
(1991) attributes the increase, first, to political reasons, "to
maintain and improve living conditions,...to improve the organizations of modern societies,...[and] to cope with growing complexity of work processes"; second, to "developments...of
knowledge itself"; and third, to the "changes in social structures
that have become increasingly apparent in the last decade." The
number of researchers, professors, students, and people hired as
human support resources is virtually innumerable, and billions
of dollars are invested in ensuring that higher education remains
qualified, equitable, and efficient. These are qualities that the
contemporary university cannot easily compensate for through
the pressing need to make education more "democratic." This
has become quantitatively more sensitive since the end of World
War II (Thorens 1992), particularly as a result of the effect of the
student movements in the 1960s and 70s (Feuer 1971; Lipset
1971).

"Before the 1950s higher education was hardly at all a field
of scholarly studies.... However, since the late 1960s higher
education has become a rapidly growing field of research, which
to a large extent has been comparative in orientation" (Husén
1991, p. 2). The study of higher education can and should focus
converging points of view on the increased number of programs
devoted to university administration (Dressel and Mayhew

1974). This task has become more complex because universities are not the only institutions in today's "learning society" that are dedicated to the production, evaluation, and spread of knowledge. There are also industrial and business enterprises and public and other organizations. None of them would claim that research is their exclusive domain; however, many of the highly specialized branches of knowledge seem to have moved out of the universities (OECD 1987).

Luckily, a forum of experts on trends in research on higher education (Unesco 1991b) highlighted the importance of constructing "a truly interdisciplinary science of higher education" based on "inter- and intra-national research." Comparative research should consider the production, dissemination, and organization of knowledge in its political, economic, and socio-cultural context. This interdisciplinary science "will develop by establishing a balance between the methodologies, methods, and techniques of various disciplines," including history of the universities, cognitive science, sociology, psychology, political science, and economics. The importance of such a study is even greater in view of the profound changes in Europe, especially eastern Europe, what was the USSR, and the Arab countries, and in view of the different situations in new countries in Africa. It could be oriented "to enable the higher education faculty and student body (i.e., future teachers at other levels of education) to perform their functions better" and to train university administrators.

In Latin America, there are two programs for training university directors: the Permanent Symposium on the University (PSU) run by the Colombian Association of Universities and the Inter-American Course on University Administrative Management (IGLU) promoted by the Inter-American University Organization (OUI). A similar program has begun in Africa and the Commission of Inquiry on Canadian University Education (Smith 1991) asserts that

> Canada should create immediately a fund for the improvement of education along the lines of the FIPSE in the United States...

[to study the] methods of delivery, results per dollar spent (productivity), methods of evaluation, and so on, tasks common to many industries in situations of similar financial stringency...[because] R&D is a tool under-utilized in the "industry" of higher education, compared to almost any other sector of the economy.

Here, I regard the topic of university administration in its widest sense. As Dias (1991a,b) states, living in crisis is not an "exceptional situation" of the university and the administration or "management of universities is also [in] transition."

Administration can be understood as an opportunity to reflect and look for possible solutions to, and future projections for, the problems of the approaching millennium. Those who are now directing institutions of higher education are responsible for future plans, which, in large part, are determinable by the operational decisions of today.

MISSIONS, FUNCTIONS, AND ROLES
OF THE UNIVERSITY

◆

The act of administration can be understood in two ways. The first, which is reflective, means that the university organizes itself. Borrowing a biological term from natural organisms, the university, as an institution, arranges itself internally so that it can fulfill its functions. The general organic structure of the university and its essential and specific part, the academic structure, thus comes about. The second sense is the more literal translation of the Latin "ad-ministrare": to minister to or serve. In this sense, the university projects its organized effort externally in service to the community.

The two views of administration provide the organizational framework of this book. Related to this concept are the missions, functions, and roles that describe the university's purpose and its institutional characteristics. The missions are the institution's goals or objectives: research, teaching, and service. These objectives can be achieved through the functions or activities that the university carries out. These can be seen as corresponding to the spread of science, to the education and training of humanity, and to the creation of society. The vigour of the university's characteristic roles, commonly expressed as corporate, scientific, universal, and autonomous, obviously results from the university's loyalty to the mission it adopts and how it understands and interprets it, and from the quality and responsibility with which the institution carries out the functions to achieve its goals and objectives (see Novakovic and Rajkoviv 1988).

Unesco (1991b) points out that "teaching and research" are the "intellectual functions" of the university. They are related to the educational mission, or "educational function," consisting of the "cultivation of the mind" and the "transmission of basic ideas and concepts." In addition, service is the "social function" or "social role of the university that provides the link between the intellectual and educational role of universities on the one hand and the development of society on the other" (Kamba in Unesco 1991d). However, carrying out these functions, no matter how they are expressed or put into practice, ought to be interactive within the university and with society (Ostar 1990).

Autonomy and the role of universality

In keeping with its missions and functions, historically the roles of the university are part of its spontaneous, original essence. The university arose from agreement and consensus between teachers and students, who were united for the corporate management of universal knowledge.

Because of the university's roles and organizational abilities, medieval society and its religious and civil authorities recognized the special privileges of each university, earned not through gratuitous concession but by virtue of internal merits. These privileges were "the institutional liberty to organize and decide on all aspects concerning" the intellectual labour carried out by teachers and students (Thorens 1992). This work was based on the high missions they set for themselves, on the responsible freedom of the thinking spirit, on the power of the higher knowledge they were seeking, and the exercise of academic liberties. This academic freedom could be universal in scope or restricted to local or regional concerns, depending on the authority that recognized such a right.

The autonomy of the university first appears implicitly in the oldest legal statute on the subject: Federico Barbaroja's *La Authentica Habita* of 1158 (Magna Charta delle Università Europea 1988; Thorens 1992) and in the university legislation that Alfonso X, the Wise, approved: *The Seven Divisions*, which was the first body of laws in the vernacular (1256–1263).

Autonomy is indispensible to the role and work of the university. Today, it is differentiated into organizational autonomy, academic autonomy, and financial autonomy. This autonomy was real and vigorous, according to d'Irsay (1933) in the "ex-consuetudine" universities, but became vulnerable and weak once the "ex-privilegio" universities became subject to the will of their founders. Throughout history, the intervention of political powers, to a greater or lesser extent, has threatened autonomy with different philosophies and different policies for higher education. Universities have also been affected by various financial pressures to the extent that they have asked themselves whether autonomy has become a myth (Thorens 1992).

The same problems have occurred with the idea of universality, which, according to Unesco Director Mayor (1991) ought to be understood in a context of "diversity" or "interdependence." He states:

> The universality of the university may be understood in a number of ways. First, the university is universal by virtue of its characteristic concern with what would at one time have been called "universals" or "essentials" and which we might now identify — with apologies to any Aristoteleans present — with first principles. Transcending the varied forms of higher education, the defining quality of the university may — I would suggest — be equated with the attempt to grasp the

principles underlying the physical and spiritual reality and, beyond that, the means of defining the nature and content of the good life.

Secondly, the university may be said to be universal by virtue of the scope of its concerns. These in principle embrace the whole spectrum of knowledge, the totality of phenomena, even if in practice a choice may have to be made concerning the range of courses offered.

A third sense in which the university may be said to be universal [is] because it is open to all those who can derive benefit from it. The university — the *universitas studii* of medieval times — is linked to the concepts of freedom of access to knowledge.

Finally, the university is universal in the internationalism inherent in the use of the common language of reason and science. Knowledge knows no boundaries, and the laws of mathematics and science are identical to all, irrespective of nationality or creed.

Universality in the four senses I have indicated seems to me to be part of the heredity of the university. However, that heredity is not static and is always to be found in dynamic relationship with its social environment.

Conclusion

The preceding views of the university's roles, functions, and, above all, missions are well documented in the 19th century, and even more so in the second half of this century. There is a desire to incorporate these themes in university work. This presupposes the existence of "the will for knowledge which is basic in human beings" (Jaspers 1970) and the will to overcome the institution's simple internal functionalism to transcend its efficient service to society. The university cannot limit itself to being an indifferent reflection, but must set the guidelines and standards for its own development.

At the second Unesco–nongovernmental organizations collective consultation on higher education, Seidel (1991, p. 32) expanded on the tripartite nature of university missions and their respective functions. He mentions the "five main functions" that "society expects its institutions of higher education to fulfill, though others could no doubt be added":

> Their first function lies in providing education and training within a structure which combines research and teaching. Secondly, they provide professional training. This is not, be it said, a recent development of the post-war period — ever since the Middle Ages universities have been preparing students for professions such as medicine, teaching and the law. Thirdly, they are research institutions, responsible for carrying out research in a broad range of disciplines, including the increasing amount of interdisciplinary work, and linked to this, for training a constant supply of qualified people for all fields of employment. Fourth, they have a part to play in regional development and also in developing international contacts. And fifth, they have a social function in fostering the intellectual and social development of society.

The Conference of the European Ministers of Education (1973) mentioned by Carton (1983, p. 5) linked the triple mission of science, humankind, and society as follows:

> The adaptation of higher teaching to social needs is the concern of institutions and individuals. On the one hand, there is no backing for the masses to have access to higher education...giving them adapted scientific, cultural and civil training, and at the same time, linking higher education to society, the economy, and practical life in order to relate, as well as possible, the right to education, the right to work, and forming the specialists that society needs.

The OECD (1987) lists nine missions:

♦ Ensure general postsecondary education to the best graduates of secondary school, and in certain countries, extramural education to adults through permanent education.

♦ Develop research and culture, with emphasis generally placed on the value, if not on the practice, of basic research, or research stimulated by intellectual curiosity more than on applied research or research contracts that represent a growing proportion of university activities.

◆ Contribute to satisfying the labour needs of a society of knowledge; because of the progress of knowledge useful for professional practice, the university has the obligation to guarantee final training and attend to the desires of people in active practice through master's courses, doctoral studies, recycling courses, and even preuniversity activities in the workplace.

◆ Provide high-level teaching and specialized training.

◆ Reinforce the economy's competitiveness and the production of wealth, especially through the engineering sciences and technology, thereby strengthening ties between the university and industry and business.

◆ The university should act as a "filtering device," for, despite the recent tendency of universities to open their doors to adults, they should select acceptable candidates based on intellectual capacities.

◆ Joined to this function of selection and degree-giving, the university should offer the possibility for "social mobility" to good students and working-class students.

◆ Serve as a model to put certain national policies into practice so that equal opportunities and the transmittal of culture and common civil norms are guaranteed.

◆ Finally, the mission and function of the university are to prepare people capable of later carrying out the "role of leaders" of society.

In 1990, university authorities from the Asian and Pacific region, meeting at the New England University of Australia pointed out that

> Higher education institutions serve their societies through their work in teaching, research and wider community service.

Their recognized functions include not only serving the productive sectors of society, but also contributing to national economic and social development, preservation and transmission of cultural heritage, the protection of the physical environment, improvement of the whole education system, the pursuit of both equity and excellence, and fostering of international understanding and cooperation.

In turn, the document, *Higher Education and National Development in Four Countries: India, Bangladesh, Thailand, and the Philippines* (Unesco 1988b, p. 1) had already stated that

Institutions of higher education have traditionally performed two major functions — teaching and research — geared to the education and training of high level manpower and generation of new knowledge. In recent years, a third function has emerged, that of extension and community service. In the performance of these three functions, institutions of higher education are generally expected to contribute to the process of national progress and development.

At the meeting of experts in Dakar, Auala (1991, p. 1), an African, gathers similar ideas expressed by different African university presidents and professors:

The role of the university in national development is a subject of much discussion in Africa today. History shows that most African nations have strived to establish at least one national university immediately after independence.... Any university worthy of its name is expected to exercise a high degree of objectivity in the search for truth and advancement of knowledge. Nyerere (1980), Kamba (1983), and Ngeno (1984) see the main function of a university as playing a crucial role in solving social problems by coming down to earth and addressing the problems of ignorance, hunger, poverty, disease, and poor living conditions facing African nations.

On our own continent we may recall the words of Dr Kenneth Kaunda, President of Zambia..."The University of Zambia is part and parcel of our society and therefore, to have any meaningful existence it must continue to be involved in that society." Thus today the university in modern Africa is committed to a sense of social consciousness and to development and nation building.

To create an African university...involves among other things: the ordering of priorities and the deciding of the role of the university in nation building; adapting the curriculum and developing new programmes; fostering staff development programmes; deciding the responsibilities of the university in continuing education; and developing research.

Yesufu (1973) sees the role of the truly African university as fulfilling the following objectives: pursuit, promotion and dissemination of knowledge; research; manpower development; promoting social and economic modernization; and promoting intercontinental unity and international understanding.

PHILOSOPHIES OF THE UNIVERSITY AS AN INSTITUTION

◆

Universities and academies

The Renaissance climate of the 15th century promoted domestic and courtly gatherings to air matters of cultural and humanistic interest. The renewed fondness for the classical era that was brewing in Italy reminded people of Academos, the Attic mythological hero, in whose fields grew the gardens frequented by philosophers — the origin of Plato's academy. Quite spontaneously, conversational gatherings of around 1400 started to be called "academies," although they were still informal, private initiatives among friends.

Nevertheless, soon the academies spread throughout Europe (d'Irsay 1933, vol. II). *New Atlantis* (1627) by Francis Bacon and his idea of the "House of Science" or "House of Solomon" stimulated the official creation of academies. Universities were starting to grant cautious acceptance to the movement caused by the scientific or Copernican revolution and the new mandate of scientific research. In 1798, Kant (1963 [1798]) summarized the difference between the two types of institutions: universities and academies. In many cases there was such rivalry during the 18th century that great scientists had to live an equivocal existence or pledge their enthusiasm to the academy that backed their new discoveries, turning their backs on the university. Because of this situation, Kant, the philosopher of Königsberg, stated that

> Apart from these corporative scholars (the universities) there can be independent scholars who, if they belong to the university, further only a small part of the complex of science and form free corporations (called academies or free societies) that are like other similar workshops, or they live in some way in a natural scientific state in which each one, as an amateur and without rules or set guidelines, deals individually with increasing and spreading science.

University models

A dilemma remains today concerning the university's missions and its respective functions: whether science should involve research or simply teaching; whether students should be taught and educated or simply trained; and how best to serve society. After universities declined in the 18th century, the fully formed modern states tried to mold the university to their principles and philosophies. Thus, the universities' characteristic roles or ways of being became diversified. They were discussed throughout the 19th century and into the 20th, the roles became interwoven and at times blurred and the situation persists.

Today, classical models or types of universities have given rise to studies and comparative approaches. Didon (1884) and Paulsen (1906) in his work on German universities established contrasts between these and the French university conceived by Napoleon in 1806. In 1808, Schleirmacher (1959 [1808]) noted the two different but neighbouring types of universities. Also in 1906, Lyman Abbot typified the three ways that academic effort could be oriented: English universities to the development of the person, the German university to science, and the North American to social development (Rudolph 1965, p. 356). Giner de los Ríos (1916, p. 108) described the three types as the German research university, the English educating university, and the French professionalizing university, with its Spanish copy:

> They oscillate around three types of universities, which for some time have started to be established in a barely predictable way: the "German" type, the "English" type and the "Latin" type. The first belongs to the German empire, to Austria–Hungary, to German-speaking Switzerland and to the Scandinavians. Russia aspires to separate itself partly from this type, which its Baltic universities belong to. The British type is seen in its pure form in Oxford and Cambridge, or modified more towards the Latin or German type in Scotland and Ireland, in new universities, and in the United States. The Latin type predominates in France, Belgium and Switzerland and in the Latin nations: Italy, Portugal, and Spain. The German university, has research and the education of scientists as its most important goal, with professional interests in a subordinate position. The English university proposes the general and higher education of its students in different areas of life and in pure knowledge, perhaps merely intellectual more than properly scientific. The Latin university, which has perhaps broken most abruptly with history, seems to be the most professional.

Abraham Flexner (1930), the reformer of medical studies in the United States, limited himself to comparing the North American style of university with the German and English ones and calls them the "classical" styles. However, recent researchers, Jacques Drèze and Jean Debelle (1968), reserve this distinction for the French, English, and German types of university, the "primary" styles in contrast to the "derived" styles of the North American and Soviet schools. The first derives from crossing the British with the German style of university, and the second from crossing the German and French styles, although Lenin's pedagogical mind imprinted Soviet education and universities with a centralist, collective, doctrinaire tinge that is subject nowadays to profound revisions as the result of perestroika and glasnost.

Having considered the philosophical substance of these five

university styles that have had an influence in different parts of the world, we can say that the university differs in the priority that each places on scientific research, on the development of the human being, or on the various forms of service to society. It is a question of preference and practical emphasis, not exclusion so that a balance among all three objectives can be achieved.

With analytical criteria, Paul Ricoeur reduces the five university types to two (Drèze and Debelle 1968, prologue). He states that although the functioning of universities in all countries is considered, it is clear that the idea of the "liberal" university on the one hand and the function of the university as a quasi-public service on the other constitute the two poles between which all current universities are balanced. This omits the fact that their legal status (private or public) brings them closer to one pole or the other. At one of these two extremes — according to the thinking of Georges Gusdorf (1964) — pedagogy submits to politics, politics is identified with the state, and education is inspected by the government. In other words, the second pole makes government approach the university to such an extent that the university seems to become confused with the state. Of course, the autonomy of the university as an institution is at stake here.

Paul Ricoeur considered that the models, English-educational, German-scientific, and American-progress, correspond to an "idea" of the university. This is especially true of the German model, as it was the German philosophers who thought most about the university and wrote most extensively about it as an idea until Karl Jaspers' writings between 1923 and 1961. In 1852, the English model was next to be formulated when Oxford professor John Henry Newman outlined it in his *Discourses on the Scope and Nature of University Education* (Newman 1959 [1852]); Cameron (1979) wrote of it, "We note this work to be the most influential (I suppose) book ever written on university education." Finally, the university in North America, with practical dynamics but foreseeable goals, had support from the philosophers Alfred North Whitehead and John Dewey. On the other hand, Paul Ricoeur contends that the Napoleonic and Soviet universities do not embody the "idea" of a university; they are a "function" placed entirely at the service of one state or another. Based on our conclusions so far, Drèze and Debelle call the first three, universities of the "spirit" and the latter, universities of "power."

A similar classification is made by MacGregor (1991) when he refers to universities that have to fulfill tasks imposed by the intervening state and to "power groups of a society" to train "ideologically-neutral professionals, prepared for practical needs." This type of university lacks "its own essence and purpose." It is a "university-workshop," like the Napoleonic university, which is not the master of its own fate. It is contrasted with the "university which is a center for social change" whose "quasi-owner" is "a political party" that uses it for "demagogical purposes." It is also unlike the "university-symbol" which is so attractive because of the benefits of prestige, privilege, and power it promises its graduates, and unlike the "university-idea" which, according to MacGregor, was well presented by von Humboldt, Newman, Jaspers, and Kerr, each in his own way.

Let us conclude this taxonomy of universities, emphasizing the mutual input that Husén (1991, p. 12) mentions:

> In order to obtain a perspective on the Western university of today one could start with the Humboldtian university in Berlin, established with emphasis on research and graduate training which first spread to other parts of Germany and then was emulated in other countries. When Cardinal Newman in 1852 held his famous lecture on "The Idea of a University," making a plea for "knowledge being its own end" and refuting the Baconian utilitarianism, the idea of research and teaching being conducted in close connection began to materialize at German universities with institutes and seminars established around university chairs.

> The idea of a university, where research and training of researchers was a main mission, materialized in the United States at Johns Hopkins which was founded in 1876 and began as a pure graduate school with emphasis entirely on research and training of researchers. Shortly before that the Land Grant

Act (The Morrill Act) had been passed in Congress, which was a break through for a new utilitarian conception of the university, some decades later followed by the extension services which revolutionized agriculture in the Untied States. The young President of the University of Chicago, Robert M. Hutchins, in the 1930s launched a "counter reformation" which should "take the university back to Cardinal Newman, to Thomas Aquinas, and to Plato and Aristotle". He succeeded, according to Clark Kerr (1963), in reviving the philosophical dialogue, but Chicago went on being a modern American university.

The undergraduate program Hutchins introduced was one designed by "secular absolutists." Students should be acquainted with absolute and timeless truths. Worthwhile knowledge was to a large extent embodied in a set of Great Books, which could be listed and defined what every educated person should know. Thanks to the devoted work by the faculty and a good selection of students the Chicago undergraduate program for quite some time was successful in training young people to become "generalists," to give them a well-rounded liberal education.

In the following section, Husén (1991, p. 14), based on Ben-David et al. (1977), describes the "models that have been more or less emulated" in the world, not only in Europe and North America:

The Humboldtian "research university," where research and teaching were expected to interact right from the beginning of university studies. Students were to gain experiences from the frontiers of knowledge and how these frontiers were extended in order to be prepared as pioneers in their respective professional fields.

The British "residential model," the Oxbridge model, is built on close informal contacts between students and professors. Such contacts are considered to be as important for the development of young people as are the attendance of formal lectures and seminars and have at Oxbridge been formalized by tutorials.

The French model of "les grandes écoles" epitomized a state-steered meritocratic society, where professionals with a particular education are regarded as an exquisite elite. These institutions (where no research is conducted) are intellectually and socially highly selective.

The "Chicago model," developed by Hutchins, was a program with a strong liberal-arts orientation. The ideal was to make the student familiar with the thinking of leading personalities in the humanities, sciences and the social sciences and to promote his ability to pursue further studies on his own and to train him to be independent and critical in his study and thinking.

In spite of this analytic examination, Husén continues by pointing out four characteristics shared by the Western university:

It has made a more or less sharp distinction between theory and practice. It has put a premium on autonomy and aloofness to the extent of complete irrelevance. It has both socially and intellectually been an elitist institution. It has tried to be an "ivory tower," as an institution whose main purpose is to "seek the truth."

Finally, Husén polarizes the tendencies between "theoretical thinking and action" which are simultaneously the "typical modes of human behavior" (Morgenthau). This is similar to the way Paul Ricoeur contrasted universities of ideas and universities of function. "Practice tries to understand the empirical world by observing it but without changing it. Practice tries to interfere in the empirical world with the prime purpose to change it" (Husén 1991).

It should be pointed out that the classical university models include some that have a specifically national character (Ferrer Pi 1973). For example, Osman (1983) points out the Egyptian model, which is the result of Islamic traditions mixed with English and French prototypes.

It should also be noted that the struggle for teaching freedom in France during the post-Napoleonic restoration gave rise to an international type of Catholic university (Aigrain 1935), the oldest of which is the restored University of Louvain (1835), followed by others, such as Notre Dame and the Catholic

University of America in Washington, and the Catholic University of Chile (1888) in Latin America. This raises the question of religious affiliation, which was anticipated by the universities of the Protestant Reformation and the Catholic Counter Reformation of the 16th century. Thorens (1992) points out that individual academic liberties may not be compatible with the principles that each university sets for itself to determine its missions as part of its institutional autonomy. There is a danger that the university's creed and nature could be reduced to a religious character, lessening the mutual respect between the institution and its members.

University imperatives

Continuing these reflections on university models, Ricoeur (Drèze and Debelle 1968, prologue) declares that the modern university is pressed to complete its missions and functions with an awareness of three factors: critical, political, and flexibly national. He asserts that, from the point of view of autonomy, university institutions have fluctuated or still fluctuate between complete academic freedom and subservience to political and economic power. This results in the deterioration of the university's moral and scientific autonomy in the face of undue external pressures that prevent it from behaving according to its own nature.

Critical awareness must, above all, be rational and ethical to judge, for example, the effects of science on people and on society (Thorens 1992). However, at least at some times and in special circumstances, it has been confused with revolutionary actions that reject anything that currently exists, including the university itself. The movements of the 1960s and 70s showed the sometimes irrational criticism of students: the university is the establishment; it must go! But it would be necessary to study each case and situation to determine when critical awareness that has got out of hand corresponds to an institutional attitude, and when it was justifiably instigated by the teacher and student body.

Political awareness, a concept with a wide variety of meanings, is revealed in very different ways in universities in various parts of the world. In Latin America, for example, especially in the 60s and 70s, students remained faithful to a principle inherited from the Reform of Córdoba in 1918: politics as a great school and school as a greater politics. This tendency in political awareness in Latin America has been, and is, most obvious in public universities. Although some think this is good, for others, politicalization that does not always coincide with the missions, roles, and functions of the university is damaging.

In a world that is rapidly becoming international and at a time when large transnational companies have criteria affecting more than the purely economic and business arenas, it is foreseeable and praiseworthy that national awareness, without completely destroying the old criteria, reflects a new concept of national sovereignty. One of these concepts is the ecological awareness that future generations also have environmental rights.

In spite of the internationalist and transnationalist winds blowing in the world, universities in the sectors most subject to political and social, industrial and technological, commercial and economic dependence have risen in defence of the cultural values of each nation.

Whatever its present-day or future situation, it is the function of the university as an institution to establish its principles, its course, and its goals. Depending on its internal convictions, the university succeeds in its task of internal self-administration to serve the external world, the social environment surrounding it.

THE UNIVERSITY TOMORROW

◆

In 1987, the Director General of Unesco (Mayor 1987) asked the university world, "Can the present-day university still become an efficient institution? Or is it necessary to create another university or another institution to replace the university, which is overwhelmed and unable to recover?" However, "this question is not inspired by doubt, because universities have not denied their future, whatever difficulties and crises they must face."

Every topic dealt within this book arises from university reflections on the future of the institution of higher knowledge, a future that largely depends on them. "University members can be those who give rise to the positive changes in the university, and they can also act as their brake" (Carton 1983). For the former, "the university must be a source of imagination and innovation" (Ki-Zerbo 1991, p. 3).

The remainder of this book is divided into parts based on the distinction between the two meanings of university administration. Although separable, the two concepts are so closely linked they should be regarded as two parts of a whole. Serving the exterior world with quality, justice, efficacy, and pertinence depends on the internal organic arrangement of the university's parts, the structures, the quality of the university's corporate action, the availability of resources, and the suitable exercise of its functions or missions. Part II deals with these concepts: structures, quality, resources, and functions or missions. Part III looks at the service the university provides to the community through disseminating culture, university extension, the relations that the institution of higher knowledge establishes with its surroundings, and its foresight in relation to the future. Part IV, the Epilogue, deals with planning and self-evaluation.

PART II

◆

THE UNIVERSITY: WELL ADMINISTERED AND WELL ORGANIZED

ADMINISTRATIVE STRUCTURES

◆

From the beginning, the university as an institution determined its mode of operation, government, and direction because some form of "institutional response must follow quickly upon academic achievement if the intellectual movement is not to be dissipated" and "perpetuation and controlled development can only be gained through an institutional framework" (Cobban 1971). Cobban maintains that the University of Salerno (1213) was short-lived because of its "failure to develop a protective and cohesive organization to sustain its intellectual advance."

The medieval universities of Bologna and Paris both developed administrative structures governed by a rector to direct student life. The state also took part in running these institutions. The growing complexity of university structure gave rise to the University of Ingolstadt's (1450) use of a rector's council, a foretoken of the councils that exist today (d'Irsay 1933, vol. I; Aigrain 1949). Over time, the university's general organic structure has become considerably more complex and the exercise of authority more difficult (IAU 1967). The general organic structure includes the academic structure and how it interacts with national educational systems.

General organic structure

Comparative studies of most university organic structures reveal similarities that can be broken up vertically into areas or fields of activity and horizontally into levels of management and authority. Arranged thus, the university also established internal relations that were qualitatively greater than the sum of the parts of the total structure. Clark (1983, p. 36) states:

> Within institutions, we refer to the horizontally aligned units as sections; the vertical arrangements as tiers. Among institutions, the lateral separations are called sectors; the vertical,

hierarchies. Sections, tiers, sectors, and hierarchies appear in various forms and combinations in different countries, affecting a host of crucial matters.

To determine what and how many areas, tiers, or fields of diversified activity there should be and their mutual relations, the university distinguishes between its basic function, which is academic and all that that includes, and the area or sector that handles the inevitable economic and financial management that affects scientific activity. There can be other fields of activity, as is the case in many universities that look after the interests of individuals and groups in the university community.

Levels of authority are determined by the policies at the highest levels: by boards, superior councils, plenary sessions, university councils, congregations, or directive or executive councils. Other levels can or do exist related to the government and direction of each area or field of activity.

Academic structures

The vertical division into parts of the general organic structure determines the university's specific, characteristic area or field: the academic area (Calleja 1990).

Academic structure is related to the total concept of the university. These relations are concerned with all areas and all levels of authority and should serve the academic function because it is there that research, teaching, and educating are carried out every day. This determines the degree to which the university provides services to the social environment with responsible, aware attitudes of criticism, with a political sense of science and education, and with a vigorous national and international spirit that is simultaneously open and receptive.

The university's inherent and respectable institutional autonomy is established in academic rigour and expressed in the continuing practice of academic liberties.

The faculty

From the start, the university laid down the elements of its academic structure, and the concept of faculty grew from the "facultas artium" and the "facultas philosophica" of the 14th century. This led to the "facultas theologica," the "facultas juridica," and the "facultas medica."

The Latin "facultas" (authoritative ability) meant not only those who teach because they are able or "authorized" to do so, that is, the faculty, but also the structural element of academic administration, a meaning close to "school" or "faculté." "Collegium" (college, collège, Kollegium), which is of medieval origin, had and still has different meanings and relations to the university.

In many universities around the world, the academic structure is arranged in faculties named after the branches of science and the humanities or professions: human, social, biological, and technical (engineering). Another suggested method of classifying the sciences was that of Francis Bacon. He proposed dividing them according to the human faculties of imagination, memory, and reason, but it would be difficult to structure an institution on such vague criteria.

The "facultas philosophica," conceived by Kant in 1798 as both pure knowledge and in-depth knowledge of the sciences, became the structural core of the 19th-century German university. There could be no place for government intervention, as the "facultas" were the realm of the "academic liberties": *Lehrfreiheit* (liberty to teach) and *Lernfreiheit* (liberty to learn). The "facultas" were concerned with the historical sciences and rational knowledge. Others, secondary in Kant's mind, were the professional faculties of the medieval university: juridical, for the preservation of goods and property according to the law; medical, for the preservation of the body and health; and theological, which Fichte vainly wished to erase from the university.

The German thinkers believed that the French universities were being broken up into professional schools, and philosophy was being reduced to the status of a course in secondary schools.

In Germany, technical professions would be the concern of other educational institutions.

D'Alambert's *Encyclopedia* (1751–1765) considered the split between the arts and the sciences to be "experimental." North American universities, however, followed this scheme in the schools or colleges of arts and sciences. This influenced the type of university degrees, so that the traditional professions of the medieval period and the modern professions derived from the human and social sciences that had been part of the university's academic structure were left to other schools and colleges. England has largely remained faithful to the system of confederated colleges.

Departments and credits

The present-day division of universities in departments started in the 19th century. Sometimes this is combined with faculty structures and sometimes not.

The department as the academic unit resulted from pedagogical and curricular causes, professorial corporative causes, and other functional administrative and financial causes. Historically, James Marsh, president of the University of Vermont in 1826, wished to inaugurate a new era for the university curriculum. He proposed that the study programs of the college be divided into four parts and that students who were not interested in working toward a professional degree be permitted to do their studies in one of the four divisions or departments, according to each student's desires. In defence of his proposal, Marsh argued that "it is certainly best for one to get a part rather than attempt all with the certainty of universal failure."

Although Marsh's idea was not implemented in Vermont, Jacob Abbot, founder of Mount Vernon School in Boston in 1828, heard about it when the faculty of Amherst College prepared two reports, one in 1825 and the other in 1827. In the first, the professors reported some doubts expressed by Harvard, where there were complaints that, while science was making advances everywhere else, the colleges were stagnant "and in danger of being left far behind, in the rapid march of improvement." The second report proposed that students wishing to devote themselves to any language, specific scientific discipline, or new profession should be able to do so without having to cover a multicourse curriculum. Thomas Jefferson had a similar idea when he founded the University of Virginia in 1824 and divided it into eight single-discipline schools or departments: ancient languages, modern languages, mathematics, natural philosophy, anatomy and medicine, moral philosophy, and law (Rudolph 1965; Weymouth 1973).

This concept of structuring by discipline or profession spread to Cornell and Johns Hopkins in 1880 and Harvard in 1890, followed by Columbia, Yale, and Princeton. Professors concentrated on a pure discipline to be researched and taught to students who dedicated themselves to that subject, without aiming for a practical profession.

Gradually, the number of departments increased as scientific advances created new disciplines and existing ones were subdivided. Each department would have assistance for its individual development. The University of Chicago led the way in departmental structuring; besides having a great number of departments, it divided those it had created previously. This occurred toward the end of the 19th century, when the "university era" in North America blossomed and university degrees led to the academic professions (Rudolph 1965). However, a critical voice was soon heard. When Alfred North Whitehead arrived at Harvard as a professor in 1925, he complained about the "departmentalization that sterilizes," and exerted his influence to end, if possible, the positivist division of the university's departments (Whitehead 1964).

Whitehead's efforts were in vain, however. Departmentalization continued, as did its complement, the academic credit, that quantified the student's performance. This system was necessary for several reasons: the elective courses pioneered by Harvard under Eliot; the distinction between "majors" and "minors"; the fact students could take courses in different departments, schools, or colleges of the university or in other universities, now or later, in regular school periods, in two terms, or in summer school; and, in short, the curricular freedom that the North American university has sought.

Objections have been raised not only about the departments but also about the system of credits. Abraham Flexner (1930, p. 59) addressed this subject:

> Although Columbia is a flagrant, it is not by any means the only, offender. Fifteen "units" are required for admission to the Colleges of the University of Chicago, of which more than one-fourth (one, two, three, or four units) may be made up of stenography, typewriting, and bookkeeping — what a preparation for the intelligent use, cultural or professional, of four college years. Home economics and agriculture — as taught in high schools — are also "accepted." Now, to be frank, there is no more sense in "counting" stenography and bookkeeping towards college matriculation than there would be in counting manicuring, hair-bobbing, or toe-dancing. One has as much to do with intelligence and taste as another.

He later continues:

> With certain important exceptions...the colleges count points and units and credits — an abominable system, destructive of disinterested and protracted intellectual effort; any one of them could abolish it root and branch without notice.

However, fortunately,

> A few American colleges are endeavouring to break away from the absurd computation of degrees by arithmetical means and to encourage both concentration and scholarship.

> [In many institutions,] by one method or another the more earnest or better endowed students are able to escape the deadly lockstep of the classroom, the deadly grip of the unit system, and to focus their energies on a limited field in close contact with the more competent instructors.

On the other hand, Bereday (1973, p. 118) accepts that

> The American credit system has been much frowned on by European academicians, and they have profoundly criticized

its lack of theoretical justification. Who can equate immersion in Plato with the study of calculus, or, worse, with a course on preparation of morticians by assigning each a three-point credit value....

The somewhat clumsy system, the first valid attempt to establish automatic equivalence, permits the wide choices in shaping individual university careers. In Europe, Britain, France, and Sweden have begun experimenting in this direction.

Bodelle and Nicolaon (1986) affirm that the "system of credits seems to the French students to be very similar to the units of value."

Divisions and laboratories

In addition to the academic structures of faculties, which sometimes join to form divisions, departments, or a combination of both, other structures emerged. This started in Gottingen in 1737, the beginning of the modern university (d'Irsay 1933). Gottingen had novel teaching and research aids: an observatory and laboratories for the natural sciences; dissection rooms, anatomical collections, a surgical amphitheatre, and a pharmacy for medical education; and a botanic garden. Once these innovations were adopted by universities worldwide, more complex general and academic structures arose, along with imaginative methods of administration. Laboratories, thought by Bacon to be places for work and learning and later occasionally constituting part of departments in the 19th century, more recently began to need substantial resources and investments.

Institutes and centres

Institutes have a more recent history. The University of Berlin, founded in 1810, was closest to the contemporary concept of an institute. Von Humboldt called them *Hilfs-Instituten* (auxiliary institutes). An institute was oriented more toward research than teaching, but was part of the university. "Humboldt's great plan," said Prussia's Wilhelm II in 1910, "in addition to the Academy of Sciences and the University, requires research institutes that are independent but integrate the entire scientific organization" of the university.

Nowadays, however, institutes vary widely. They may be university hospitals, farms and experimental agricultural plants, and even other university units devoted to research that goes beyond the limits of a single discipline or profession and includes fields of interdisciplinary work for the study and solution of problems such as public housing and energy sources. The teaching offered in institutes is customarily linked to research, and the students are generally in graduate programs. Institutes do not normally grant degrees but certify to faculties or departments that the students have done the required work.

Institutes possess a certain autonomy in relation to the university. They have their own rules and financial and administrative function. They even have legal recognition and independent income. In certain cases, they work with a fixed staff or personnel hired for specific projects undertaken in cooperation with public and private entities. The institute can be like a research extension of the faculty or department, but it maintains relative independence.

A more recent, postwar concept is that of a centre that does not do as intensive research work as an institute but regularizes certain teaching activities in a more informal educational setting. Centres are connected with such industries as computer and information systems and can offer services outside the university. It is not unusual for centres to have as much independence as institutes.

In reference to laboratories, institutes, centres, and other similar entities, Ikenberry and Friedman (1972, p. *ix*) maintain that

> Following World War II, some institutions, particularly the large, complex universities began to move beyond departments...[and] these new organizations employed professional personnel with similar if not identical qualifications; many were very clearly engaged in the work of the academy — teaching, research, or service.

In other obvious ways, however, they were quite different. They didn't focus on a single discipline, as did departments. Funding tended to come principally from grants and contracts with foundations, governments, businesses, or industries, and not from the traditional sources. And there seemed to be a tentativeness to the whole enterprise — less permanence of programs, staff, budget, and other resources than one tended to expect in departments.

The new structures proved to be attractive to faculty members, administrators, and donors. Once a minor and generally insignificant appendage, institutes grew in number and scope of operations in universities and colleges until they controlled a significant segment of the programs and resources at many institutions and rivaled departments in numbers. As they multiplied, they tended frequently to become centres of controversy. Split appointments, different budget constraints, different policies, and different values widened the gulf between departments and institutes on many campuses. In short, the data suggest that the strength of the departments and disciplines is inversely related to the power and autonomy of institutes.

Considerations and conclusions

Universities use flexible levels of management to create academic structures. Institutes and centres are part of the university and are integrated in various ways. Are they part of the university or in the university? Do they belong to the university simply because they are close to it? This raises the question of what is the university as an institutional unit in contrast to the "multi-university" (Kerr 1963).

Critical to university administration is the problem of each university's successful design of its general organic structure. This should be simple and sufficient in its elements, flexible and effective in its actions, and easily intelligible so that the structure responds to the ideal of every bureaucracy: to increase efficiency to the highest possible level and reduce to a minimum the inconveniences and annoyances arising in any type of organization.

One question is that of the number of authority figures and their positions, and whether individuals or councils should be the decision-makers. Some universities have a collegial government, but whatever the structure the aim should be to avoid unnecessary delays in making and carrying out decisions. This occurs when decisions depend unnecessarily on several councils, committees, or chains of command.

There is often a problem over the proportion of academic to lay members in councils and their affiliations — the university's founding body, the government, or private enterprise. As the assignment of functions is equally difficult, the three important characteristics needed for the university to function normally must be applied: sufficient simplicity in structure, flexibility, and clarity in design.

Universities should distinguish between legislated cogovernment and the academic and scientific comanagement of researchers, professors, and students. Successful pedagogical systems are ones propitious to cooperation between research and teaching.

The many additions that have swollen the university's academic structures and hence its general structure, the increasing interest in "problem-oriented programs" and service to the community, the continuing interest in interdisciplinary work as well as a desire for innovation explain the worldwide trend toward new structural concepts of the university. Interdisciplinarity began in the French reform of 1968 and 1969 with the Unités d'enseignement et recherche (UER) at the same time as departmentalization. Twenty years later, the question still is whether the UER, or the Unités de formation et recherche (UFR), are the same as departments, or if they are part of a new structural element (Boumard et al. 1987).

Among the university's recent interdisciplinary academic structures, such as in Bochum, Germany, Sussex, England (CERI 1970), or Norway, there are three main groups. The first is the professional–entrepreneurial, in which students attend an institute, centre, or laboratory that prepares them for practical work, because academic preparation is not enough. Second, the entrepreneurial and social structure has similar aims. Students spend time in work situations, in family, municipal, or regional community groups, or in different organizations in political and social life. Finally, there is the pragmatic structure or practice, which prepares the student to study and solve problems affecting society, such as collective behaviour, life and health, or habitat, which covers housing, relations, communications, and the environment.

In every case, it is worth remembering the original sense of the word university. Rashdall (1936, vol. I, p. 4) says:

> The notion that a university means a "universitas facultatum" — a school in which all the faculties or branches or knowledge are represented — has, indeed, long since disappeared from the pages of professed historians; but it is still persistently foisted upon the public by writers with whom history is subordinate to what may be called intellectual edification. However imposing and stimulating may be the conception of an institution for the teaching or for the cultivation of universal knowledge, however imperative the necessity of such an institution in modern times, it is one which can gain little support from the facts of history. A glance into any collection of medieval documents reveals the fact that the word "university" means merely a number, a plurality, an aggregate of persons.

The university should not be defined quantitatively by the number of faculties, departments, laboratories, institutes, centres, or programs it offers nor by the number of areas of knowledge or professions it covers. It should be defined qualitatively by the clarity of its missions, its vigour in carrying out its functions, and the roles that win it recognition and esteem. The fact that, today, there are specialized university institutions does not reduce the prestige of those with a wide academic spectrum.

Given the special character of the United Nations University, which is less oriented to the systematic advance of the sciences and professions than to the pressing problems of humanity, its academic structure presents its own difficulties. The sciences and academic disciplines are classified like the professions. This is not true of the presentation, study, and solution of the problems afflicting the world.

National higher education systems

García Garrido (1992, p. 13) writes:

> It is well-known that the national systems of education were set up as the consequence of two important historic circumstances, which were in turn closely related: the coming of the Industrial Age and the development of the Nation-State as a determining political structure. Until that moment, which occurs at regular intervals in most countries, education had only been familiar with institutionalized forms of a limited range which also lacked a link to each other. Education, even though it had individually formalized or systematized institutions as a support, lacked a global *system* to unite them, to insert them in a coherent and harmonic whole. It was like a planetary chaos which lacked a star around which the planets could organize themselves in order to form a real system. That star, without a doubt, was the Nation-State. The institutions, which until then had been scattered and roving, had to find their definitive orbit, their own space, their close link within a system that would make collisions impossible and not leave dead space.
>
> For most of the Western world, the detonator that set off the process was the French Revolution. Nevertheless, it should not be forgotten that in some countries — England, for instance — things evolved differently, perhaps with less pomp and vehemence, perhaps more gradually, but with equal determination, for deep down, it was the birth of a new age — the Industrial Age — which spurred on the change in some countries as well as in others.
>
> From the very beginning of the 19th century, we can observe the determined will of the new nations to construct their own school systems. From that time, Ministries of Education or political–administrative units of a similar character began to emerge in different countries. At first, the educational institutions did not display an excessively all-embracing interest. However, the interest would increase throughout the 19th

century, it would rise sharply after the beginning of the 20th century, and it would become very strong, even overwhelming, after World War II.

Garrido continues by saying that since the "educational system...was the most prominent cultural product of the Nation-State, it has been simultaneously used by it as an instrument of its stability and development...and [has] begun to highlight national aspects above, and even at the cost of, the peculiarities that are particular to the underlying communities." But while the "tendency to nationalization" has been so pronounced, there has also been a "growing display of uneasiness because of the size acquired by the national systems of education." The system has, therefore, probably grown to its maximum size and will start automatically to reduce (García Garrido 1984).

Clark (1983, p. 1) believes that

National systems of higher education gather together a good share of those individuals who develop and disseminate the intellectual heritage of the world. Important through the centuries in training professionals and political elites, these centres of knowledge, growing many times over and multiplying their activities, occupy an ever more crucial place in the 20th century. Yet we fail to do them justice. For a long time scholars did not take seriously the province of their own commitment. While disciplined perspectives developed on the economy, the polity, and such realms as the social-class system, only occasional comments by professors or retired rectors were mustered on the workings of systems of higher learning. After 1960, problems of expansion and discontent elicited much public and scholarly attention, but in ways that were fragmented and fragile. The research agenda centred on immediate issues and episodes as government and other patrons sought answers to problems of the day. The dramatic events of student political action drew much comment but left behind little serious literature. Notable, as attention freshened, were the scholars with new perspectives who came into the study of higher education in many countries, but all too briefly and soon to wander away: organizational theorists to gaze awhile upon the odd ways of universities and then return to the business firm; political scientists to assemble some essays on

government and higher education and then go back to traditional political institutions; economists to measure some
inputs and outputs and speculate on benefits and costs and
then find other topics for their tools; sociologists to absorb
education in the study of stratification and forget about the
rest. In addition, much research has been limited to a single
country, but then freely used to assert what the academic life
is like everywhere. Continuing *comparative* analysis has been
left to a few. Thus, while measurably richer in ideas and facts,
the emerging serious literature on higher education leaves
much to be desired.

Clark divides the field of national systems of higher education horizontally and vertically, as we did university structures,
to begin a comparative study. Again the question of the exercise
of authority is raised.

Systems and authority

Starting at the bottom, the first unit in the academic structure of
educational institutions is the faculty, then the department, laboratories, institutes, centres, and others. The second institutional
level consists of universities and other institutions in postsecondary education. The third level, which is less defined because it is
very recent, corresponds to multicampus, confederated layouts,
where the institutions either have a central government or enjoy
relative independence and autonomy. The fourth level is found
in government and state spheres of higher education policy.
Finally, there is a growing transnational or international level that
consists of agreements made by several countries for educational
purposes, such as the programs of COMETT, ERASMUS, LIN-
GUA, FORCE, and TEMPUS promoted by the European Community. Although neither the Treaty of Rome nor the Single
European Act specifically mention education, there have been
community-level movements oriented especially toward higher
education (EC 1991).

The ways of exercising authority vary because of the difference between authority based on knowledge, which is stable and
can be increased by scientific mastery, and directive, administrative, or governing authority, which depends on the result of

elections or appointments that invest authority for temporary, previously agreed-upon periods of time. Bocheński (1979) calls the first kind of authority "epistemological" and the second "deontological." Although both types of authority should be agreed upon at all levels, epistemological authority, which dominates the lower levels, contrasts with deontological authority, which has greater control in the upper levels (see Weber 1967).

Indeed, at the first level it is clear that authority is based on knowledge. Professors, because of their scientific and pedagogical quality, have a recognized, accepted command over their students and colleagues. There is a mutual recognition because each professor is protected in his or her field by the academic freedom to teach and do research, to criticize, to be creative, and to contribute personally to the advance of knowledge. It has been like this since the origin of universities, and it is or should be like this today because the basis for autonomy lies in the power of knowledge and the freedom of the thinking spirit. Even at this level there should be room for direction, which is necessary even in "chair-based" systems and even more so in departmentalized and collegiate systems. For this reason there are deans of faculties and schools, and directors of departments, institutes, and centres.

At the second, institutional level, there should be balanced agreements between the epistemological authority, which deals with the everyday task of the academic structure, and the deontological or bureaucratic authority of the institution's general structure. There should also be balance between the educational institution and the pre-existing entity from which it arose: the state, business enterprises (nowadays more frequently the case), churches and religious denominations, or private or social initiative, because, whatever the founding organization, it must respect the university's inherent autonomy.

There are different degrees of bureaucratization of higher educational institutions depending on the relative positions of the deontological authority and the epistemological authority. In addition, the organic structures of the university organization and government can influence the type of authority that is dominant. This can depend on the people involved and whether there is a collegiate form through councils with a well-thought out composition.

As for the university's external relations with its originating source, at least three situations can be outlined. The first is that of universities founded by a stable entity, in which case it is customary to have a council rather than a governing body, to which people from both the founding entity and from the university belong. In the medieval university, a key figure in this link was the chancellor.

Another situation is that of trusteeship, overseership, or regentship, which, following the English tradition, was established at Harvard (1642) when the Massachusetts legislature gave the recently created college a board of overseers with "full power and authority to make and establish all such orders, Statutes and constitutions as they shall see necessary." Later, in the state universities created in the United States in the 19th century, "a governing board of externally chosen non-academic citizens" became the usual way in which the university conceived its authority as "legitimately public and yet largely autonomous" (Clark 1983). Epstein (cited in Clark 1983, p. 117) stated that "the board exercises authority in the name of the people of the state, but it is not as directly responsible to the will of the people as are governors and legislators. And it is not, in principle, as directly responsive to governors as are most state agencies." The system of trustees, which is typical of North American universities "has served as an instrument of institutional aggrandizement, linking the interests of specific constituencies and the participation of influential citizens, generally from business, to the welfare of the individual college or university." Nevertheless, the influence of the trustees "has varied across US enterprises, and has shifted over time as first administrative authority and then faculty control was strengthened. Its influence has also become problematic...as state and national governments have increased their supervision. In contrast, the period since 1960 has seen trusteeship grow in Latin American systems, particularly in private universities.... Notably, some of the non-trustee systems of the European continent began in the 1970s to search for quasi-trustee ways of associating outsiders with institutions...to relate higher education with society" (Clark 1983).

The third situation is that of institutions set up by individuals, family groups, or groups of citizens. These universities develop their institutionality themselves using any of the methods that seem appropriate.

At the third, multicampus level of authority, the three situations described can repeat themselves. The trustees' influence can be expanded, divided, or even reduced in direct relation to the number of campuses in a particular university group.

The fourth level, that of political, public, and governmental spheres, depends on the historical relation in each country between the state and education in general and higher education in particular; the concept of education as a public service; the status of a university professor or director in terms of the law; and the means of financing. This is reflected in Ricoeur's poles: "idea" and "function." However, in practical terms, there are at least three ways of distributing deontological authority.

In most European countries, there are carefully balanced relations between faculties or collegiate groups that exercise their intellectual power and the official bureaucracy of the ministry of education or other ministries and state agencies. This is the formula in France, Spain, and Italy and originates in the Napoleonic tradition. It reached its extreme in the USSR after the October Revolution and more so after World War II under the Communist Party. Germany's case is different because of the political, federated organization of the states and because of the greater awareness of the academic freedom to teach and learn: Lehrfreiheit and Lernfreiheit. As a whole, the continental system has a very weak concept of institutional autonomy.

The British style is very different as the epistemological authority of faculties has been combined with a very reduced influence from trustees and administrators. Each college and university sets up its own norms. In addition, as professors never form part of the bureaucracy, it is not possible to speak of a formally constructed system at the national level. During the 1960s and 70s, a Department of Education was developed with powers similar to those of ministries on the continent. The University Grants Council (UGC) — nowadays the University Funding Council (UFC) — was created, and the legislature and upper agencies of the executive branch began to establish higher education policies. "With this trust, the power contest moves toward the European mode of professors versus the state apparatus" (Clark 1983).

Unlike the British style, in North America the power of the trustees over the university is much stronger, as is that of university administrators over the authority of the faculty. As stated by Clark (1983), this is because

> The mechanism of the chartered corporation, used historically by many hundreds of independently established units, meant separate boards of trustees, each fully in charge of its own institution, and, sooner or later, creating its own administrative staff, from president to assistant dean, to "run" the place. With faculty authority developing late, largely in the 20th century, and thus within the context of the established powers of trustee and administrators, the faculty forms of personal and collegial authority did not achieve the influence they had in Europe and British modes.... The emergent departmental form both dampened personal authority and had to blend the internal collegiality of the department with its place in a larger structure that was decidedly more bureaucratic than that found within the European and British modes.... No national bureau had an important role and the private institutions, in the 19th century, became entirely independent of state officials; the leading public institutions had their own boards of control and chartered autonomy.

With similar criteria, García Garrido (1992) classified education systems according to degree of centralization and decentralization. He considered France

> The clearest model of educational centralization operating in a country with a democratic system of government, [in]

countries of Southern Europe [Italy], in spite of the boom
experienced recently by the regions and the regional administrations [Portugal, Greece, and Spain].

Garrido also looks at the countries that were "the heirs of
Communist centralism"; the Arab countries in which "the
administration...is centralized and is endowed with overly large
powers" (Unesco 1978); the Latin American countries, which are
influenced by the Napoleonic tradition; and some of the new
countries in Asia and Africa.

Calleja (1990, p. 31) clearly described situations that afflict
centralized systems, their consequences, and possible solutions:

> Since bureaucracies are frequently based on a mentality of
> control and confrontation between the individual and the
> Administration, such growth has in many cases produced even
> greater inoperativeness. Social energies are lost in the zeal for
> suspicion, which ought to be replaced by an attitude of coop-
> eration. The experiences resulting from bureaucratic reduc-
> tion carried out in this line by certain countries shows the
> feasibility and efficiency of this new approach.

> The design of the organizational structures and the orientation
> of their functioning must go from a reference based on distrust
> to one backing the person and based on trust. It is not a
> question of appealing to all citizens to be just and beneficent.
> It has to do with something more serious and realistic: the
> certainty that all capacity for innovation and adaptation flows
> from free, responsible persons. If, instead of placing all types
> of obstacles to block their emerging vitality, the fields of
> community action are left open and a strategy of incentives
> and help is formulated, it is immediately confirmed that
> human freedom is the original, irreplaceable creative force.
> Otherwise, the neatness of the motives that mutually neutral-
> ize each other is upset, triggering conformism and the absence
> of social courage.

The government of education systems in countries with a
similar political tradition has a regionalized or federative nature:
Switzerland, Germany, Canada, and Australia. The United
Kingdom, which according to García Garrido (1992) has a very
particular system of "difficult, careful balance," and the United

States with its "varied organization from the base" are also in this tradition. Finally, García Garrido mentions the education systems with a decentralized tendency, such as those of Austria and Japan, the "linguistic regionalization" of Belgium, and the "Nordic proposals" of Sweden, Denmark, and Finland.

CONDITIONS OF UNIVERSITY CORPORATE ACTION

◆

Some of the topics dealt with in this section could be applied to the levels of authority into which national higher education systems have been divided. However, my intention here is to discuss the conditions of corporate action so that the university can be governed in the most effective way.

The administrative structures are the visible face of the university. They are not an end unto themselves no matter how well described they are in statutes and regulations or how beautifully drawn in catalogues and guides. They should be conceived of entirely in terms of the effective action expected from the corporate nature of the institution of higher knowledge. Today, this is necessary for fair competition.

At the same time, effective action depends on the coordinated action of the parts into which the university is divided for functional reasons. Thus, as has already been said, the horizontal division is by levels and the vertical is by sectors. This should result in a true "com-position" of coinciding efforts, and not an anarchic "dis-position" in which intentions and directions differ. Far from strengthening the institution's natural autonomy, this would make it vulnerable to the heteronomy of external pressures. We must, therefore, examine the links that help the university's institutional cohesion (Perkins 1967) and their participation in the whole.

Links for internal cohesion

Among the links for internal cohesion is, of course, the university's guiding principles to achieve its goals or mission. They are a "prima lex" constitution because the noble initiatives that created the universities come from humanity's great ethical and social values, and the university institution integrates them with its heritage and future directions. The university maps out its own course.

It is argued that the university should not have any principles, since this would be opposed to individual academic liberties and to the rights of conscience and opinion. This does not allow for the university, as an institution, to exercise its autonomous right to determine its own principles. It is a question of mutual respect: that of the university not to force its principles on its members, and that of those who freely join the university knowing its principles. Self-decision, inspiration, directionality, or orientation are valid, legitimate concepts that the university wished to have of humanity, of science and of service to society, although it is each institution's duty to be, ontologically speaking, first a university and, later, an inspiration. If it were otherwise, it would do poor service to the principles it upholds.

These principles, in turn, should inspire the statutes that, together with the operational regulations, form another link of internal cohesion. The principles must take into account the legal, political, and social rules of the university's environment and be able to criticize them, where necessary, as the university is not only a reflection of society but also sets an ethical standard.

There must be a delicate balance between academic liberties and the proposal for the ruling principles of the university institution. Without such guidelines, however, the university would sail adrift according to the whims of the helmsman on duty.

Participation

Given the university's corporate nature, participation is a necessary condition for effective, coordinated action. As the word indicates, participation means to take part in the comanagement of all the diverse university activities. Participation implies sharing, not only distributing duties and responsibilities.

Participation can thus be understood in both the wide, general sense of nonformal or informal participation, and participation that is formally structured through the sectors and collegiate bodies of government. The two types of authority, epistemological and deontological, come together but in different proportions for academic comanagement and cogovernment. The former is more vital the greater the participation permitted by the pedagogical, teaching, and research methods that the university adopts and develops in its everyday life. Cogovernment is, in most cases, reduced to precise, concrete acts of deontological authority in the different levels of educational systems and in the levels of the university's "general structure" and "academic structure."

There are three major problem areas with the university's government or cogovernment: the make-up of councils in those universities governed by the principle of collegiality, the character of participation and expansion, and the system chosen for making decisions.

The make-up of councils

The two types of authority, epistemological and deontological, converge in a scientific or technical criterion for membership. It is hoped that those who sit on councils are people knowledgeable about the issues and capable of knowing about other problems the council might eventually have to deal with.

Besides this fundamental criterion, others usually taken into consideration are the juridical criterion, which determines who ought to be a member, ex officio, of the council; those with professional representation, such as professors or students; those who should be members for social reasons, such as lay members; and those who participate because of continuity in government policies, such as the predecessor or successor in some post. Thus, a council does not usually re-elect all its members at a given time.

The nature of participation

In a council, the nature of participation can be divided into the merely representative participation of those who, for example, elected the representatives and participatory participation, which is not limited to the interests of one group and extends to looking after the common interests of the entire university institution. Carter (1980, p. 106) expresses the distinction in the following way:

> The question of "who should participate in the government of a higher education institution?" can be answered in two quite different ways, one concerned with the "interests" of the participants and the other with their "contribution."

After drawing up an extensive list of possible groups that could provide "interests" and "contributions" to a university council, Carter (1980) states:

> Even allowing for the possibility that one member could represent several interests...,it is difficult to see how a satisfactory governing body could be created from so many interests. Some would require several representatives.... Considerations of balance would then require several representatives under other heads, and the total would rise to a hundred or more. With a very large governing body, the initiating power tends to pass to unacknowledged groups of officers meeting in private. This produces a divergence...between the formal and the informal structure of government, which eventually may lead to misunderstanding, suspicion and conflict.

After these well thought out remarks, Carter limits the range "of those with evident competence to make a significant contribution to the decisions to be made" to

> Educationalists, including experienced teachers and administrators from the institution itself, from other similar places, and from the school system.... Educated men and women, and

especially those who are brought into contact with higher education because of their interest in general cultural matters, or as employers of graduates, or as users of research or others services.... Managers who can advise on the management of the institution's affairs.... To a limited extent, students, since (despite their lack of experience) they may have relevant things to say about the needs and aspirations of their successors.

Carter concludes:

Any structure of government will evidently be a compromise, but, given the danger of producing an unworkably large Council, it seems best to give the principle of competence priority over that of representativeness. Even so, there are problems of finding appropriate "constituencies" to appoint those who serve. Members of local authorities, for instance, are "representative citizens" only in a special sense: they are representative members of the group of those citizens who are prepared to engage in political activity at a local level. Similarly, students appointed to governing bodies may not be representative of the majority of students, who opt out of the political process; there has sometimes been a heavy over-representation of extreme left-wing groups. Any scheme of government must, if it is to be plausible, do its best to solve this problem of "constituencies."

Decision-making

There is frequently a difference here between participation that is informative, consultative, and decisive. It remains to find out where and how this process of expansion of participation comes about in the university's organic composition, and if it is complete. If not, then we are referring to decision-making.

This matter is delicate and can lead to conflict as deciding is the turning point in the process of reflection and maturation of reasons and arguments. After the decision is made, there is a gradual spreading, carrying out, and supervision of the subsequent executive acts.

Clark (1983, p. 132) comments:

"Decision" is increasingly a weak concept for describing aptly the flux of activities that engage officials, even on the top rungs. Those normally described as decision makers or as authorities, in public office, for example, "recommend, advise, confer, draw up budgets, testify, develop plans, write guidelines, report, supervise, propose legislation, assist, meet, argue, train, consult" — but *decide*? Decisions typically take shape gradually, without the formality of agenda, deliberation, and choice. With numerous problems and issues to be dealt with simultaneously and over a protracted period of time, such small steps as writing a memo or editing the draft of a regulation, each with seemingly small consequences, gradually foreclose alternative courses of action and imperceptibly produce a choice. Such accretion occurs particularly when there is a wide horizontal dispersion of responsibility combined with a vertical division of authority. The balkanized authority of the academic system provides a setting in which authority is rarely pinpointed in specific persons or found in clear-cut policy actions.

The distinction between informal participation and formal authority runs through Clark's thesis. The principles of the university and its future planning should come into play because they are guidelines that determine how the decisions will be carried out. In every case, there is the problem of whether to arrive at these decisions through votes or opinions, or by consensus. In the first case, once the decision has been discussed and it has been verified that the needed quorum is present, it is then agreed what proportion of votes are needed to carry a decision and who is qualified to vote. With consensus, however, there is an attempt to reach harmonious agreement in the governing body even if unanimous agreement cannot be reached. Consensus runs on common persuasion whenever possible, and not the imposition of the majority point of view over minority points of view. It is based on the principle that the presiding person is "primus inter pares"; the office enables the director to sound out and lead the different thoughts of the "equals" to a final decision. Concerning this, Brown (1982, p. 106) says:

> Collegiality requires...that legitimate acts be identified with the participation of all members of the collegium. Action is not determined by a vote in the ordinary sense; it is the outcome

of an emerging consensus that may be formalized by a vote. Representation denies most members their collegial right to speak; and on matters of academic policy, one individual cannot commit others.

The distinction between the two methods is clear, but carrying out either can entail undeniable difficulties. For this reason, there is considerable research on how to obtain consensus (Sasaki 1981) in contrast to obtaining a majority of votes, which is quite well covered by the usual practices in representative and participatory democracies. In addition, research has been conducted on the advantages and disadvantages of one or the other method for making decisions.

Consensus usually stimulates more discussion of the issue to clarify it; on the other hand, a majority vote is centred on the moment of decision, which is hardly the point for reflecting and discussing. Consensus tends to unite, whereas the triumph of the majority over the minority creates confrontations that will make subsequent execution more difficult.

Beckmeier and Neusel (1990) describe the majority vote as "behaviourist," accentuating the behaviour of those who decide each case; consensus takes into consideration the fact that the moment of the decision is only a single point in a process involving objective reasons and circumstances. However, both attitudes are compatible and fit together.

Consensus requires the previous development of a common business culture, or university culture, in our case, that is open and comprehensive, that sets the scene so that all can concede something for the sake of obtaining a goal and the institution's progress. The procedure for consensus makes everyone more willing to accept joint responsibility in decisions that for some are not ideal; it is better to share the risk that is an inevitable consequence of every decision (Ouchi 1982, p. 54).

Whatever the method, lack of knowledge concerning the proper nature of university administration leads to decision-making that is usually blurred with theories and practices that come from politics, ideologies, emotional attitudes, and partisanship, especially if the composition of the university councils is influenced by external compromises and less fitting ambitions than the academic nature that should distinguish them.

Moncada (1971) comments that, with only a few exceptions, universities do not show the same degree of concern about the efficiency of decision-making as businesses. Because of competition in the market, business enterprises are more accustomed to making quick decisions. In contrast, university directors are not normally very bold administrators. They look with disdain on everything that comes from dynamic business practice; they teach it but do not practice it. Holding firmly to their principles, they tend to postpone the discomfort of making urgent decisions, and they entertain themselves with prolonged teleological discussions; or, faithful to the dictates of the discipline, science, or profession they master and prefer, they break up into factions, putting aside the interests of the institution as a whole. Moncada (1971) cites Corson (1968) who affirms that decision-making in the university becomes complicated due to the exclusive fondness of directors and professors for their preferred discipline; this is less likely to occur among business people.

Finally, cogovernment is frequently understood as the representation of so-called university bodies in the councils that direct the institution; these bodies include professors, students, graduates, and, in some cases, support personnel. This scenario is typical in Latin American universities. It originated in the Reform of Córdoba, Argentina, in 1918, which conceived of the university corporation or community as a "republic of equals." Its immediate antecedents lay in the First Congress of Students that took place in Montevideo, Uruguay, in 1908. In the Reform, autonomy was conceived of as being founded on the political principle of democracy and not on the freedom of the thinking spirit, the power of intellectual knowledge, or the exercise of the academic freedom to teach and learn (Tunnermann 1979; Delich 1991; Todd Pérez 1991).

This type of thinking did not include the benefits to the university of academic and corporate comanagement by professors and students as, for example, in the union of teaching and research (the latter was of little concern to the reformers of 1918). This led to severe struggles for a type of cogovernment more oriented to obtaining purely administrative power. The confrontation between members of the university has prevented them from achieving the university's real self-government, which is the product of true participation. Instead it has led in many cases to the university's "nongovernment," which has resulted from submitting the process of decision-making — not to the rationality of consensus but to the randomness of majority vote as in participatory and representative democracies. In this respect, without directly alluding to Latin America, García Garrido (1992, p. 237) notes:

> With the desire to serve democratic ideals effectively, schools have tried to incorporate typical characteristics of democratic functioning: assemblies, meetings per section or group, participation in the schools' government, control of management, votes, elections, looking at contrasting points of view, etc. In this way, educational systems should be called "democratist."

There is no reason to confuse educational activity with political activity, although both need mutual support. The case of Africa is similar as Taiwo (1991, p. 9) writes:

> By far the most striking reform that has taken place in university administration in Africa today is the democratization of the traditional committee system employed by universities world-over for university governance. It is satisfying to note that inputs are today sought from the "grassroots" in the governance of many African universities. This involves not only the staff but also the students. For example, at Ife as in most Nigerian universities and in Lesotho, Swaziland and Botswana, the recruitment, review and promotions of academic staff are initiated from (and in most cases by) academic departments/units within the universities. And not only this, aggrieved staff members have avenues for airing their complaints. It is significant to note that this privilege is not restricted only to members of staff in African universities; students, as a right, in their capacity as members of the university community, serve on various university commit-

tees. The story is even carried a little further in Botswana where student representatives serve on the university Senate, the highest academic organ of any university. This story is also true of [other] universities in Southern Africa.

Concerning Poland, Wierzbowski (1988) says:

For over 20 years we may observe a stronger or weaker pressure of students to be allowed to participate in the management of universities. Students are intent on getting a portion of the powers exercised by rectors (chancellors, presidents) and deans. In some countries students have been granted some powers and admitted to participation in the management of universities. In others, students are still treated like school pupils. A lot depends on the tradition of universities, the political climate, the average age and the economic situation of students.

All this relates to the day-time students, who are most active at universities, usually politically very radical and unstable. Recent years have changed the role of universities. As a result of this, the system of management of universities is again entering a period of transition. The diminishing role of government subsidies in the universities' budgets requires a more active role in the economy, by closer ties with industry. To achieve this, the management of universities must shift to a model closer to the management of a commercial corporation, leaving traditional models of governing universities behind. Also, the idea of permanent education changes the image of average university students. More postgraduate students are admitted to the universities. They are older and more experienced. Their needs and expectations are different.

This changed situation of universities creates a new challenge to the system of university management. It creates a contradiction between the requirements of efficiency and the expectations of students.

On the issue of student participation in the cogovernment of the universities and academic comanagement, no one has the last word. The different modes and experiences are very particular.

RESOURCES

◆

Corporative, participatory action depends on the resources available to the university, including institutional organization with the general organic structure and the academic structure as its basis. This efficiency, in turn, depends on a normal functioning in which human resources (directors, professors, students, and support personnel) and material resources play a fundamental role.

Some historic illustrations will point up the origin of the university's human resources and its traditional functions, and the qualities the university nowadays expects in its professors, students, and support personnel.

Human resources

Human resources can be divided into several groups, the first of which is the directorial resources, with the rector at the head. There was no such figure to restrict the free activity of maestros and students in the 12th and 13th centuries when spontaneous university groups arose. However, since they were professional associations, as soon as universities took on an institutional form, some type of deontological authority became indispensable. Rashdall (1936, vol. I, p. 162) describes the origins of Bologna:

> The title of rector was one which only began to be applied to various civic magistrates and officers of guilds after the revival of Roman law studies in the 12th century. It was a term commonly used as the Latin equivalent of the Italian "podestà," to denote the elected chief magistrate or dictator of a Lombard town. It was also used of the head of a whole federation of cities, or of the head of a single guild. In the guilds the term rector is especially employed where the society was placed under the government of a single head, instead of (as was frequently the case) under a plurality of "consules" or other officers. All the associations of the word suggest a concentration of corporate power in the hands of a single

individual. From the guilds the expression was borrowed by the universities, as it had been borrowed by the guilds from the constitutions of the towns. The same was the case with the university "consiliarii," who are first heard of in 1224. In fact, the whole organization of the university was exactly parallel to that of the guilds, of which it formed merely a particular variety; the organization of the guilds themselves was in Italy largely a reproduction of the municipal organization of the cities. The guild, whether of scholars or of members of a political party or a particular trade, was a civic state in miniature, a "civitas in civitate."

Concerning the rector's functions:

The jurisdiction of the rector was in the main derived from the statutes voluntarily enacted by the members, and from that formidable oath of obedience to them and to himself,... [and] at the same time the rectorship was from the first looked upon as something more than the mere presidency of a private society.

In other words, the rector was considered the "caput universitatis," or the head of the corporation as the idea contained in Roman law was understood and applied to guilds, but with little or no power over academic affairs, that is, no epistemological authority.

At Oxford, the rector was, strictly speaking, the chancellor who served as the head of the university and represented local ecclesiastical power. In Paris, he began as a mere guardian of order among the "nationes" (Murray 1982). In the *Seven Divisions* or legal codes of Alfonso X, the Wise (1843), which according to d'Irsay (1933, vol. I) contain the oldest university legislation, the existence of a rector, who on many occasions is a student, is mandated together with an academic authority, as in Salamanca: the "maestrescuela" or schoolmaster. However, this dual figure disappeared in 1422, and the rector also became the highest authority in the academy, with the exception of certain functions that remained with the chancellor or "cancelario" (Rodríguez Cruz 1975).

Rashdall (1936, vol. I, p. 326) and Verger (1973) state that deans date from 1264 at the University of Paris:

At first the deans appear to act side by side with the rector rather than in obedience to his authority; though from the first the initiative and superior importance of the rector is plain enough. During the heat of the great conflict with the mendicants (1250–60) which contributed so much to develop the importance of the rectorship, we hear of no disputes on this head. When the tie of a common enmity was removed, the superior faculties seem to have awaked to the fact that they were falling under the authority of an official not elected by themselves.

Over time new components of the university's general and academic structures were created to meet the demands of the modern university. More directors were appointed in whom the two types of authority, the epistemological authority of knowledge and the deontological authority of the organization, were balanced. According to d'Irsay (1933), the university is simultaneously idea and order.

Nowadays, especially in the biggest universities, the rector, chancellor, or president is an impressive figure. The university has both intra- and interorganizational functions. In the former, the internal bureaucracy is such that it is unclear whether the rector is dependent on the council or the council on the rector. The interorganizational functions are concerned with domestic or foreign persons and legal entities. The rector's functions can also be considered from a social point of view: keep the student body calm, make sure professors are fulfilling their obligations, and keep the city and neighbourhood happy. From an administrative point of view, the rector should make the following resources available: staff or human resources; physical space and time; books, informational aids, and equipment; material, physical, and technical resources; economic resources; and the good reputation of the university. Henry L. Ashmore (1979) preferred a humorous approach in pointing out the qualities and virtues rectors need to carry out their functions: "A recent listing of required characteristics for a presidency included: wisdom of

Solomon, strength of Hercules, cunning of Machiavelli, spirit of David, beauty of Adonis." He forgot to mention the patience of Job.

Finally, Barzum (1969, p. 107) lists "the many offices with the specialized, unmergeable functions" of a rector:

> Alumni affairs, street policing; architectural plans; contracts for new construction; proposed gifts; government grants; fund-raising drives; dormitory rules; prospect or sequel of riots; extension of insurance and other fringe benefits; status of lawsuits; setting tuition fees; supervising standards of admission; studying effects of proposed federal and state legislation; appointing committees; issuing or revising guides and manuals; salary scale; income and budget estimates; announcements to the press; participation in conferences; proposed institutes; adding or phasing out divisions of instruction and research; allocating space and permitting alterations; planning major renovations; ensuring radiation safety; renewing labor contracts; relocating neighbors dispossessed by new buildings; holding scholars against raiding; mechanizing routine by computer; replacing and promoting administrators; preparing council, faculty and trustee meetings; revising current budget and preparing the next; meeting demands of government auditors; responding to proposals for exchanges and affiliations; awarding honorary degrees; organizing anniversaries, ceremonials, lectureships, and other public functions.

The requirements for a good rector need consideration: should the rector, or other officials, be academics as well as managers, or more the latter than the former; should they come from the heart and soul of the university or be a newcomer; should the rector be appointed by the university, from among its own, or be imposed from outside and for such unfortunate and harmful reasons as official bureaucratic appointments, political pressure, and governmental interference.

Some universities rely on the names of distinguished rectors and presidents to determine a future course of action. In North America, for example, we find the names of Eliot at Harvard, Gilman at Johns Hopkins, Harper at Chicago, White at Cornell,

Agnell at Michigan, Barnard at Columbia, Folwell at Minnesota, Star Jordan at Stanford, Adams at Wisconsin, and Wheeler at California. There is also Unamuno at Salamanca. The anthology of great university rectors has yet to be written.

There are many types of university organization but, undeniably, a university administration suffers from blunders and impermissible meddling in the designation of authorities.

Appointment of the rector or university president

There are three basic methods of designating a rector corresponding to the three institutional organizational methods in universities. First, a rector's or president's appointment can be the prerogative of a governing council; it can also depend on juridical, constitutional, or legal norms by which an official has the responsibility for appointing and removing a rector; it can be left to electoral processes in the university involving professors, students, and in some cases, other university bodies; or it can be the result of decisions made in "claustros," or assemblies. Second, a body of trustees or regents appoints the rector, or this authority is given through elections at the faculty level.

In the third situation, either of the above methods or a combination of them is used. For example in Ecuador, Peru, and Venezuela, the election of a university president depends on assemblies or university councils, which include representation from professors, students, and graduates. In Panama, the university council, the least representative of these legislative bodies, elects the president.

Professorial resources

The academic vigour of the university depends greatly on its professorial resources, that is, the academic or pedagogical staff. The titles at the original medieval universities depended on the degrees granted; the "licentia docendi" gave authorization and permission to teach, the "doctorado," which like the previous title is based on the Latin word "doceo," and the master or "magister," from the Greek root "mag," were based on degrees of knowledge.

The origin of these titles and degrees and the current problem of preparing university professors will be dealt with later. First, we are interested in issues concerning academic staff that are the concern of the university administration. For example, should researchers necessarily also be competent professors? Should the emphasis be on first-class educators who are filled with enthusiasm for research and keeping up-to-date, or on researchers by trade who are almost exclusively dedicated to research?

More important than ratios of researchers to teachers or conditions of work is the administrators' responsibility to make all the teaching staff feel a sense of belonging to an institution where moral, intellectual, and educational values prevail above all. If these values are neglected, however good the educator, the quality of the instruction suffers.

An everyday, ordinary professor is not the same as a real master teacher of science and life. But how is a great teacher made and where does such a person come from? From the university where he or she learned to be a master teacher, or from the more or less fortuitous practice of the profession?

Student resources

Concerns for the quality of teaching in educational and university administration reinforce the idea that the purpose of the university is to educate, not only to train a student for a profession. Canovic (1988) maintains that educating is an action that should take into account the subjectivity of each student who is, after all, a human being.

> The subjectiveness of students and their position in the process of study is not a mere form deprived of content but a variable condition characterized by the growth of certain qualities which are achieved through systematic effort and the implementation of all relevant scientific discoveries. The students' subjectiveness is a multivarious problem underlying which are activity, independence and creativity which are increasingly becoming the dominant elements of self-instruction and research activities. This is a process that begins from the very start of instruction and continues throughout the educational process. At the level of higher education it should

develop into something approaching the ability for self-instruction and scientific research.

A student-subject is an accomplishment of fundamental significance for him as an individual but also a guarantee of his assertion as a valuable and useful member of the community. He becomes a strong personality with a sound basis for his further intellectual growth and creativity.

If we give due consideration to these matters, we will be doing justice to the quality of student resources. This raises the question of whether the university should be open to everyone or whether students should be selected for superior ability. This presupposes the democratic principle of equal opportunity for all students to apply for entrance, which will hopefully be in effect throughout the world. The call for equal opportunities in education in general and for university education in particular is constant, but it is well known that no matter how much it is defended or sought, equal opportunity depends on cultural and economic constraints that are difficult to overcome. Although the elitist university is undesirable, the university has been, is, and will be selective. This debate is a burning, emotional issue. It would be convenient to think that elitism is always to be rejected because it carelessly excludes many people from the educational processes. Selectivity, however, rationally accepts that although everyone has a natural right, capacities, effort, and circumstances place each person at a different level of social activity, and no one is sacrificed (Berger et al. 1985).

The criteria of quality and quantity in relation to student resources are inseparable from variety and heterogeneity. Carton (1983, p. 28) states:

It is evident that not only in Europe and the United States student heterogeneity is displayed, with special shades of meaning, in the different disciplines and professions. The phenomenon has become very noticeable since the 60s and can be explained, with slight regional differences, by the expansion of secondary education, the importance assigned to continuing education as a result of socio-economic business policies, the increasing importance assigned to social ascent as a result of university degrees and the need to prove one's professional mastery to society; the increase occurring in relations between countries, especially in favor of developing countries; and the greater felt need to prepare persons for the study of problems and their solution.

The Colombian Association of Universities is currently engaged in national research on the polyfaceted "profile" of the university student.

Education should be governed by the criterion of merit rather than social origin of wealth. Candidates should come from any cultural and social background as long as they have a sufficient basis for education. There can also be other arguments for admission of the best.

At the basis of this discussion lies a practical question that has made the traditional system of "numerus clausus" necessary, either absolutely or relative to some fields or professions. This has led to the establishment of entrance examinations or tests, which in some countries of Latin America are government run (state examinations). Whatever the response might be to the well-known desire for open and universal opportunities, every educational process, whether formal, nonformal, or informal, has to be for what is superior.

Nowadays, the growth of modern mass communication facilitates an active awareness and promotes student mobility, which was also characteristic of the original university. Ishumi (1990, p. 12), in reference to African universities, recalls historical examples from Hetland (1984):

> Do you recall names like Athens, Constantinople and Toledo? In different centuries these centres of learning attracted people from far and near. At other times and on other continents there were similar centres, for example in India, Egypt, and Timbuktu — the small desert town in today's Mali. Such centres of learning were intellectual fora, international in nature with a transcending understanding of national and cultural borders. We have all heard of the "wandering" scholars, students and researchers of former times, travelling far and wide to seek the best scientific environment, discuss with and learn from

famous colleagues, and receive stimulation and reactions to new ideas. They left their homes and beloved ones to undertake strenuous and long-lasting journeys in pursuit of wisdom and truth.

Ishumi continues with his own reflections based on Davison (1964):

The scholarly activity of international dimensions...would include the historical study travels of man such as the Persian Al Mas'udi (Abdul Hassan ibn Hussein ibn al Mas'udi) to the east African seaboard in the 10th century for a study of the socio-political and economic life of people in what was described as the land of the Zanj (from the Horn down to Mozambique). It would likewise include Ibn Battuta (Muhammad ibn Abdullah ibn Battuta) to Mali in West Africa and Kilwa in East Africa, India and China in the 14th century, as well as Leo Africanus, a north-African scholar, to the School of Timbuktu in the 16th century, for a deeper taste of book learning and for an account of the civilization of the Western Sudan and the political and economic structures of the Songhay empire.

International student flows in modern times, though now wider in scope and multifarious in objectives, build on the traditions of the early times in the one respect of a search for dialogue and intellectual stimulation. This remained one prime motive throughout the centuries up until the first half of the 20th century, when "scholarship overseas" assumed further roles beyond the very original one.

After the end of colonial rule, for most African countries in the late 1950s and early 1960s, it was realized that actual productive areas and potential investment areas in the newly independent nations were increasing at a rate faster than the availability or training of local manpower to produce the targeted goods and social services. The limited number of their local (nationally-based) educational institutions — even when operating at full capacity — were not adequate enough to cater to a fast development of skilled high- and middle-level manpower required to harness and propel the anticipated production processes. Overseas scholarships, then, ceased to be viewed merely as a process of dialogue but rather more as a practical means, and a short cut, to training and deploying of high-level human resources.

At the same time, concern about transfer of technology from industrialized to less advanced nations was beginning to surface. Debate centred on the argument that it was not enough to transfer ready-made machines, equipment and packages alone, but rather to match this with a conscious sponsoring of training of personnel in relevant and appropriate theoretical and applicational areas. Without such a match, it was argued, dependence of developing nations upon developed industrialized nations would not only be total but it would also be perpetual.

Among countries of the eastern–southern African subregion, Kenya provides a classic example of the trend of international student travel from home-base to countries and centres abroad for reasons beginning with the initial search for cultural–intellectual dialogue and developing into wider practical concerns for social and economic development.

In 1988, the Copernicus Project (Cooperation Program in Europe for Research on Nature and Industry through Coordinated University Studies; Unesco 1989c) was created by the Conférence permanente des Recteurs, des Présidents et Vicechanceliers des Universités européennes with mobile groups of students. It sets in motion the program's objectives, which are contained in the acronym that reminds us of that wise Polish scientist.

Student welfare

Student welfare in its broadest sense is part of the administrative structure of the university. The activities, programs, and services devised for students are part of the university's organic structure. As the university as a whole is designed to educate, this should also be true of student welfare and of those who direct and coordinate it.

University *activities* are often considered to be the cultural, social, artistic, or sporting events; university *programs* are designed to assist poor urban and rural communities; and *services* cover the everyday needs of the student body, such as residences, meals, and medical and dental services.

Activities have a special relationship with the university's educational management. Analyzing the North American student environment, Searle (1967) identifies the following areas of interest that he calls the five student cultures: the culture of fraternity and brotherhood, which is most frequent among undergraduates; the professional culture; the intellectual and scientific culture; the political culture; and the artistic culture. There is a certain correspondence between these student "cultures" and the university "imperatives" or aims discussed above.

On the other hand, Arthur Chickering developed seven what he calls vectors for student growth and maturity (see Casebeer 1991).

♦ Developing competence: the physical, intellectual, mental, and social competencies needed for a maturing person.

♦ Managing emotion: a means of self-control of the individual in social and cultural situations, the avoidance of explosive behaviour, and sexual advances perpetrated on other students, and faculty as well.

♦ Developing autonomy: a product to develop one's self regulation and one's own value system.

♦ Establishing identity: to be understanding of one's physical and sexual self.

♦ Freeing interpersonal relations: a respect, and tolerance of others to develop mature and intimate relationships with students and others with whom she or he may come in contact.

♦ Developing purpose: developing a direction for one's life interests and one's life style.

♦ Developing integrity: a congruence between belief and behaviour, and thus personalizing of value.

Searle does not explicitly mention physical culture and sports, while Chickering includes them in "physical

competence." There does not seem to be a great deal of discussion
on the educational importance of physical culture. Each university does what it deems necessary, convenient, and possible
according to its interests and resources. Flexner (1930) started
an ongoing debate about sports in North American colleges and
universities:

> [Colleges] are all mad on the subject of competitive and
> intercollegiate athletics...the colleges...could, given the cour-
> age and intelligence, frankly tell the world that their problem
> is infinitely complicated by giving loose rein to the athletic
> orgy in order to amuse and placate a populace, largely consist-
> ing of their own graduates. There is not a college or university
> in America which has the courage to place athletics where
> everyone perfectly well knows they belong. On the con-
> trary,...proportionately more money is spent on college athlet-
> ics than on any legitimate college activity. The football coach
> is better known to the student body and the general public
> than the president; and professors are, on the average, less
> highly remunerated. Does the college or university have to
> endure this? Of course not. But it does more than endure: it
> "advertises."

Recently, with financing from the Knight Foundation of
Akron, Ohio, a committee presided over by Theodore Hasburg,
President Emeritus of Notre Dame University, and with William
C. Friday, President Emeritus of the University of North Carolina
as its vice-president, produced a "draft of reform" for the sports
system in American universities. "The problems facing college
sports are relatively obvious: too much money, an over-emphasis
on winning, and too little concern about educating athletes."

There is usually little discussion about the educational
importance of activities and programs, but many university
administrators ask what services should be provided for students.
Many feel that students not only have the privilege of a superior
professional preparation but also often demand innumerable
benefits.

However, a more legitimate and general concern is the
administration and equitable distribution of the human and

material resources available to the university. Ideally, university faculty should be educators in the broad sense of the word and share the principles that govern the university and the way it understands its missions and functions and puts them into practice. The faculty are part of the educational community and in some cases, are also part of the university's governing bodies and even have the right to vote in the election of authorities and dignitaries.

D. Carrier (1990) adduces other arguments for the import-ance of the "support staff," both in universities and in all business and management:

> Processes are becoming much more complex, not only in terms of the tools being used which are increasingly more sophisticated, but also in the organization of the work itself.... Tasks are becoming more and more interactive and comple-mentary, and thus the work force must be considered less as individual but more as an important and integrated group. To meet these needs, the first priority is to take account of urgent social demands. The overall level of expertise continues to rise; at the same time, the requirement of individuals and those of the productive sector converge to press for an unprecedented development of the missions of higher education; in terms of numbers and content, and in terms of the social, economic, and international environment.

Material resources

The material resource of the university's physical layout has a visible, obvious importance. Like the institution, it has had secular development. Originally, the university hardly had any physical connotation: "Its strength lay in its poverty," Rashdall (1936, vol. I) asserted, and maestros and students moved in search of more agreeable situations. There was little or no oppor-tunity for students to say, "See you at the university" as they do nowadays. Nevertheless, human activities require physical space, and medieval architecture provided them with cloisters, churches, housing, pleasant urban retreats, and cobblestone paths along the Seine. It is said that Irnerius declaimed his speeches on juridical science outdoors, having climbed to a street pulpit in the corner of the big piazza in front of the Basilica of Saint Stephen, and that Alberto did the same in the Palazzo Publico of Bologna.

Everything indicates that in the early days, universities did not have their own definite sites. It was not until the 14th century in Europe that the movement to build structures for universities began, along monastic or civilian designs. The medieval urban boom led to the title of "university cities," which some cities deemed an honour. The first legislation pertaining to the physical location of universities were the seven legal codes of Alfonso X, the Wise. By the end of the 15th century, the idea of the university as a fixed place became more accepted, although the concept of university architecture did not really develop until the Renaissance style in the 16th century.

Scientific development and the appearance of new elements in the general and academic structure of universities necessitated changes in university buildings. In North America, the concept of "campus" arose at the end of the 18th century. While designing the University of Virginia, Thomas Jefferson described his goal as the creation of an "academic villa." As described by Turner Venable 1985, p. 4):

> The word "campus," more than any other term, sums up the unique physical character of the American college and university. When it was first used to describe the grounds of a college, probably at Princeton in the late eighteenth century, campus had simply its Latin meaning, a field, and described the green expansiveness already distinctive of American schools. Charles Dickens in the 1840s was struck by the appearance of Yale, with its buildings erected in a kind of park...dimly visible among the shadowing trees.... And Le Corbusier, after traveling in America in the 1930s, observed that "each college or university is an urban unit in itself, a small or large city. But a green city.... The American University is a world in itself."

Nowadays, campus is the word used worldwide to refer to the physical university spaces even if they are in the heart of cities. The concept of "school ergonomics" used by Mialaret and

Vial (1981, vol. IV) in which the technical resources of a campus, such as laboratories, equipment, resources for so-called educational and pedagogical technology, or computer resources.

However well designed a campus might be, the most important aspect is the people it serves. Similarly, the functioning of the general organic structure and the academic structure of a university depends on the quality of the persons involved. University administration is more complex, but simultaneously more stimulating, because it involves intelligent people, who for that reason are in the university. Administration must never take precedence over the academic liberties of *Lehrfreiheit* (liberty to teach) and *Lernfreiheit* (liberty to learn), of which the German university has spoken since the 19th century. This is one of the great differences between the university as a human enterprise and other enterprises.

Economic and financial resources

One of the problems that has been with universities since their beginnings is that of obtaining and handling finances. As Thorens (1992) points out:

> The university's complete autonomy was questioned from the moment the tuition and fees paid by the students weren't sufficient enough to pay the teachers. The pecuniary requirements of a stable, sufficiently well-paid staff of professors as well as the need for buildings and libraries obliged the university to stay in fixed locations and to depend on the benevolence of the Church and the princes in their villas.

At first, there were officials in charge of collecting and assigning funds. After the 14th century, foundations could be set up to finance universities, but there was a danger of limiting academic freedom (d'Irsay 1933; Aigrain 1949). Nowadays, a few universities have set up a foundation with a vice-rector or vice-president at its head. In very large and complex institutions this makes sense; but, it is bureaucratic excess in the rest.

Eicher and Chevaillier (1992, p. 7), whose opinions are shared by Neave (1992), argue that

> Throughout the world, the financing of education is in a serious (and dramatic) crisis...not limited to the problem of meeting the obligations of society to provide some minimum amount of compulsory education to their students. This minimum does not assure the preparation of an appropriately trained labour force in a world that is increasingly technological and in which a competitive economy requires the replacement of traditional production processes with ones based upon sophisticated labour and capital. The rapid growth of post-compulsory systems of education is no longer a luxury, but a necessity for industrialization and economic development. Properly trained engineers, managers, professionals, and high level technical and administrative support personnel are crucial to the establishment of efficient industries and government services and thereby to the generation of employment for those with only compulsory schooling....

> Top financial priority should be given now in all countries to the higher levels of the school system. Basic education is still far from being universal in many less developed countries,...and, in many instances, its quality has been deteriorating, sometimes drastically. Where this is the case, basic education does remain a priority and its part in the education budget should, if anything, increase.

> But expansion and improvement of post-compulsory education (PCE) is considered to be crucial in industrialized and semi-industrialized countries and is, in the long run, a condition for the development of the poorest countries, especially if we remember that PCE takes many forms, including not only university-level education, but also, in many countries, upper secondary level education and post-secondary options such as short course technological institutes, community colleges, as well as training programs run by industries or trade unions.

The current financial crisis in education is exacerbated by the fact that world population is rising exponentially with ensuing demands on educational systems. This crisis was foreseen in the 1950s (Coombs 1971), but today it is aggravated by a "doctrinal crisis." Eicher and Chevaillier (1992, p. 9) state:

> The tremendous expansion of education in the 1960s was made possible by the fact that most governments put a great deal of public resources into that sector. They reacted so positively and so quickly because the then dominant economic theory presented education as a highly profitable investment.
>
> By the mid-1970s, this excessive optimism and the compulsion to give first priority to education in public budgets subsided substantially when, with the rise of graduate unemployment, the capacity of educational systems to produce graduates geared to the needs of labour markets was questioned, especially in developing countries where many accused the existing school systems of imitating the programmes of the former colonizers. The capacity and the willingness of public decision-makers to allocate resources according to social preferences was also challenged by new economic theories. All these new trends converged towards a more critical view of education and a reduced willingness to increase public financial contributions to its development, thereby making the financial crisis more acute.

The "doctrinal crisis" has repercussions on the current attitudes toward educational planning and institutional evaluation. However, there are three main participants in the current financial crisis in education: government, society, which includes students, and the university itself.

In general, state and government support of public universities is considerable, with a preference in each country for what is called the national university. According to the political organization of a country, whether federalist or unitarian, the provinces, states, or departments contribute in different ways to the support of their respective universities. Some countries recognize to a greater or lesser degree and some ignore altogether the fact that private institutions also have legitimate rights to public money. "Within the limits of available financing, it is the responsibility of government to adequately fund the [total] higher education system" (Unesco 1992a). If justice and equality come into play, human, material, and financial resources should be distributed fairly. Not everything should go to one or a few universities, because the result is a distribution that parodies equal justice and creates imbalances that are intolerable for society.

Although it is the state's duty to provide for higher education, it is also a responsibility of society in general and of productive enterprises in particular that benefit from the students trained in the university (Stubbs 1990). This social conscience seems to be more firmly rooted in North American universities than in the original European schools. The Colonial College, founded in 1636, was inspired by Emmanuel College, Oxford. Its name was changed to Harvard in 1638 because of the donation made by a wealthy citizen to the newly created institution. Another example is Yale, where Cotton Mather suggested to Elihu Yale that a generous donation would be "much better than an Egyptian pyramid." Today's philanthropic customs arose from this old-fashioned origin, and graduates, business enterprises, and foundations all participate, stimulated by the possibility of tax breaks.

A similar social awareness toward education in general and higher education in particular ought to become widespread throughout the world. Private enterprise and nongovernmental organizations should be able to recognize and value higher education initiatives as a justifiable financial investment, as often mentioned in scholarly journals.

On the other hand, the university also has duties (Unesco 1992a):

> It is obvious that higher education institutions are responsible for the *effective* and *efficient* use of the scarce resources allocated to them by government and society. But scarce resources go beyond financial provision; they include capital investment and staff time and expertise. All this puts a good deal of pressure on the managers of higher education institutions (including senior managers), but many higher education managers come to their tasks with little or no training. Here, international agencies and higher education institutions in countries with stronger management traditions can help.

International agencies can serve as a catalyst to the creation of higher education management *training programs* through bringing expertise in this area together on an international level. Such agencies can also act as clearinghouses for information on management problems.

There should be programs for training university administrators so that they can understand the history and nature of the institution they are running, its missions, roles, and functions, its organizational structures, and its future prospects. There should also be programs designed to train those who are in charge of obtaining and managing the university's material, economic, and financial resources. In both types of programs, especially the second, it should be pointed out that higher education is not expensive but costly; although understood as an expense, it is simultaneously an investment in human resources that shapes the cultural and economic development of nations. The university is a nonprofit institution and, especially in countries with limited economic resources, it is necessary to make adjustments according to circumstances rather than copy more expensive foreign models and to develop strategies to "do more with less" (Schütze et al. 1992).

In general terms, Eicher and Chevaillier (1992) believe that the government and society both have roles in the education crisis, but "mixed financing is better than either exclusively public or exclusively private financing." This leads to their question:

Should mixed financing imply a dual system of schools, public schools being financed through public monies and private schools receiving their support solely from private sources? Our conclusion is that mixed financing is advisable for both public and private institutions.

However, two more questions arise. The first relates to the subsidies provided by the government: should the money be given to the institutions or to the students who attend them? The answer, of course, depends on the situation. The other problem refers to the private subsidies coming from firms, philanthropists, and, in developing countries, foreign aid and how these subsidies should be given and received. Eicher and Chevaillier (1992) believe that this type of help "should increase in many countries" and that "it should be provided according to varied contractual arrangements."

A fifth question concerns the cost of education to the student, including the cost of living while studying. What is preferable: grants, loans, or a combination? There is no general answer to this question.

Finally, even assuming the convenience of mixed financing, is public or private financing preferable, and to what extent? Such a delicate dilemma cannot be answered easily because there is a crossover of specific conceptions, interests, and situations. "In market economies, competition among buyers and sellers and between the two groups is supposed to lead to the best possible use of available resources" (Eicher and Chevaillier 1992). However, in the case of education, many economic norms are not fulfilled in the trade-off between quality and quantity. What is the interest of governments, and what is the interest of the private institutions or people who ought to be responsible for the costs of education? "The students and their families have no way to evaluate accurately the quality of teaching. Private suppliers could therefore be tempted to increase the quantity...even though this has an adverse effect on quality" (Eicher and Chevaillier 1992). It is frequently forgotten that education has unavoidable obligations to culture, which is often ignored to give priority, sometimes exclusively, to more immediate benefits to industry and professions. However, the ultimate outcome of education is spread over time and can be affected by many events, most of which cannot be foreseen (Council of Europe 1989).

Another argument concerns fees. The argument for token user fees is based on the opinion that people are inclined not to appreciate what they do not have to pay for and consume free goods indiscriminately and wastefully. When a fee, however modest, is collected, the value tends to increase and the university's internal efficiency is promoted.

The financial situation of universities is a given item on the agenda in any meeting or conference on higher education. There is particular reference to additional sources of financing which ultimately come from the state, from the society being benefited, and from the use universities make of what they receive.

It is preferable to talk about "new means" of obtaining income that are earmarked for the institution as such, for carrying out all its activities, for paying staff, and to help students get the education they need. In any case, whether we speak of new income sources or new means of obtaining income from the same sources, it is important to point out, as does Neave (1992, p. 4), that

> The question of resources will always be central to higher education for the simple and unavoidable reason that changes in this area carry with them a type of snowball effect. Change the system of financial allocation and the delicate balance of authority between academics, institutional administration, and government will also most likely find itself altered — in which direction is a matter of circumstance. But this balance is unlikely to remain entirely the same as it was in the past. It is this aspect of the balance of power or of shifts in co-ordination at institutional level which is often underplayed — or perhaps underestimated — by the proponents of the diversification of funding sources.

On the other hand, Neave also points out that

> One of the frequently made arguments trotted out in favour of such diversification [of sources] is that it allows the institution to maintain a higher degree of independence than would be the case if it relied wholly on the pennies of the Prince. The more diverse the sources from which an institution gathers its funds, the less the leverage any one of them may effectively bring to bear on the institution. Such is conventional wisdom. It is based on an older adage that when two workers chase one employer, the employer controls workers and wages. When two employers go head hunting after one worker, the latter has the whip hand. When a university seeks its finances from multiple sources, it may the easier impose its terms on each of the competing interests.

There is considerable documentation on the "new sources of financing." They can be categorized according to whether they are started by the state, society, or the university itself.

There is a tendency to leave a good part of higher education in the hands of private initiative rather than the state. In addition, professional taxes have been proposed that would tax the person benefiting from the education received or tax the institution that employed that person, and there would be tax exemptions for any kind of help given the university. The creation of sponsorships, the awarding of grants, and the state's assignment of goods for the university's benefit and for it to manage are other means that have been proposed to make government action in financing higher education more bearable.

As for social action, donations, assistance, and subsidies are encouraged from individuals, legal organizations, and especially foundations, of which there are many in the world. Obtaining help from social institutions and from government organizations is another means of obtaining a relatively stable income, depending on the circumstances.

Beyond the gradual increase in tuition that the public or private university justly claims for the services it provides to its students, institutions of higher education also turn to other means of increasing their funds. These can include offering services to businesses and to the general public through continuing education courses; contracts, particularly for research and advising; production of bibliographies, for example; and royalties from technological transfers from their laboratories to industry and the marketplace. In this area, some think it feasible for the university to be converted into a productive enterprise for its own benefit. The academic administration does not always agree with income redistribution so that the more self-sufficient programs subsidize those requiring greater investment of economic resources. Different types of cooperation — regional, national, and international — among universities and with other types of institutions are a useful resource for shared financing in offering courses, providing services, or in research projects.

Occasionally, universities launch special projects, such as new buildings, the purchase of equipment, the establishment of centres or institutes, bibliographic collections, for which a special public relations or fund-raising organization is of enormous help. These bureaucratic tools are necessary for all types of institutional relations and for carrying out financial planning. Necessary arrangements between the state, credit organizations, and the university, besides making the preceding proposals possible, facilitate the establishment of educational credits for the student's benefit or for the system of educational vouchers proposed by Friedman (see Costa 1991).

Koso-Thomas developed a scheme similar to the above means of university financing which he called the University Central Fund. His suggestions were summarized by Eicher and Chevaillier (1992), with approximate pre-evaluation of results in terms of efficiency, equity, resource broadening, and administrative costs (Table 1). To sum up (p. 31):

> The optimal financial setting for higher education, which could be extended with some important qualifications to upper secondary education, seems to be the following: *public*

Table 1. Evaluation of different methods of funding education.

Method	Efficiency	Equity	Resource broadening	Administrative cost
Specific grants to institutions	+	=	= or +	–
Vouchers to students	+	=	+	–
Tuition fees				
Token fees	+	=	+	–
Substantial uniform fees	+	–	+ +	–
Substantial variable fees	+ +	– –	+ +	–
Full-cost fees	+ +	– –	+ +	–
Financing by business				
Contribution to teaching	+	= or –	+	–
Research services	+	=	+	–
Educational payroll tax	+	= or –	+ +	–
Endowments and gifts	=	?	+	– –

Note: + +, very good; +, good; =, average; –, poor; – –, very poor.
Source: Eicher and Chevaillier (1992).

financing, which should be predominant and should consist of a mixture of: (a) a basic unrestricted block grant to institutions ensuring a minimum of security and continuity; (b) specific grants negotiated between each institution and one or several public bodies, phased over a period of several years, subject to interim evaluation and renegotiation; (c) income-related grants to students, helping covering both tuition fees and maintenance; and (d) guarantee to student loans. *Private financing*, in the shape of: (a) fees (basic tuition fees, uniform and substantial) and additional specific fees for special services, freely set up by institutions, within limits; (b) business contributions, which should be limited, in the public and publicly subsidized sector, to the financing of continuing education and training, practical training included in the curriculum of regular degrees and applied research, and which could be made compulsory in part through a payroll tax earmarked for education; and (c) gifts and endowments, which could be made easier by changes in tax regulations (but are likely to remain nominal in the short run for countries where they are not rooted in tradition) [Figure 1].

Of course, each country will have to make its own choice according to its own constraints and political stance, but the logic of the present situation should lead them all to broadly similar choices.

Obviously, not all the suggestions are applicable in all circumstances. Each university should choose those that might be promising. This requires accurate research and, of course, foresight and evaluation of the results obtained. Eicher and Chevaillier (1992) tell us:

Everything considered, the diversification of the sources of funding of post-compulsory education institutions is a distinct possibility, but it would not be without consequences on their organization. Diversification generally strengthens their autonomy, but it also supposes a stronger management, for it increases the difficulty of achieving the consensus.

But it should be emphasized that changing the source of funds also strongly affects the working of the system as a whole or that of each member institution. The effects of various innovations introduced in a given system can be assessed according to four criteria.

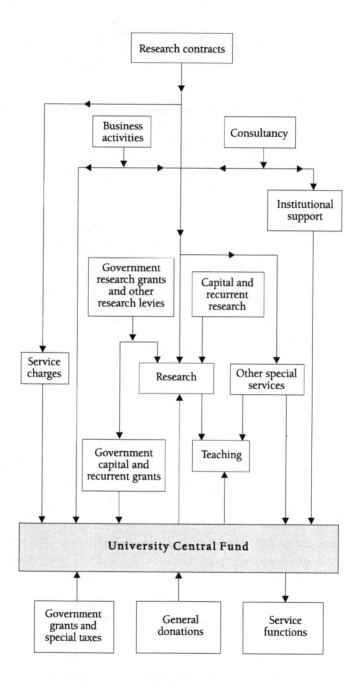

Figure 1. Proposed diverse funding for institutions of higher education.

Efficiency and *equity*, the two traditional criteria of welfare economics. *Resource broadening* potential, that is the capacity to generate new resources by bringing in new categories of fund providers or by inducing existing contributors to increase their funding. But new modes of financing may entail *administrative costs* which may lower the net intake. If we consider, for instance, a system financed mainly through public unrestricted grants to institutions, the average effects of the main financial innovations can be summarized in the table below [Table 1]. In some cases, the outcome cannot be foreseen without knowing more details about the way changes are implemented.

No single source scores high according to each one of the four criteria. The same conclusion would be reached if one started from a different initial arrangement. Two conclusions can be drawn. First, the final choice depends on the weight the final decision-maker gives to each criterion; second, a combination of different sources is in most cases to be preferred to a single source of income.

This theory, as we have already seen, is shared by Neave.

FUNCTIONS OF THE UNIVERSITY

We have already discussed two of the three concepts frequently used to state the university's functions or missions. Now we must turn to how they are administered from inside the university.

The functions are research, teaching, and service, which assumes the university understands, will develop, and makes use of these three key words and their mutual relation. This occurs in agreement with the principles and philosophy governing the conduct of each university as it pursues its missions and aims.

The research function

Research in universities is administered for various purposes: scientific development and the politics of research and science; research areas and the selection and maintenance of lines of research in the university; technological research; and the student's development as a creative researcher. Some of these topics are related to the functions that each university assigns its departments, institutes, and centres. However, technological research and the student's development require special consideration.

Technology

The concept of technology, its requirements, effects, operations, and implications, should be given special attention by the university as an institution. Technology can be defined as the science of industrial arts. But industry, in its turn, means unusual diligence in creative and useful work. Thus, technology can mean the science of how to do things; the application of science to techniques, or science combined with action and action combined with science. The expressions techno-science and science and technology imply a certain conjunction between the two fields, with technology as the result.

"Technology has been defined as the application of science to technics; in other words, as applied science" (Goffi 1988). However, Goffi also presents J. Beckmann's definition (1777), which conceives of technology not as

> A technique that works for the contribution received from the sciences, but as a systematic and rational study of technical procedures. Technology is the science that shows the treatment of natural products or knowledge of the "métiers" [arts and crafts]. Instead of showing only how the instructor's customary instructions and procedures should be followed in workshops in order to produce a product, technology provides deep instruction according to a systematic order that, through real principles and sure experiences, allows us to find the means for attaining the proposed goal and to explain and take advantage of the phenomena that appear during treatments.

Goffi continues: "In the first definition, technology *is a* special type of technique (a *scientific* technique). In the second, technology *takes technics as its object for study* (it is the science of technics)." However, "these two approaches appear to be complementary more than incompatible; what brings them close together is the discarding of the notion of technics as a more or less efficient routine, for the instructor's procedures are replaced by the engineer's calculations." In addition, "if technology is applied science, there is also a *circulation*, both of science in the direction of technics and of technics towards science." In the words of Daumas (see Goffi 1988), "Technology is located between science and technics, and it is characterized by their mutual penetration." Moreover, "it would be absurd to think that the development of techniques would be systematically subordinate to the development of the sciences. Techniques, even nowadays, are not only applications of sciences as if these had always preceded techniques." Over the course of the preceding centuries, the sciences "have received a lot from techniques, and this still occurs nowadays." In short, in the circulation between science and technics, the latter has frequently taken the initiative" (Vessuri 1991).

There is a sense in which technology can encompass the profound reasoning of the being and acting of things. It is also the source of how things originate, grow, and develop, of how they produce and reproduce themselves, and of the way in which beings behave.

The original sense of the word technology refers to that which is physical or mechanical. However, there is also the realm of living, organic beings, of human and animal organisms. From this we have biological and medical technologies. Technology can also deal with human behaviours, both collective and individual, for, although bound to the sphere of the natural sciences, technology has already delved into the social and human sciences: educational technology, social technologies, and political technologies.

The philosopher Ismael Quiles (1984, p. 43) describes the two first senses of technology, the physical or mechanical and the biological, as follows:

Material things occur to me in a particular way that essentially does not depend on me to change. I have to handle the material things in the world according to what they are; otherwise, they do not respond to my desire.... As deep and marvelous as the advances in the transformation of science and technology in the use of nature might be, it is only an insignificant portion that man is able to modify, always respecting and taking advantage of nature's laws. We transform nature using her own laws.

However, although technology is scientific, it is always practical. Whereas there might be simple techniques or explanations, technology implies a certain magnitude or importance. Indeed, it is common to speak of "big science" and of "high technology," which leads one to think that there must be minor or intermediate technologies, or simple techniques. In the nonscientific world, we keep the simple, traditional, and obvious ways humankind has of guiding and making use of natural forces or materials, without using them for spectacular undertakings and without causing significant modifications in them. This is the opposite of what happens in big science, high technology, and advanced technologies, all of which do entail significant change.

Research and development

Given the practical character of the technological power of human knowledge, its effects are all the more expansive and enveloping in direct ratio to the sizes and dimensions of technology. They are inseparable from the concepts of change and development, with unavoidable emphasis on economic power. Technology has revolutionized organizational, management, and socioinstitutional models (Pérez 1991).

For this reason, research and development (R&D) is a phrase that frequently appears in combination with so-called great technological agents. These have led to astronautics or cosmonautics, electronics and computer science, and to the management and transformations of macromolecular chemistry, nuclear energy, and biological engineering. Some of these great agents have unfortunately been placed at the service of bellicose technology and have all in turn somehow contributed in their own way to the "technification" of life and cultural, social, and political individual and collective behaviours. This is true not only in the countries that produce technology but also in those that import the technological product.

Technology, science, and university education

Alvarez (1991) and Biljanovic (1988) both discuss technology and its relation to university education and development. Alvarez describes the relation between knowledge and power:

> The recent history of international conflicts, the springing up of new poles of power in the world and the changes that are occurring in every sphere of human life as the result of science and technology surpass the predictions that philosophers and historians made in the past about the importance of knowledge as the source of power.
>
> The economy's center of gravity actually moves inexorably from the production of goods to activities related to services, information, technological innovation, and, in general, the intensive use of knowledge.
>
> One of the lessons that resulted from almost half a century of struggle for Third World development is that the success that some countries are achieving is due more to appropriate policies, institutional capacity, human competence, flexibility and stability than to rich natural resources or geographical location.
>
> Aristotle would have been hard-pressed to imagine the infinite possibilities of *practical knowledge* in society when he distinguished it from *speculative knowledge* based on its end goal. While the goal of the latter is knowledge for its own sake, practical knowledge would be oriented toward the production of some concrete work (technology, for example) or the correctness of an action (the formulation of a policy). Practical knowledge, besides the help of intelligence, requires the help of other faculties of the spirit, such as the faculty for carrying out something or the faculty of production (entrepreneurial capacity) and the appetite for action; the truth criterion for this type of knowledge would be more than the confirmation of a theory, since it deals with acting effectively on things and on persons. This concept is a precursor of the present-day

methods of applied research and operational research and of the growing emphasis on the utilization of science by all kinds of institutions.

The most advanced enterprises and governments from all over the world devote more and more resources to research and development projects, whereas centers for research and training are becoming increasingly involved in activities that traditionally were outside of their boundaries, opening new possibilities for alliances between knowledge and power in a wider sense.

In turn, Biljanovic (1988) writes:

The main trend of technological development today is the shift from the classical technologies based on raw materials and energy to new technologies based on knowledge. This trend gives to knowledge the strategic importance which in the past was held by ores and oil. Knowledge becomes a dominant factor of technological development. Knowledge is the product of scientific research and educational activities. Both these activities are naturally linked to the universities. Therefore, universities are directly responsible for the technological development of every country. This responsibility existed in the past, too, but now it is emphasized more than ever before. On the other hand, reproductive knowledge typical for the era of classical technology, is now replaced by creative knowledge typical for the era of high technology. This fact calls for a profound transformation of the universities. The model of the new university should be built in the triangle of technology–education–science; mechanisms which will make the functioning of this triangle possible should be activated.

Different technological operations can be the recuperation, improvement, modification, or transformation of technologies for social benefits; the production of original or imitative technologies; innovation, which introduces something new into an existing technology; or the adoption, adaptation, and appropriation of foreign technologies. These are all transfers of technology from one place to another, one medium to another, or one culture to another.

However, transfer can also mean the delivery of technological invention from the laboratory or workshop to industry, and from the latter to the marketplace. In this sense, universities, business-ess, and the social environment use technology to work together to promote new enterprises and create new jobs (Hull 1991).

Finally, there is the concept of "blending." Not long ago, E.F. Schumacher (1989) showed how simple techniques could be used where more complex technology would create difficul-ties. Humberto Colombo (1985) declared himself a supporter of old-fashioned "technological blending" which, while maintain-ing its tradition increases its efficiency by using new technology.

There are many different technological operations, and it can be difficult to achieve the right combination of traditional, simple techniques and technological advances so that the powerful and new does not destroy the small and simple. There are techniques and technology that are intermediate, convenient, and necessary even in parts of the world that are highly developed.

Ethical implications of technology

To conclude the topic of technology, we should consider the ethical implications of the educational missions of the university as an institution (Ortega y Gasset 1965). Science and advanced technology are no longer morally neutral because of the good and evil they cause with their advances. We must accept the view of Ortega y Gasset (1965) that

> Starting with the atomic bomb, escalating with the new challenges of today's technologies, a seeming ethical neutrality of the scientific endeavor is beginning to be questioned by the community of scientists and by society as a whole.

Above all, the present and future of human life and every-thing that sustains it are connected to scientific and technological advances. The very life of the universe is present in the birth and development of science and philosophy, and as humanity recog-nized and respected the value of life, it moved from barbarism to civilization.

Technological advances, if not threatening human life itself, are threatening the ecology and the environment that sustain life. If the delicate interweaving of the biological complex of the universe is harmed, it will be difficult to restore its vital equilibrium. It is a legacy that current generations should save as a right for future humanity. This reflection leads us to think that science and technology must have a religious aspect. Anheim (1992) states:

> Theology, that is, reflection on God as he reveals himself to Man and thus "reveals man to himself," has something in common with technology. They both challenge us to reflect on the ultimate purpose of our lives and consciously to dedicate our life's efforts toward its fulfillment.... Today's theology can gain from science and technology new and deeper insights into the earthly reality, insights which can help to understand God's revelation in a deeper manner. Technologists have every right to expect from theology answers to questions of meaning and orientation toward the ends of technology, its place within the broader aspects of human life and its service to mankind. Questions about its humanizing and de-humanizing effects, about the ultimate meaning of the technological endeavor beyond what can easily become an eventually self-destructive self-fulfillment must be answered by the united effort of the scientist, engineer, philosopher and theologian. Since all these disciplines reveal various aspects of Man, they can complement and enrich each other. If humanity and its future are existentially threatened by technology today, as many maintain, there is both a logical and a moral imperative to listen to each other and to work together to mitigate the danger.

Technology is full of the promise of development and an irreversible sign of the times. However, although it can help us to live, it can also create confrontation and fear. Where technics prevail, it is said, there is danger, in the highest sense of the word; but where there is danger, that which saves is born.

The university as an institution should be aware of the complexity and loftiness of its institutional missions and of the delicacy and accuracy with which it has to practice its functions of research and serving, critically, politically, and nationalistically. It must also be aware of its mission toward people as the basic element of society who produce science.

Technology and education are controversial subjects

(Unesco 1989a). The new computer and communication technologies mean much more nowadays than the invention of the printing press meant in the Renaissance or encyclopedists meant for the Enlightenment. They affect socioeconomic development and should, therefore, be accessible to the whole population as a new cultural element and form part of the pedagogical and preparatory repertory of universities. At the same time, it should be noticed that the high costs of rapid technological advances increase the disparities even within the countries producing and controlling them, and they increase the distances between developed and developing countries.

The teaching function

The teaching function of the university is inseparable from the educational and developmental task of anyone wanting to reach higher goals. The university gives the highest level of education, as it is the last stage or component in the formal educational system.

Education is inconceivable if it is directed toward that which is inferior. It should always be directed toward higher objectives even at the primary and secondary levels. The university should give the last push to the continuous ascent of every educational process. The teaching and educational mission of the university as an institution for the integrated education of the person must keep in mind the following considerations. The teaching function is not limited to the everyday contribution of the scientific disciplines. It must form the student's understanding of the discipline of intelligence and the discipline of an intellectual life, without limiting it to the learning of a "science" detached from its repercussions. Teaching should open unified paths to knowledge in the human mind to attain the ethical aims that justify scientific development and to show the student, in the words of Morin (1982), that

> The human sciences are not aware of the physical and biological characteristics of human phenomena. The natural sciences

are not aware of their inscription in culture, society, and history. The sciences are not aware of their responsibility to society. The sciences are not aware of the hidden principles that have command over their lucubration. The sciences are not aware that they are unaware....

For this reason there arises the urgent need for a science with an awareness; the time has arrived to become aware of the complexity of all of reality — physical, biological, human, social, political — and of the reality of complexity. The moment has come to become aware that a private science of reflection and a purely speculative philosophy are insufficient. Awareness without science, and science without awareness are mutilated and mutilating.

The cultural development of students takes more than making them informal beneficiaries and admirers of cultural values, for they have to be builders of personal, social, and national culture. Education is more than measured doses of "general education," so pleasing to the taste of the North American educational system. This has been the case under Harvard University's leadership from the 19th century to its most recent proposal of a Core Curriculum (Keller 1982). The student should rather receive a liberal education that promotes humanity's full command of its potential and a selfless love for truth. This is better understood in the unified knowledge proposed by John Henry Newman (1852; see also Cameron 1979).

The student's preparation for a profession should not be reduced to merely satisfying demands in work organization and distribution. This is the commitment the university has been assuming almost imperceptibly since the Industrial Revolution. It has become more acute with the recent fashionable custom of human resource studies and projects. A student's education should not consist of projects tailored simply to fit the size of the job, dispensing with his or her spiritual, intellectual, and moral development. The university can fulfill the needs of society in general and business in particular if it produces students with a high level of personality development.

Every man and woman's faculties, strengths, and habits

should be developed to work for justice. The university has to try to establish relations among intellectual, cultural, and altruistic development. According to the universal, multisecular precept of giving each person what is his or hers by human right and respecting this right, it is inferred that personal liberties end where the next person's rights begin. The basis of the political development that the university as an institution is obliged to provide as part of its educational function is the practice of justice with individual and community rights.

The university, in short, has an educational mission that is not limited to, but goes beyond, the simple transmission of the courses listed in what is sometimes referred to as the visible curriculum that is taught at prescribed times and in prescribed schedules. There is another curriculum that could be called a hidden curriculum underlying the university's educational commitment. It assumes the undefinable and imprecise task of providing profound and full learning.

Some teachers have an ontological intention to develop a person's learning to be and learning to become. Others actively work in education with the intellectual, comprehensive, and creative capacities of the student: learning to learn, learning to understand, and learning to create and produce. The social nuances of education, such as learning to coexist with others and with nature, which is the basis of all life, learning to adapt, and learning to become leaders are also included. Finally, there is learning to discover the moral and eternal transcendence of human faculties and actions.

University pedagogy

I use the expression "university pedagogy" (Beridze 1990), although it may be inadequate as it is "etymologically absurd and does not cover the entire field" of such an important matter (Unesco/CEPES 1985). This is why authors such as Knowles (1969, 1985) prefer the neologism "andragogy."

The topic of pedagogical types in universities, which is closely related to the quality of professorial resources, is easily traceable to the development of the teaching sessions of the old schools and the nascent university during the medieval period. They later produced the teaching and research seminars at the universities of Halle and Göttingen in the 19th century (Paulsen 1906).

Although today the large numbers of students make seminar teaching more difficult, the university should concentrate on teaching and research seminars as its most effective teaching methods. They help unify research and teaching and stimulate full learning and personal development (Tot 1988).

In general, university teachers increasingly recognize that as educators they must have a double competence: an academic one in their respective fields and a pedagogical, or rather, a psychopedagogical and ethical competence (Unesco 1990f). On the other hand, however, it is alleged that there are subjective and objective obstacles that confirm the estimation made by Jean Demal, the president of the Association international de pédagogie universitaire: "Up to now we can notice an inverse ratio between the pedagogical training of teachers and the level at which they teach, from primary to higher education" (Unesco/CEPES 1985).

"Although auto-didactics generally characterizes university pedagogy" (Carton 1983, p. 30), pedagogical training deserves special attention except where this has been the object of investigation and specific training, for example, in graduate programs. Rodek (1988) proposes the following points for consideration:

> The school and organized study are currently at a cross-roads. We are witnessing an increasingly obvious transformation of the school system for, in the society of the future, the school and the university will not and cannot be the sole places of study.
>
> A broader notion of study tends to suppress the traditional concept of instruction. It is usually described by the following syntagms: from strictly guided study to independent study; from mural to extra-mural study; from early study to life-long study; from adaptive toward anticipatory study; from individual toward social study; from national toward global study.

> Whereas traditional study is mainly oriented toward guided study achieved through teaching, guidance and teaching are important for the new concept of study only in so far as they are a function of independent study, of learning to study. Under contemporary conditions, we should insist on future-oriented studies, studies that will be in the service of man and society (anticipatory study). New information and communication media can make a major contribution to anticipatory studies. Their application in pedagogy comes fully to expression only in the context of innovative and anticipatory studies.

It is not only the European universities with a long history of tradition that organize seminars on university pedagogy. "The preparation for higher education personnel, which for some time has been carried out in English-speaking countries, has extended to French-speaking countries, following the example of Zaire and the Ivory Coast" (Unesco 1991a). Taiwo (1991, p. 3) says:

> In pedagogy, for example, there has been some re-orientation of university teachers' attitude toward teaching. And on its part, university administration has made funds available to some extent for the modernization of teaching techniques at the university level. Concerned with the need to improve teaching and examining skills of her lecturers with a view to getting better student results and in consonance with practices in the developed nations of the world where internship programmes have been mounted on regular bases since the turn of the century.

Taiwo points out that recently, the University of Ife, Nigeria (now the Obafemi Awolowo University)

> Perhaps became the first university in West Africa and probably in Africa to launch an intensive one-term orientation course for new lecturers and professors...which was expressly designed to familiarize new teaching staff of the University with their teaching chores [and] covered detailed examination of faculty and departmental objectives vis-a-vis a discussion on planning various courses and instructional objectives of the University.

The initiative at Ife, because of its "desirability," was "replicated" by many African universities, e.g., the experiences at

Abidjan in Côte d'Ivoire, at Botswana, Lesotho, Swaziland, Zambia, and Tanzania (Taiwo 1991). Taiwo (p. 6) adds:

> Apart from efforts that have been made by African Universities in improving the teaching effectiveness of their lecturers, another innovative reform that is worthy of mention is the application of technology to teaching with the sole purpose of facilitating learning. Teaching techniques have been modernized in many an African University in the last decade to a point that one is tempted to talk of revolutionization of pedagogy by technology. And it would be fair to conclude that teaching has become "gadgetry" today in the typical African University. For example, language laboratory carrels and closed circuit television facilities are common sights nowadays in many African Universities. Educational television studios, photographic and cinematographic units are also common educational facilities to be found today within the four walls of many African Universities; and so also are video-tape recorders/players and overhead projectors. These educational gadgets and more have become the order of the day nowadays in our University setting that many African Universities have institutionalized units to cater for teaching aids within their environment.

At the third international workshop for pedagogical improvement on the continent and in the Caribbean, Havana, September 1989, university pedagogy was the subject under debate. It has, among other factors, "the unusual growth and transformation of university centers" and the "expansion and democratization of higher education" that ought to go hand in hand with "quality." This requires that the professor continually raise the level of his or her knowledge, through continual up-dating and training and that the teaching–education process has a solid scientific basis, using methods that facilitate learning by heterogeneous groups of students (Unesco/REDESALC 1989).

The Asian and Pacific regional workshop on the organization and management of teaching–learning units in universities held at Tribhuvan University, Katmandu, Nepal, in 1988 (Unesco 1989d; see Adams 1987), started from a clear principle: almost universally, academic staff members have, in varying proportions, dual responsibilities of research and teaching, for which the university ought to prepare its professors because the question is no longer whether academic staff development is necessary, but how it is to be achieved.

To justify such an urgent goal (Unesco 1989d, p. 3):

> Within the turbulent and rapidly changing environment of higher education, academics find themselves under pressure to contribute to the growth and development of knowledge in their respective fields, to provide intellectual leadership in the community and, at the same time, to ensure that their courses and programmes are relevant to the developmental needs of their respective societies. The combined result of these pressures has been to emphasize the need for continuing professional development by academic staff. It is increasingly recognized that the rate of growth of knowledge in most fields is so fast that university faculties are everywhere confronted with the need for continual upgrading and renewal in their disciplinary areas.
>
> In addition to this, and despite the widespread belief that all that is required of a good university lecturer is a sound knowledge of subject matter, teaching itself is becoming more complex and demanding. Students, anxious to succeed and to better themselves through education, are making demands on their instructors for relevant, up-to-date, well-prepared instruction. Methods of assessment have become more sophisticated with increased reliance on both qualitative and quantitative indicators of student learning. New technologies have influenced teaching: the use of video, computers, self-paced learning materials and even distance education. All these factors combine to place new pressures and demands on teachers already burdened by static or declining budgets, large enrolment and changing curricula.
>
> [As a practical consequence, and] recognizing the need for structures to promote academic staff development, institutions throughout the region have undertaken a variety of programs that differ in detail but are nonetheless united in their common concern [for] the improvement of teaching, improvement of research performance. evaluating teacher effectiveness, enhancing students' learning competence, institutional research and investigation, awareness-raising and

dissemination of information, maintaining a resource centre, and mobilizing resources.

There is great diversity in the range of approaches adopted by institutions to facilitate academic staff development. When they are reduced to their bare essentials, most approaches fall into one of the two categories: they either rely on an individual or a small group acting as a committee, or utilize a formally structured centre, department or unit.

In the case of the approach based on individuals or groups, again this subdivides into two categories: separate groups or individuals with a concern for staff development or some formally constituted unit may be located either inside or outside a School of Education. These various possible structural arrangements have been summarized in a single diagram which is reproduced below [Figure 2].

Concerning the inclusion of an academic staff development unit in the university's general structure, workshop participants said:

The unit should be permanent and also independent so as not to be disturbed by too much unwanted interference or constant change. Its roles should be that of a facilitator and co-ordinator rather than a controlling body.

An academic staff development unit should be client oriented and responsive to the needs of academic faculty members, it

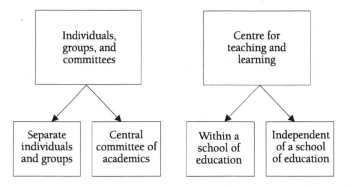

Figure 2. *Structure for academic staff development*
(*source: Unesco 1989d, p. 19*).

should be small in size yet effective. There should be a core or nucleus of permanent staff, but it should also draw upon the services of staff from other departments, faculties and even outside institutions on an ad-hoc basis. It should not be so formal in its administration that it inhibits effective functioning.

Related to the question of where the unit is located and its nature is the issue of whether it is basically responsive (reactive) or whether it initiates changes of its own accord (proactive). The reactive unit is generally answerable to a representative committee and responds to the requests made via the committee [Figure 3].

There is no direct connection between the unit and its clients, and if there are no requests forthcoming (even where change and improvement are clearly called-for), there is nothing for the unit to react to. This is probably the greatest drawback of this model because it presupposes a greater degree of critical

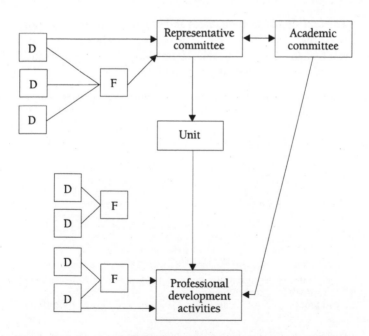

Figure 3. A reactive staff development unit: D, department; F, faculty
(source: Unesco 1989d, p. 27).

self-awareness and personal responsibility for academic development than many staff and students may possess.

The alternative is the proactive unit which, in addition to responding to requests, also initiates activities or development studies and interacts directly with academic staff [Figure 4].

Such units may have an advisory or consultative committee and take it as their responsibility to generate awareness of teaching and learning issues, and to raise the consciousness of staff, students and administrators. They seek to get people to recognize and solve problems, which, although they are real, may not be perceived by the organization's members themselves.

Krismanic (1988) points out:

The increased number of students which is not followed by an adequate increase in the number of teachers does not allow for a tutorial system and makes necessary a search for some institutionalized form of assistance, available to students as

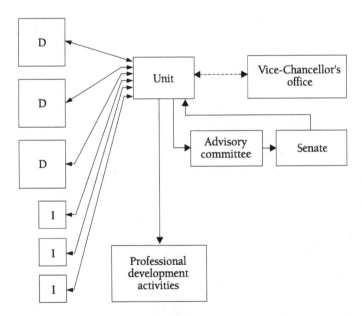

Figure 4. A proactive staff development unit: D, department;
I, individuals (source: Unesco 1989d, p. 28).

well at the beginning as in the course of their studies. Psycho-logical counselling and organized informative communication with students could compensate for the lack of individual contacts with the faculty, enhance students' adaptation to the higher level of education and increase the efficacy of their work.

Brauer and Bieck (1988) mention the pedagogical conditions required for the teaching and study of the modern science and the importance of training students to master scientific methods, learning methods, in the face of the extraordinary growth of knowledge now and in the future.

Audiovisual and computer-assisted instruction

Audiovisual aids and computers have become important instruc-tional media in pedagogy and university teaching. The word audiovisual has been fashionable since the 1940s, and now has a variety of meanings: photographic production; radio broadcast-ing; designs on overhead transparencies; television in its diverse forms; the magnetic or adhesive board that requires the teacher to do the audio portion; magnetic tapes; fixed or moving images; ephemeral Hertzian messages; and sound and slide presentations.

There is a continual stream of new teaching methods, but they have not yet overcome traditional procedures. Developing universal criteria for classifying audiovisuals is an impossible task. In some cases, the teacher controls the machine directly in the classroom; in others, the person teaching is subject to the mechanical whims and rhythms already programmed into the device. Occasionally, the machine is allowed to surpass the message.

In some cases, the teacher might be distanced by the machine, but good teachers know how to preserve face-to-face, intelligence-to-intelligence, and heart-to-heart communication. With mechanical audiovisual means there is always the risk of staying with what is purely instructional.

There has been discussion about the degree to which audio-visuals complement or replace textbooks. Audiovisuals can entice the student and teacher to such an extent that the former loses his love for reading and the latter gives up to the producers of audiovisuals too much of his or her capacity to think about, invent, create, and explain concepts.

The final classification for audiovisuals deals with the degree to which they estrange the student from direct manual contact with objects (Table 2). It is not the same to see the flower, stem, leaf, and root on a screen as it is to touch and feel them. Watching a plant grow in seconds through the art of luminous projection is not the same as planting it and lovingly caring for it so that it will thrive and bear fruit.

These are all things to think about because audiovisuals are relatively new. It is difficult to pinpoint when they originated as visual aids. Humans scratched cave walls when teaching. The medieval artist cast stained-glass windows to teach the history of salvation. Chinese shadow figures were useful for Fénelon to teach the Dauphin of France, and Comenius introduced graphic language into texts to be studied. We are indebted to the 19th and 20th centuries for the chemical, electronic, and mechanical processes that made cinematography possible. However, as today

Table 2. Classification of telecommunications technologies.

	Noninteractive	Interactive
Audio	Radio (primary carrier) Radio (subcarrier) Audiotape	Telephone Audio teleconferencing
Video	Open broadcast television Cable television (one-way) Videotape Instructional television fixed service Satellite television (one-way) Slow scan/freeze frame television (one-way)	Microwave (point to point) Cable television (two-way or viewer-response) Slow scan/freeze frame television (two-way) Electronic blackboard Satellite television (two-way) Video teleconferencing
Computer		Computer-assister instruction Computer-based instructional management

Source: Lewis (1983).

there is very little lapse between an invention and its use pedagogically, audiovisuals can be used in education at a distance to give more students, in scattered areas access to information.

The technical explosion in the area of audiovisuals helps us face the challenge of the explosions in science and knowledge, in worldwide demography, and in the yearning for educational democratization and continuous education.

Expressions such as "programmed teaching" are used along with "computer-assisted instruction" or "teaching machines." There is a wide variety of methods for self-instruction in which different processes stimulate the student's activity and permit him or her to control and verify the learning process. "Programmed teaching" depends on a method of organizing and programming steps based on individual effort and dates from 1806. A mechanical device was created by S.L. Pressey that permitted the learner to push one of four keys to see if the questions that had been previously prepared had been correctly answered. If the key corresponding to the correct answer was pushed, the machine presented the next question, and so on. Skinner's theories had a lot to do with his compatriot's invention.

"Computer-assisted teaching" appeared in the United States in 1958, and its development runs parallel with the development of computer systems. In the 1960s, governments became aware of the importance of this resource and manufacturers designed and produced tutorial programs, guided exercises, tests of adaptation, and simulation programs.

Once again, we can ask ourselves about the formative and educational value of these and other procedures. We cannot completely deny their validity (Unesco 1989b, 1991c), but there is a danger of confusing education with instruction and of ignoring social and communication aspects, which are so necessary in the formative processes.

Modern society is often called "the knowledge society," "the information society," and "the communication society" even though there has not been a complete consensus about the true meaning of these expressions. "Dictionary definitions appear circular" (Ploman 1991). In the face of such inconsistent concepts, he recalled the deep questions posed by T.S. Elliot: "Where is the wisdom we have lost in knowledge? Where is the knowledge we have lost in information?" Cleveland (in Ploman 1991) added another perceptive question: "Where is the information we have lost in data?" What is certain, Ploman continued, is that although "throughout history societies have evolved practices and rules for the generation of knowledge and for the flow of information," knowledge, information, and communication, as they are used today and in whatever way they are understood, have generated the "emerging information society," conditioned by a series of imbalances in technology, in applications, as much as in conceptual approaches. All have a direct bearing on the management of knowledge, which arises from its unequal production and proceeds to its unequal use, mastery, and practice, until we reach an "imperialism of instrumental rationality."

Carried away by the desire to restruct Soviet undergraduate and university education, Timina (1988) reacts by warning:

> While developing automation, computers, artificial intelligence and the like, man must not turn into an appendix of technology or fall prey eventually to his own intellect, his own spiritual underdevelopment.

Interdisciplinarity

Seminars are probably the best setting for interdisciplinary research and teaching. Although the concept of interdisciplinarity is not new, it has recently aroused renewed interest (Gusdorf 1963, 1977; Luyten 1970). Interdisciplinary studies should be synergistic in that the subjects' interrelations mutually reinforce one another and the outcome is greater than the sum of the parts. Carton (1983, p. 34) states:

> After the sixties, the debate on interdisciplinarity has become considerably enriched; proof of this is the Colloquium organized by CEPES (Colloque sur l'interdisciplinarité dans l'enseignement supérieur en Europe, Bucharest, 1981) and by Unesco. It was there that it was established that "interdisciplinarity" had to be defined in relation to "disciplinarity"

and that the former was understood as "a constellation in which more than one discipline are involved" and which is also located in the research domains and in educational contexts.

A similar concern led to the conferences and discussions promoted by CERI (1970).

Carton (1983) also states that joint disciplinary interaction

Can go from the simple communication of ideas to the mutual integration of directorial concepts of epistemology, terminology, methodology, procedures, data, and the organization of research and teaching, the areas in which this interaction is of such importance. In turn, an interdisciplinary group is made up of persons who have received training in different domains of knowledge (disciplines); each person possesses his own concepts, methods, data and terms.

Luyten (1970), with his historical vision, and Popovic (1988) and Oyen (1988), with a critical attitude, point out that the university's structure is not always conducive to interdisciplinary studies. Popovic says:

The attention of the academic circles has been turned, already for a long time, to various atomizations of branches of science and art which increase the expansion of specialization of high education. In this respect, we found out an interesting contradiction in our universities: every important breakthrough, every important step forward in a science and every important achievement in the field of arts destroys the barriers and the differences between various branches of science and arts and between those newly established disciplines; still, the institutional effect after such achievements tends to divide and to atomize even more the system of high education by an elaborate network of different specializations. After every progress, after every achievement, the scientists and artists divide themselves into increasingly narrow specialties, each of them having its own rules, languages and values. The model of curricula at the universities obviously missed the opportunity to reflect the links between various fields of knowledge, and therefore leads increasingly to the wrong direction, and thus becomes the expression of retard and of hindrance to any progress.

It is important to note the following: if we do not have an educational system which can secure the linkage between experience and knowledge, which can not provide data about such links, if those data are scattered everywhere, like in the present model of academic "fields" (domains, departments, chairs) we can not even notice that we lack such data. In such a case, is it possible to give complete and correct information about ourselves and about the world we live in, or do we keep proving our own dogmas?

Oyen (1988), moreover, says:

One fundamental aim of science, reflected in teaching as well as in research, is that of demonstrating how variation in phenomena under observation may be reduced through explanation. However, the structure of scientific institutions appears to have the dysfunction of encouraging the formation of discipline "territory" whose occupants must act as defenders against intruders and, not uncommonly, against the closest neighbors who compete in a market of scarce resources that which is to be explained may well have a location within a particular discipline, but science is not well served if that which provides the explanation must be sought, for such structural reasons, within the same discipline boundaries.

The Canadian report on university education (Smith 1991, p. 69) states something similar:

The issue of disciplinarity is also vexing. While knowledge is organized by discipline, it is seldom applied that way in the solution of practical problems. Such solutions tend to require perspectives that draw on more than one discipline and often require teams of individuals with different kinds of expertise. In preparing people for the solution of practical problems, therefore, universities face the conundrum of how to provide a broad education with an appreciation of interdisciplinary approaches when the material to be presented is organized and taught within disciplinary boundaries.

Real interdisciplinarity means more than teaching several subjects in conjunction. It is perfectly possible to find relatable disciplines or cross-disciplines with all or some of the subjects in the curriculum. This cross-disciplinarity undoubtedly produces better and more integrated pedagogical results. Two or more disciplines can mutually support each other because of the methods they have in common. They can also join together and form a new discipline — isomorphic interdisciplinarity — such as biochemistry. Or they can unite the disciplines of a particular profession, such as the disciplines of education, of social education, of administration, or of health. This is known as auxiliary interdisciplinarity (Boisot 1970; Heckhausen 1970).

The study and solution of complex problems, among them that of ecology, by interdisciplinarity helps to prevent seeing them solely from the point of view of disciplines and professions that work independently without obtaining agreement on solutions or plans. This is known as compound interdisciplinarity, given the variety of viewpoints that must be agreed upon to reach successful solutions.

Given the vast number of conflicting situations in which university professionals are involved today, universities should encourage the academic practice of interdisciplinarity as a way to develop the student's capacities for understanding. "Even if it is true that interdisciplinary programs abound in universities, it is the disciplines that continue to offer the framework for recruiting and promoting persons and for the confirmation of knowledge" (Weiler 1991). However, "interdisciplinary research" is indispensable because it "responds in the most ample way to reality and prepares professionals for the development of new leadership" (Schlemper 1991). Interdisciplinarity is "a response to the theoretical–methodological atomization of reality. It is a style of work both in theoretical aspects and in empirical research that rests on an integrating, overall vision, although this does not mean that the specific profiles of each discipline are lost" (Castro 1991). Only through the interaction of disciplines could there be a healthy response to problems such as those posed by Ki-Zerbo (1991): "health, nutrition, habitat, civic education, and human rights."

This social commitment of the disciplines and specializations is related and emphasized by Carton (1983, p. 36):

> If the internal evolution of scientific thought is considered, we can verify a double movement after the passage of a few years: that of the creation of new disciplines situated at the union of two or more existing disciplines and, vice versa, the search for trans-disciplinarity through the use of concepts that are similar to the models or structures. This second movement can be explained by the students' demands to bring science and socio-economic realities closer together and, simultaneously, of certain university environments to get out of their ghetto.

Both movements explain the distinction Carton makes between endogenous and exogenous interdisciplinarity. The former is based on the production of new knowledge and pursues its more or less explicit ambition of "the unity of science." This is a legitimate goal integrating curricula and promoting new types of research and teaching outside thre usual structures. However, society's problems, such as jobs, urban growth, health, or transportation, do not necessarily fit into university disciplines. Dealing with these problems through interdisciplinary studies is exogenous interdisciplinarity.

This makes the university think about what its training contract with its students should be and what ought to be "the knowledge prepared for/with/by the preparers and the students. In fact, the university can limit itself to increasing its circle of initiates through the broader admission of new candidates and through the invention of new pedagogical formulas.... It really opens up when there is a radical change in the types of intellectual production" (Carton 1983), and it is important that all students who are admitted are aware of this. Instead of requiring students to accumulate a certain amount of knowledge to obtain a degree, the university ought to discover what the community is lacking and where it needs help. It is time to renounce the myth of the democratization of university studies and "for the university to concern itself more with its role in the preparation of democratic knowledge. By posing the problem in this way and looking at it from this perspective, interdisciplinarity makes much more sense."

Computer resources support modern university administration. Although their educational results are frequently questioned, they are at least a useful instrument for interdisciplinary work.

Education for creativity

Research, which has been emphasized since the 19th century, is commonly in opposition to the teaching and educational mission because of different philosophical positions. Since the early 19th century, ideologists in German universities raised the precept of research linked with teaching to "awaken the idea of science in the most outstanding young people" so that, in the process of learning, "they would investigate, invent, and present scientific knowledge, gradually producing it" (Schleiermacher 1959 [1808]). Fichte (1959 [1807]) supported this idea when he criticized teaching based on memorization as "more an act of suffering than an activity of the spirit." He advises that "education at the university is the process of preparation for work that is rich in contents, precisely through participation in the spiritual life that is aroused there"; that "this preparation does not consist of dividable contents" and that "precisely with the principle of linking research with teaching, a second principle is that of joining research and teaching with the process of formation."

Von Humboldt (1959 [1810]) agreed with both these thinkers when he denounced the French plan to leave teaching to the university and research to the academies. Humboldt proclaimed that "science ought to be sought unceasingly, almost as if it could in fact be fully discovered," for "all is lost forever if one renounces the task of enthusiastically seeking the truth, or if one were to imagine that it is not necessary to create science from the deepest part of the spirit, or if we thought that science could become alienated into pieces of knowledge, some of which are placed next to others."

Nevertheless, with the increase of scientific research, Paul de Lagarde, a professor at Göttingen, deplores the fact that the university, wishing to be both a research academy and a teaching school, has become only "a very imperfect type of teaching establishment" (de Lagarde 1959a [1878], b [1881]. Among other reasons, this is because of the difficulty in finding good teachers and good researchers. This is a functionalist objection that Max Weber (1959 [1919]) also puts forward when, in speaking to the students at the University of Munich, he distinguishes between the "internal vocation" toward science, which is natural to the scientist and researcher, rich in inspirations and ideas sustained by an enthusiastic intelligence, and the "external vocation" that characterizes the professional and the professor.

In the two postwar periods, the positions of two philosophers can be contrasted. Max Scheler (1959 [1921]) advocated the distinction between the institution that proposes merely professional education in different specialties and new research institutes closely connected with the old style of universities and academies, where the most outstanding researchers would transmit the knowledge of the era, not only to students but also to professors in different professions. They would consider current progress in research. Scheler does not advocate breaking up research and teaching, but rather proposes a new postsecondary system.

After World War II, Karl Jaspers (1970), on the other hand, returned to the "idea of higher education, which is simultaneously useful for research and teaching as a unit; it requires the freedom to teach and to learn as the condition for the responsible independence of all teachers and students; it rejects simple pedagogical practice and exclusivist specialization. On the contrary, it develops the unity of the sciences in lively communication and spiritual combat."

This debate over the relation of research to teaching still continues. There is more concern over what is researched than who does the research. There are universities that do not consider research as part of their mission. Others separate it from teaching and consign it exclusively to institutes or centres. A third alternative is to try to make room for it in the course of daily academic activity.

Just as important is the research itself or what is researched, the concrete product that, in turn, can be external. The university should plan the lines or fields of continuing research that it selects, that give it prestige, and that allow it to compete in the research market.

The aim of linking research with teaching has the significant benefit of producing internal effects in the minds of the researchers who also teach, which in turn affects their students, if they are inspired to discover more than what they are simply required to learn through obligatory assignments.

The researchers involve both the teacher and the student. Some object that emphasizing research causes teaching to suffer and can even affect students' progress. It is contended that it is impossible for professors to be first-class teachers as well as notable researchers because the two vocations, the internal and the external that Weber spoke about, are conflicting and irreconcilable. However, this is not necessarily the case, as the professor well knows and the true maestro best understands. If it is necessary to teach to live, the professor must try to become the complete "university man": the scholar with an internal vocation for his or her science and discipline and an enthusiastic intelligence from which inspirations and ideas emanate. The professor must not allow the vocation of the researcher to overcome the external vocation of teaching, but combine the spirit of searching that feeds the life of understanding.

This way of being a university person is the equivalent of the professor–researcher who works hard at teaching, but not only at teaching. The opposite side of the coin is the researcher–professor who works harder at science. About the first, Emerson (1840) says:

> [Colleges and professors] can only highly serve us, when they
> aim not to drill, but to create; when they gather from far every

ray of various genius to their hospitable halls, and, by the concentrated fires, put the hearts of their youth on flame.

Both types of university person know how to overcome the four most frequent objections to the alliance between research and teaching: time, because the researcher's dedication to the university is part-time, or if full-time, overloaded with hours in class; space, because there is no office or physical place for work; technical or instrumental, because the information media and the university's laboratories are deficient; and finally, salary.

The report of the Commission of Inquiry on Canadian University Education (Smith 1991, p. 31) presents a typical, practical description of the relations between research and teaching. The report accepts the fact that

> Universities are believed to be institutions of teaching and learning wherein research is performed and wherein the teaching is done by persons engaged in continuing scholarly activities. This arrangement persists because it is felt to be desirable that teachers and students both be in a learning mode with an enthusiastic desire to expand their understanding.

> [Nevertheless,]...a trend from the United States has been imported into Canada, namely a situation where the quantity of research publications is more important to the careers of university professors than is the excellence of their teaching. At many universities teaching excellence is not accorded the same importance as research publication with respect to decisions concerning hiring, tenure and promotion;...new challenges with respect to the organization and delivery of teaching services are being responded to sluggishly;...actual teaching hours of full-time permanent faculty have remained stable or have declined, even in the face of the challenge of dealing with larger student–faculty ratios; and...few steps are taken to ensure the acquisition and improvement of teaching skills among new and existing members of the academic profession.

Whatever the objections to the alliance between research and teaching, the educational function of the university ought to be the winner. The objections are worthwhile, and can and should be attended to by the university as an organized institution, and also by the researcher, who would do well to have read the history of important, creative individuals who did not at first always have everything they needed to achieve their research goals.

The unity of research and teaching is a consequence of the corporate effort of professors and students, united through their research. Von Humboldt (1959 [1810]) quite fittingly expressed it as follows:

> If there is a certain relation between professor and student in schools, there is another, completely different one that exists in the university: there the former does not exist for the latter; rather, both exist for science; the presence and cooperation of students is an integral part of the task of doing research, which could not be carried out as successfully if they did not support their professor.

It is also true that knowledge of pedagogical methods, such as teaching and research seminars, and the effort to overcome obstacles associated with interdisciplinary work, create an environment in which different types of alliances between research and teaching can bear fruit. This supposes that university professors act in the pursuit of findings, although they might not be researchers by trade, and they instill this in their students. "A teacher who is not involved in research becomes rapidly outdated and the very notion of higher education is no longer valid" (Lemoyn de Forges in Unesco 1991c). For this reason, Ishumi (1990, p. 25) says that

> The distinction between teachers and researchers at higher, especially university levels, is not very valid. For, at such a high level, the transmitter or imparter of knowledge, or teacher, is supposed to be at the same time the producer of information and knowledge through the use of varied techniques of research. And any serious and worthy researcher is duty-bound to disseminate the results of his/her research labours to the many others for the sake of wider knowledge, informed policy formulation and meaningful practice.

In this way, a stimulating climate for research — Ishumi calls it a "research culture" — is created in the university because research as a concrete act only occurs if it is nourished by an inquisitive attitude of searching and finding.

This is the climate and environment that satisfies the research mission of the university. In addition, they develop and form the students' inquisitive minds. When they see things the way they are, but with an inquisitive, penetrating, patient, and reflexive spirit, they ask, "How could things be otherwise, and for what legitimate purposes or benefits?" Eventually, students achieve the illuminating synthesis, which is the productive, creative moment.

If research, which has been so emphasized since the beginning of the 19th century, can be maintained as the intrinsic mission and function of the university and not conflict with its educational, teaching mission, it cannot be made to depend solely and extrinsically on the research market. In this respect, we have a clear warning from the Ministers of Education of the Member States of Europe at their second conference in 1975 (see Carton 1983).

Education and complexity

The cognitive explosion surrounding us and the speed of development in different branches of knowledge create problems. One of these is the way in which work is often fragmented. Another problem is the rapid and almost unforeseeable succession of social changes combined with the intricacy of national, international, and supernational relations. These are some of the factors that, while making the tricky practice of the university's academic administration and the student's integral formation difficult, also spread uncertainty in both. This is the result of the complexity of the modern world, which some might even call chaos. Although this planet seems more complex day by day, the human mind can cope if it nourishes itself with the serenity of the thinking spirit and does not only see uncertainty and a chaotic situation.

The teaching and formative function of the university as an institution is to develop the student's capacities to confront the complexity that surrounds us and to provide him or her with the basic ethical principles with which we all agree (Unesco 1992b).

PART III

◆

TO ADMINISTRATE
IS TO SERVE

The complexities of university administration can be condensed into the following types of service: to culture, through the professions, through university extension services, through institutional relations, and to the future of the university as an institution.

SERVICE TO CULTURE

◆

H. Carrier (1985) asks, "How can the surprising situation of culture in present-day social language be explained?" More than a hundred countries have created ministries or official institutions in charge of the protection, support, growth, and strengthening of culture.

Of course, culture has always coexisted with humanity. The ancients spoke of "humanitas" and "civilitas." In the 17th and 18th centuries, faithful to the classical humanism and civil spirit revived during the Renaissance, it was suggested that everything humanity does to enrich its own nature and institutions and to improve its attitudes and behaviours should be included under the term "culture," a word related to the Latin "colere," which means to cultivate with love. All this is inseparable from knowledge gained for its intellectual capacity and from the treasures of artistic and functional beauty we use and enjoy for our own benefit (Scheler 1972).

The universals of culture

On the one hand, there are the manifestations of personal culture and collective culture: linguistic, political, and social culture; scientific and erudite culture; ethical and moralizing culture; and religious culture. On the other hand, there is objective and expressive culture, which includes the "belles lettres," fine arts, and the great achievements of humanity: literature, drama, music, sculpture, painting, handicrafts, architecture, landscaping, physical culture, sports, and even the culture of leisure and relaxation, tranquillity and rest, silence, and prayer. These are delicate objects that reunite us with the cultural behaviour of people in society and with the eternal importance of cultural values.

Cultural spheres, or cultural universals, are so called because of their extension throughout time, or history, and their spatial dispersion throughout geographic regions. All are contained in the concept of civilization, which if reduced exclusively to political and economical perspectives, reveals a categorical difference between the developed world and the Third World.

The human being and culture

People take part in the various forms of culture such as erudite culture, learned culture, or inherited culture; they grasp it and assimilate it as a guarantee of stability, and, most importantly, transform it in the process of creating and building cultural values. In this sense we can speak of anthropological culture, or of human culture.

Since 1982, Unesco (whose C stands for real, objective culture and cultivated, erudite, personal culture) moved closer to anthropological culture and the protagonist of all culture: humanity in society. However, it did so without dropping its initial efforts. Unesco (1982) stated that

> In its widest sense, culture can nowadays be considered as the cluster of different spiritual, material, intellectual and affective traits that characterize a society or a social group. In addition to the letters and the arts, it includes lifestyles, the basic human rights, the systems of values, traditions and beliefs.... Culture gives man the capacity to reflect about himself. It is what makes us specifically human, rational, critical, and ethically committed beings. Man expresses himself through it, becomes aware of himself, recognizes himself as an unfinished project, submits his own realizations to discussion, unceasingly seeks new meanings, and creates works that transcend him.

A year later, in a colloquium sponsored on the social goals of higher education (Unesco 1983), Third World participants insisted that "their cultures not only be taught" but be "converted into fertile ground in which all the actions of preparation, education, and research in cultural forms can take root" to create a "national awareness" and to better "participate in universal culture."

Similar concepts were understood and accepted in the constitution of the Second Vatican Council, *Gaudium et Spes.* Unesco's declaration had precedents in the *Cultural Charter of Africa* (1976) and the *European Declaration on Cultural Objects* (1984). Such international approval concerning culture was echoed in the declaration by Arab countries, which was worked out within the framework of ALECSO, the cultural organism of the Arab League (Carrier 1985).

The university and service to culture

There are signs of contemporary uneasiness concerning culture, because societies have now noticed that their survival is dependent on the cultural sphere and on ways of approaching culture, but they find that this is already almost lost. This creates confusion as people find themselves without a secure base and lacking spiritual support.

The confusion can be attributed to the effects of technological advances, to the disenchantment caused by social, political, and economic systems, to the failure of so-called models for development, and to various other factors that the university should analyze. The university cannot be content with reflecting the societies surrounding it, casting aside its principal commitment to being their model and pattern, for only in this way will the university serve culture.

University research and culture

The course taken by university research has a lot to do with culture. In this regard, H. Carrier (1985) states:

> In our changing societies, the very objective of university research has yet to be defined. If on the one hand research is becoming more and more specialized and fragmented, which is necessary in order to make scientific analysis advance, there is another research requirement that unceasingly seeks to unite and integrate knowledge and the evolution that is profoundly transforming our institutions and our civilizations. Moreover, if scientific research is being divided among universities, governments, and enterprises, and if this exodus occurs in regard to universities, it is sufficient reason to redefine the type of research that corresponds to universities as academic institutions. It is true that universities should support the scientific policies of industrial States, but at the same time they should protect research that is the most disinterested, most basic, and most linked to cultural needs. This research can not be planned based only on economical logic, the importance of which, without minimizing it, should have its limits. Another type of logic should also inspire universities, namely a logic based on cultural perspective. What we ultimately defend is the status of free intelligence in society. As Jaspers said, "The idea of the university is the idea of our intellectual existence."

Pajin (1988) points out that "The university is per definition a mediator between cultures" in a "vertical (historical) strata of cultures, and in various horizontal (intercultural) sections, under the motto: value the past and understand the present, to create future."

A document from the Asian and Pacific region (Unesco 1990b) emphasizes culture as service when it says: "Along with teaching and research, service to the society is now a well-accepted function of higher education institutions." This function is one that "goes beyond immediate pragmatic and practical needs; they preserve the cultural heritage of a society and provide a form for objective debate about pressing philosophical and ethical issues."

Carton (1983, p. 26) adds:

In such a perspective, the university is called upon simultaneously to recognize the emergence of new cultures in society
and to integrate them to the activities of formation and
research, the safeguards of its analytical and critical capacities.
This cannot occur except through the university's support for
the cultural participants given the task of constructing the
society of tomorrow; through the university's call to these
same participants to make room for the multiform ways of
practicing and expressing contemporary cultures; and
through the university's enthusiasm for the cultural creation
of those who participate in it: professors and students.

SERVICE THROUGH THE PROFESSIONS

◆

It is said that people are not only the users but the builders of
cultural values. Consequently, the university provides an
immediate service to individuals and social groups through
professional work.

The professions and trades

The distinction between the liberal professions and the service
industries or trades dates back to the old distinction between the
social duties of a free person and the tasks of servants and slaves.

When the masters' and students' guilds were solidified in the
12th and 13th centuries, the universities granted a special posi-
tion to the juridical profession as a service to justice, to the
medical profession as a service to health, and to the theological
profession as a service to a society. Historically, the liberal arts
and trades and professions connected with them were not
included.

Historians believe that during the Renaissance the university
placed more importance on the person than on the person's
practical actions. Although the progress of the natural sciences

began as a result of the Scientific Revolution, it was after the Industrial Revolution that many technical trades were elevated to the category of university professions once it was established that they had the scientific basis that was by then indispensable. This phenomenon started at the end of the 17th century in France, when educational institutions were created to train skilled labour.

However, the gradual transformation of many trades into professions with university training grew dramatically in the 19th century. Technical schools multiplied, and schools and faculties of civil, agricultural, and manufacturing engineering, as well as schools dedicated to the veterinary sciences and agriculture, were opened.

The modern professions

In the shadow of the research and subsequent scientific development that followed the industrial and commercial boom, the modern professions arose, including those of administration.

The relations between the professionalized university and trade organizations grew and, as a result, the highest level of formal education became divided into institutions with different characteristics. Nowadays, we use the term postsecondary educational systems to denote higher education or the "third level" of education. Within this category, the university continues to be dominant. Postsecondary systems are best defined by the nature and degree of the academic functions carried out in them, rather than because the student has finished secondary-level studies.

The modern professions did not, however, remain closely tied to the university's academic organism in the same way. Several of the professions arose out of the university and prospered together with the university until their long-standing scientific tradition was attested to, or the university kept them separate from its secular academic structure. As a consequence, today's postsecondary systems in different countries around the world still have biases. This is especially evident in the universities that arose in the 19th century. In some of them, technical and technological institutions created early in the 19th century raised their academic level at the same time as the growth in technology increased their size and importance.

Many of these still maintain the designation of technical or technological institutions and have not changed their name to that of "university." Many "national systems of education" and postsecondary systems, have been the result of historical, social, cultural, and educational evolution. They were not conceived of with an organization already in place, but had to be flexible to respond appropriately to the gradual, unpredictable changes in education. Even later legislation prevents the necessary educational flexibility. For this reason, the following discussion on scholastic systems of education and on possible theories of postsecondary systems will be more useful for analyzing, classifying, and understanding situations than for planning, legislating, and strictly regulating the changing flow of education. The word "system," if understood as a set of norms and laws, cannot adapt to changing times and circumstances.

"School" and formal educational systems

This quick introduction to modern professions links them with postsecondary educational systems and institutions. In its original semantic sense, the word school means rest, relief, intellectual leisure, training in spiritual things. In classical antiquity it began to mean lines or ways of human thinking and, at the same time, the institutions of the Hellenistic Age, which were the cradle of literature and culture.

The liberal arts of the ancients and the "Greek paideia" (Jaeger 1957, 1974) were the basis for these scholarly institutions (Galino 1973). When monasteries and cathedrals took over the educational institutions they were still called schools. Many historians see the origins of the university in these schools.

Once the term school was institutionalized, it came to mean formal education in contrast to informal or nonformal education in society and at home. However, Mialaret and Vial (1981) maintain that the origin of formal educational systems became a real part of the social system. Schools became better modeled during the long period after the Middle Ages until the first secondary-level high schools were built; that is, from the 16th century until the Napoleonic legislation of 1802 and 1804 (Mesnard 1956).

Systems of formal education were rare before the 18th century (Archer 1982, 1984). Their structures were developed in the 19th century according to the way states, governments, legislatures, and society influenced them with their diverse philosophies and policies of education. These schools developed even though education, of all social activities, is the least amenable to legislation and the least manageable by public powers. Teachers and their classrooms are one of the few remaining sovereign spaces in which the norms issued from the celestial heights of a ministry do not arrive if the teachers do not open their doors.

The formal educational system is made up of three levels: primary, secondary, and higher education. Preceding the first, the preschool level (kindergarten, escuelas de párvulos, nursery school, école d'infants) was instituted for many reasons: greater knowledge of developmental psychology; advances in psychopedagogy and improvements in pedagogical methods; earlier formalization of the nonformal processes of education; and the changes in the family structure because of women's entry into the work force.

From classical times, science has been an important part of any educational system, but since the Scientific Revolution of the 16th century and the Industrial Revolution of the 18th, it has become crucial. This became even more clear in the 19th and 20th centuries as, especially at the secondary and higher levels of education, one role of education is to prepare students for professional job demands. Along with the traditional classic or academic secondary school programs, technical, industrial, commercial, and agricultural programs have been developed.

The concept of postsecondary eduction is relatively recent and arose because of philosophical, social, political, and economic factors as well as for educational reasons. There is a fairly rigid division between the arts and the sciences, especially the technical sciences that lead to work in the crafts and trades.

After the 18th century, the word technology became current in the language of philosophers and educators (Goffi 1988). The universities became more concerned with preparing students for the professions and the work required by the growing production, industrial, and service businesses. Universities became aware of their research and technology–creative mission. To educate increasingly meant entering into a formal education system that would open doors to the rising social classes, as well as to women. Theories began to be developed on "human capital" together with economic and financial capital. In the 18th century, the higher levels of education became more diversified with such schools as l'École de Ponts-et-Chausés in France and other specialized professional institutes.

The need to diversify higher education and the tendency to do so continued to gain force. Scheler (1921) insisted on the need for institutes of higher education other than universities. In the United States, Flexner (1930) declared that the increasing demand for higher education necessitated new institutions that should be considered as elements of a higher educational whole. The character of the universities should be preserved in the system because of the quality of their academic programs and students. Drèze and Debelle (1968) add that "the problem of the mass can not be proposed or thought of only in terms of the University but also in terms of a diversified set of higher institutions." In Latin America, Latorre (1980) affirms that if "the heart of higher education is in the university, its momentum remained in the 19th century" and that therefore, "another series of higher institutions" with a more limited reach began to arise.

Recently Unesco's Centre européen pour l'éducation supérieure (CEPES 1990, pp. 20–22) stated:

> It has often been contended that the very survival of universities for some eight centuries demonstrates that higher education has been able to adapt to change and to introduce

innovation, but at its own pace. This pace has accelerated over the last two decades. Higher education systems are no longer closed systems aiming at the development of intellectual elites, isolated from changes in society, regulated by their own professional ethics and bounded solely by regional, or national environment. Most institutions have had to diversify their range of activities and 19th century boundaries between universities and other institutions of higher education have become increasingly blurred. This blurring both leads to and results from the assimilation of institutions which previously had separate and distinct missions. The diversification of educational needs, combined with persistent resource constraints over the last 15 years, have also given rise to many initiatives in the public and private sector of education as well as in business itself. These "corporate programmes," especially those developed by larger firms whose role in Europe is increasing, now constitute a wide range of offerings both at post-secondary and at post-graduate levels. All of this contributes to the development of a "competitive market" for education amongst the different types of educational institution and the training schools of corporations which is conducive to innovation. Any measures which will increase the mobility of people and of resources will also reinforce such competitive structures.

Within a democratic philosophy of educational provision, which aims at improving equality of opportunity, universities and other higher education systems are being considered increasingly as part of a broader system of "post-secondary education", capable as a whole of satisfying a wider range and a greater volume of educational needs. These needs are both a response to and a stimulation of greater diversity in demand arising from differences in socio-economic background, age, sex, ethnic origin, cultural background, secondary education, professional experience and in capacity to work and/or study on a full-time, or on a part-time basis. This diversity of demand has to be matched by a corresponding diversity of provision. A post-secondary system should embrace all institutions providing education which follows on from completion of secondary schooling, whether for the young people who have just left school, or for adults who already have experience of working life. It would include universities, other public sector higher education in institutions which are more professionally orientated, private schools and colleges and the "corporate" sector (including specific institutions attached to ministries or foundations) providing internal courses at different levels for its own employees. It would also include "open universities" and other distance teaching arrangements.

Such a system requires a larger diversification of missions, structures, norms and rules, pedagogy, resources and competitive strategies. It should also facilitate the mobility of students and of faculty from one institution to another. It would call for an organization of teaching and certification, possibly on a modular basis, which would permit students to transfer on pre-determined conditions between institutions and courses of different levels and receive appropriate academic credit for their previous studies. Such an arrangement would not only serve a process of lifelong learning, but, if adopted on a community-wide basis, would be supportive of the mobility of EC citizens. Interactions of this type between different levels and styles of education and between institutions which are themselves competing with one another require the support of firm, appropriate and well-articulated policies of cooperation. They require, too, more adequate strategies on the part of the institutions so as to ensure an overall better use of scarce and costly resources.

The extension of distance learning techniques and their appropriate use in training are seen as particularly significant assets within a post-secondary education system of the future. The wider application of these techniques tends to be constrained by a belief that they are awaiting significant breakthrough in communication technology and that they are separate systems, not to be integrated with conventional teaching and study structures. There is a need for a much better appreciation and understanding of the role which can be played by such methods within higher education systems, of the wide and varied base on which they rest and of their applicability within the framework of existing technology. Development work on this aspect and on the joint production of compatible teaching materials should accompany that which is taking place on the technological aspects.

Regarding the diversification of educational opportunities at the higher level from demographic and sociological points of view, Zagefka (1989) rightly states that the multiplicity of names for postsecondary institutions makes it difficult to see that they are not universities. This study explores the situation in Argentina, Côte d'Ivoire, Indonesia, Morocco, Mexico, the Philippines, and Senegal. In each of these countries, there is no consistency in institutional names, whether they offer short- or long-term programs for preparation in the professions or trades, or in pure or applied disciplines.

Theories on postsecondary systems

Postsecondary institutions with a long historical tradition as well as those of more recent origin specialize in certain vocations. This fact assists in tracing a theory of postsecondary systems.

Although some institutions or universities specialize in providing preparation in the liberal arts (human, social, and natural sciences), others concentrate on the practical intellectual professions. Some universities decide to work in only one field of knowledge, one of the professions, or one area of research; others, however, prefer to diversify their scientific, professional, and research spectrum.

Although most universities and educational institutions seek to prepare a person to perform in various sectors of society, a few train students only for specific activities and vocations: civil servant, member of the armed forces, pastor, or priest. Some universities stick to the traditional rigour of pedagogy with the student in the classroom, while others, either totally or partially, turn to modern methods of nonformal education with open universities and distance education.

Some universities pay more attention to formal research in one or more areas of social and human sciences, philosophy, and the natural sciences and mathematics. Other institutions carry out their research mission to fulfill their interest in developing a questioning attitude and creative capacity in all their students, rather than allowing a few well-known professors and students to carry out specific projects. There are also universities that concentrate on graduate studies or specialized programs, whereas others work harder on the sound, creative preparation of the undergraduate student. Finally, there are universities devoted solely to the scientific–technological area; these are often called industrial or technological universities, or polytechnics.

There are so many names for postsecondary schools that it is difficult to compare nonuniversity institutions. Their diversity is so great that it is risky even to attempt to develop theories; for example, Bereday (1973) speaks of "the militancy of the mushrooming sub-university institutions." Nevertheless, it can be illuminating to make the attempt, as I will do later.

In Australia, one speaks of colleges of advanced education; in the United States there are junior colleges, 2-year colleges, and community colleges; in Canada there are community colleges; in Germany we have pedagogische hochschulen, kunsthochschulen, fachhochschulen, and others; in some African countries, and in France, there are grandes écoles; and in many countries there are technical schools, polytechnics, or technological schools (Zagefka 1989).

Among universities, not all agree on their purpose. However, the institutions in postsecondary systems may be classified by their origin and legal status (public or private), autonomy, academic expansion and degrees offered, length of programs offered, type of programs, demographic criteria, or whether they offer distance education or require student presence. More important than these are two closely connected criteria that seem to be the most valid for determining the nature of postsecondary education systems and the academic programs they offer. They are defined by relations between science and technics and between educational institutions and the oganization and division of work.

Regarding the first criterion, when something is taught in an educational institution, it is taught for a specific reason. In other words, the content of the course can be oriented toward four typical sets of professions — social, human, biological, and engineering or technical — but at the same time there are different goals — educational, pedagogical, and training.

The goal can be research in any of its forms: theoretical research and reflective inquiry, which take into account any necessary distinction between pure research and research with potential for application. In such an all-embracing context, "matters such as patents and the distribution of results income between the institution, the research centers and the individual concerned" should also be covered (CEPES 1990, p. 19).

It is evident that these and other types of research, from an institutional point of view, belong to the universities that devote the greatest efforts and resources to research. In the United States, this work is done by Research Universities I and II, according to the classification of the Carnegie Foundation for the Advancement of Teaching, or in Japan and several other countries, by those institutions recognized as having a serious research vocation. The doctorate and the master's degree that are more research oriented than professional are granted to the student for the work done and correspond to intellectual or academic professions.

Some institutions concentrate on training for the professions. Universities named as such, liberal arts colleges, professional schools, Grandes Universités, Écoles Especiales, Hochschulen train in the areas of health, engineering, or the human and social professions. They usually offer bachelor's degrees, professional degrees, and other equivalent degrees, as well as master's and doctorates, especially if they are professional.

The technological institutions have eminently practical and applicable goals; they seek the technological interaction between science and technics, high technologies and intermediate technologies. In other words, the scientific research foundations of institutions, such as institutes of technology and, in some cases, polytechnics, have practical applications. Doctorates, master's, or bachelor's degrees from these institutes are technological.

Finally, practical or technical institutions are oriented toward the trades or arts, the practice of which does not require any deep scientific foundation beyond some basic knowledge. These institutions have a wide variety of titles and offer certificates rather than degrees. In some cases, given the level of the programs offered and the background of the students, these institutions do not belong to the postsecondary system. Unesco (1978) speaks of "vocational education" and places it in the last levels of secondary education. The programs are usually short.

It is easy to see the relation between these four goals and the organization of work that has gone from the old, spontaneous, informal social distribution of human occupations and duties to their scientific reorganization and what is now called scientific–technical distribution of work organization. There is now, therefore, a need for trained scientists, academicians, and highly trained technologists; for professionals to carry out necessary services for individuals and society; and for support staff.

Burton R. Clark (1983, p. 16) expresses the relation between intellectual preparation and work in the following way:

> No one has yet found a way to slow the division of labor in society. No one is about to find a way to stop the division of knowledge in "academic" society. From the substance follow certain basic aspects of form: tasks and workers are grouped according to bundles of knowledge. The basic tasks, teaching and research, are both divided and linked by specialty: professors are similarly divided.

Cyrill O. Houle (1981, pp. 41, 42, and 45) says:

> In the professions, theoretical knowledge may be approached by the practitioners in either direct or indirect ways.... A characteristic of a professionalizing vocation is that its practitioners should seek to be able to use theoretical bodies of knowledge to deal competently with a category of specific problems that arise in the vital practical affairs of mankind.... The roots of this practical body of knowledge lie deep in the theoretical fields of inquiry, and therefore the two can never be wholly distinguished from one another. But the professionalizing process requires the building of a substantial body of supporting knowledge which practitioners can use in undertaking practical affairs.

Alberto Moncada (1983) writes:

> The fact that all work requires a certain abstract disposition and intellectual capacity, has led to the division of work that

governs the modern job market and the progressive devalua-
tion of sheer, physical force. Parallel to this circumstance there
is another, the complementarity of capital in the shape of
machines and artificial energy. Almost no work can be done
with only the hands, and a measure of the relative importance
of trades is precisely the quantity, the quality, and the sophis-
tication of tools which are required for each one of them.

In 1971, the OECD published *Vers des nouvelles structures de
l'enseignement post-secondaire* and, in 1975, Ladislav Cerych published his study, *Access and Structure of Post-Secondary Education*.
There are different ways of classifying postsecondary systems
according to how each institution fits into one of the four types
analyzed here. Each postsecondary institution specializes in one
or several of these areas and may thus have an integrated or
segmented postsecondary style. However, both styles can be
combined in what could be called mixed styles that lead to a
certain homogeneity of the component institutions.

This is a very general theory that can help us to understand
polyfaceted tendencies and realities. The most obvious of these
are, first, that the research and professional institutions are
integrated in universities. Second, although there is a subtle
distinction between the professional institutions, which are very
typical of universities, and the technological institutions, which
are considered nonuniversity, they are, in fact, often integrated
in universities. Moreover, in systems where the word university
was legally reserved for specific educational establishments,
nowadays, institutions that are often not recognized as universities (such as the Fachhochschulen in Germany) carry out work
that is comparable to that of universities (OECD 1987). Finally,
practical institutions are often integrated with technological
institutes or those that do not belong to the postsecondary system
of educational institutions. Carter (1980, p. 9) writes:

> What, then, is the difference between a university and a
> polytechnic or other college? Although they tend to teach a
> different mixture of subjects, and a different mixture of levels
> of course, these characteristics will provide no definite divid-
> ing line.... The universities have a far greater commitment to

research, but the polytechnics are not at all pleased to be regarded as purely concerned with teaching. The universities do nothing significant except for higher education and research, and at one time it was asserted that they could thus be distinguished from institutions which had a (supposedly beneficial) spread of advanced and non-advanced work. However, the non-university sector now contains many institutions which have virtually none of the lower level work.... Many polytechnics have sought to escape from "lower level" work, and there have been few cases of imaginative development of 2-year general education, as distinct from vocational courses.

The OECD (1987) asserts that in England and Australia there is a binary integrated model that "implies a complete separation between non-university establishments and universities, with different administrative regulations and sources of financing. The proposed courses have a wide range of choices, levels, and professional preparation," even up to doctoral work. However, Lord Bowden (see Kerstesz 1975) feels that "this extraordinary collection of institutions to educate our young people after they leave elementary school has acquired an apparent cohesion, that it evidently doesn't have, by being assigned the name of binary system. All these institutions that are not universities make up the public sector of the system." Gabriel Frangnière (1974) notes that binary integrated models are preferred in England and Canada, especially in Ontario, and that the tertiary integrated systems — three types of postsecondary institutions — are seen in the United States. Clark (1983, p. 63) says:

> Vertical arrangements of institutions and sectors are of two sorts: high and low placement based on level of task, a hierarchy of sequence; and ranking based on prestige, a hierarchy of status, which is often but not always closely related to the first. The first form of hierarchy comes from sectors having tasks that cover rungs in the educational ladder, with the sectors themselves then taking up location at lower and higher rungs, lower ones feeding higher ones. For example, in the United States, the typical tripartite differentiation of state systems has a basic vertical component: the community college is coterminous with the first 2 years in the basic structure of grades; the

state college overlaps those years and extends upward to take in another 2 or 4 years, through the bachelor's and master's degrees; and the state university overlaps both of the first two institutions and extends upwards another several years to the doctoral degree and postdoctoral training. For transferring students, the feeder sequences run strongly from the first to the second and third, and from the second to the third, as students move upward through levels of training that are assigned differentially to sectors.

Altbach (1980), Nagai (1981), and Thomas (1985) consider the Japanese postsecondary system as also being binary.

Frangnière (1974) also adds that Norway follows the mixed systems, and that homogeneous systems are particularly the rule in Germany and Denmark. The French system, originating in the écoles speciales, tend toward a uniprofessional segmented system.

Training for the professions

This review of the origin of the modern professions and the postsecondary systems of education brings us face to face with the problem of the professional world today. It is necessary to classify the professions acording to types of work (see, for example, Anonymous 1984).

First, let us differentiate between professional training received outside postsecondary systems (for example, in secondary education or on the job) and usually oriented toward the purely practical aspects of a trade not requiring academic work, and the professions connected with university and other postsecondary educational institutions. For our purpose, the professions in this large second category are important. Within the category, we can once again distinguish between the intellectual or academic professions that are connected with the sciences, such as biology or mathematics, in contrast to the practical intellectual professions, such as medicine and engineering, which are in the service of the individual and society. We also differentiate between technical professions, some of which are close to trades, and the technological professions, which come closer to the high levels of technology. In addition, we distinguish between the less scientific, spontaneous professions that can be carried out even without prior academic preparation, such as administration and business management, and professions that require careful scientific and academic preparation, such as the health professions. Finally, we differentiate between the professions that are related to culture (literary, artistic, scientific, and social) as opposed to definable, professional services.

These criteria for classification, and several others that could be adopted, are useful for several reasons. Above all, they indicate which professions require careful, constant, and close vigilance by the government or other social institutions to check their competence and which need only checks by human resource studies. These have to be carried out without encroaching on the right to work and the individual liberty to choose a trade and profession.

The concept of "new professions" seems ambiguous, but it arises from the new demands resulting from the organization and division of jobs, from the transformation of trades into university professions, and from modifications in the professions, all of which require that academic structures be adaptable and flexible (Unesco 1990a). Moreover, as graduate programs are research based, this tends to create hierarchal structures in the professions.

Degrees and titles

The Latin word "titulus" meant a kind of prerogative in the medieval university, such as the right of ownership over acquired knowledge, which enabled one to teach, as is clearly indicated by the words "magister" and "doctor." With the rise of the modern professions in the 19th century, the titles preserved part of their medieval meanings, for example, PhD, MA and MSc, and BA and BSc, denoting a titular hierarchy (doctor, master, and bachelor) and the type of knowledge involved (philosophy or the love of knowledge, or the arts or sciences).

Titles and their subsequent hierarchy have always been used to show the degree of knowledge and ability attained, to ascend the social and cultural ladder, and to enjoy substantial benefits. The knowledge the title attests to may have become outdated, but the title remained as evidence of the hierarchical heights attained.

When universities were first founded in Latin America, the three classical professions, theology, law, and medicine, also started. They were developed from the Renaissance scholars of Salamanca and Alcalá de Henares, models on which the colonial foundations were based. When the modern professions rose from the Industrial Revolution, they formed part of the professionalized universities in the Napoleonic style in the late 19th and 20th centuries. Civil and agricultural engineering broke up the process established by these models. The social professions and those related to business appeared much later in Latin American universities. Similar processes have occurred on other continents, depending on the university style inspiring them.

In addition, the diversification of postsecondary systems is something so recent that it still does not exist in many parts of the world. The distinction between the liberal or university professions and arts and trades has not been clarified. For this reason, universities are overburdened with preparing people for both types of work, whereas many institutions of higher education have not been able to decide what their real role is. There is also a lack of clarity concerning technology, which is still often confused with mere techniques.

The professional training provided by the universities of Latin America continues to be predominantly oriented toward the professions we have called practical intellectual, and only since the second half of this century has there been interest in the intellectual or academic professions. This development has largely been due to the influence of the North American university, which also encouraged graduate programs, the majority of which are professionalized, and the adoption of the North American system of university degrees, which now extends around the world.

Professions and work

At the beginning of the Industrial Age, the division of work was still quite simple and limited, and the university could easily meet the demands of the workplace. By the 19th century, the gradual process of professionalization had begun. However, with scientific and technological advances and increased specialization, the relation between the university and the workplace gradually became untenable. The university could not adapt to the fast-changing demands of the developing industrial world.

There are so many professions that it is almost impossible to classify them. Today, the rate of scientific and technological advances and growth in the computer sciences has caused many professions to be modified along with the necessary university training.

No one denies that economic, political, social, and educational factors influence the prevailing rate of unemployment and underemployment in the industrialized and developing worlds. But it is necessary to recognize that the swift advance of the sciences and the differences caused by the fast changes in the organization of work and the professions explain the number of unemployed, with variable but worrisome proportions.

Torsten Husén (1987, p. 14) outlines the historical development of the problem:

> In feudal Europe, when the nation states were formed and central governments needed trained civil servants, priests, and so on, the new class of professionals was drawn from the homes of merchants, artisans, and farmers, not primarily from the nobility. Thus a certain upward social mobility was initiated through grammar school and/or university education, and was further strengthened at the early stage of industrialization, when basic formal education was required for an increasing number of sub-professional jobs. The emerging

class of industrial workers had at best access to only primary education, provided by legislation in many European countries by the mid-19th century.

The next stage in the emerging industrial countries was one in which post-primary education increasingly became the privilege of the new middle class and the traditional upper class. A very small proportion (some 1 to 2 percent) of young people from working-class homes had access to pre-university or university education. There was an ingrained feeling that this category of young people did not "belong" in higher education.

A third stage was reached after the Second World War, when the "enrolment expansion" occurred at the secondary and tertiary levels. In the course of a few decades the coverage of formal education was considerably increased, by making secondary education available to virtually all young people up to the age of 18. But in a society on the threshold of the post-industrial stage, with an expansion of "intelligence industries" and with growing competitiveness on the employment market, the impact of home background, in terms not so much of physical as of cultural capital, became stronger. A meritocratic society entered the scene.

Husen continues: "The pattern of linkage between education and employment has in certain respects evolved differently in the developing countries." The current problem of unemployment led to Dore's (1976) work on education, qualification and development, because employment and "unemployment tend to be closely associated with levels of formal education."

Seidel (1991, p. 36) specifies three points of tension in the relations between academic life and work.

[The first one occurs] between the subjects studied and the labour market, on the one hand, and the subjects studied and the progress of knowledge on the other. The labour market changes so rapidly in the wake of new scientific and technological developments that it does not always make sense to adjust the objectives and the volume of the subjects studied immediately to changing economic developments — as employers, of course, often demand. In countries with a planned economy, the linking of student admissions to the capacity of the planned labour market to absorb them has proved a complete mistake, as has the over-specialization of courses of study. Future developments linked to the labour market must take account of the growing division of labour on the one hand, and on the other, the emphasis on basic training.

There is in addition, a conflict of principles here: are the nature and number of the subjects studied to be determined by the labour market, or should these be determined by the academic system itself? Universities also have to offer courses that will ensure a sufficient younger generation of academics for their own needs and for the progress of scholarship, even though at a particular time, or even in general, these subjects may be of little interest to the labour market or the economy. Other considerations not connected with the labour market must also play a part in course design, as must the wishes and interests of the students and other social needs.

[The second point of tension] concerns the length of the courses and the working life-time. Roughly speaking, one may say that the length of the working life is decreasing, while the length of studies is increasing. In most industrial countries a heated debate has flared up about whether courses are much too long or whether young people are being deprived of opportunities in life too quickly — which is another way of interpreting it. In Europe alone, the difference between the United Kingdom at one end and Finland at the other is extreme. The conflict is between the economic arguments put forward by employers and those responsible for state finances, on the one side, pressing for shorter courses, and on the other, the demands of thorough academic training and the development of learning. How is this conflict to be solved? I can see two possibilities. The universities must agree to place much more emphasis than they have done up till now on forming generalists and less on training specialists. This means they must be willing to recognize that, in principle, life-long further training must be given a central place among study objectives, and they must be equipped to meet this development. In the long term, the proportion of those studying at basic level will decrease in favor of those engaged in advanced studies. Business and industry will also have to accept this principle. The trend in this direction varies in the different European countries, with the northern countries being more willing to accept it than those in the southern and Mediterranean area.

Seidel adds that the institutional diversification of postsecondary systems that offer programs of varying lengths emphasizes this second point of tension. Finally, the third point of tension occurs because

> [What] society has to face, and [what] calls for a political decision, is the cost of the higher education system in relation to total national expenditure. I know this also raises the question of how much a society is willing to invest in its schools and universities. There is no scientific answer to the question: where should the emphasis lie — basic research, applied research, development? That is an open question. Universities or polytechnics? That too is an open question. But the balance does seem to be shifting in favor of the polytechnics; shorter courses for generalists, longer courses for specialists. So a plausible answer might be shorter courses and the forming of generalists. The two questions we have to answer therefore are: what will our graduates do afterwards? and, what is the country prepared to invest in learning? By which I mean not just education and training but also research. We have seen that the complexity of our social structures requires the presence of many qualified young people. To my mind this is one of the basic conditions of existence for modern societies and consequently they can make no better investment than the creative young people at their disposal.

The contemporary university appears bewildered by the problem of relating in the best way possible to the complex division of labour and to its task of training professionals. However many distinct professions there may be, these are problems that also affect many university systems.

In the 1950s, or perhaps a little later, when the wave of educational planning spread, it was accompanied by a fondness for "human resource studies" on the part of many governments and consequently by the universities. These studies were not used to ensure that professionals were trained for typical trades and jobs, neither were people trained to follow research in science and other sectors of human, artistic, and social culture.

However, the adoption of models for stable political and economic systems, the erroneous assessments in medium- and long-term planning, the lack of reliable data, political instability, and vacillating indices of economic development have led to a loss of confidence in the predictions of human resources, even in those spheres where they were preferred by governments and planning offices (Harris 1992).

Unesco's (1988a) report on long-term planning in higher education coming from the Asia–Pacific region is eloquent on this point:

> From a manpower perspective, the crucial question is whether the supply of graduates is matched with the demands of the labour market. But manpower planning is not itself an exact science. Manpower forecasting is based on predictions of economic and industrial growth and the predictions can be grossly incorrect. Manpower planning is subject to forces outside the control of the forecasters, and national economic activity is, in part, controlled by international trends and interests. Neither manpower planning nor the HEIs can be blamed totally for a mismatch between graduate supply and market demand. On the other hand, the money spent on higher education represents an investment by all citizens — some of whom will receive little or nothing in return — in the future of society. This investment is wasted when the skills and talents of the highly educated cannot be put to productive use, and it is probably misappropriated when the most highly educated leave the country for more lucrative employment elsewhere.

Another Unesco document (1990b) from the same region, besides insisting that "the prediction of labour market needs is at best an inexact science," asserts that "the question and problem of manpower supply must be a shared responsibility between higher education institutions, government, and commerce and industry" because "planning and action by one of these three partners in isolation from the others is bound to produce serious distortions in terms of the type and quality of manpower supply" and, at the same time, "grave consequences both for the individual and the economy."

Mitrovic (1988) considers the problem from another point of view and blames the "classical university model" which

> Has shown not to be adequate and flexible to react to new individual and social needs, and to initiate a new distribution and integration of human work and creativity. The modern university is at the intersection between the old and the new world, between a system and a movement, between the classical division of labor and a new one which is being constituted on the basis of the scientific and technological revolution. Therefore, the current university crisis is one of the expressions and the causes of the society's crisis, imposing radical changes both on the university and society in order to achieve an optimal industrial and social development and to realize the humanistic civilization project of the social development in the world.

> The modern university has to free itself from the lethal embrace of the state, but also from a pragmatic pressure of industrial corporations which accompanies the classical division of labor. It has to open much wider and faster to the future. It has to become a generator of a new division of labor and of more humane forms of living culture. Scientific laboratories have just started to create a modern division of labor, while the reproduction of cadres in the economy and society must have a different starting point and criteria.

Nowadays, and with the future in mind, "We must raise our education to the world level of quality" (Brunsko 1988). Brunsko continues:

> Instead of the predominant orientation to the training of personnel for specific jobs, we must create skilled people who will be able to be retrained several times during their working life. Permanent education is now of paramount importance. Therefore, the modern university faces a dilemma: to prolong the studies, or to organize various forms of education and training after graduation?

In turn, Iredale (1991, p. 4) looks at the topic of professional preparation revolving around the labour market in this way:

> The manpower model (or impact of higher education institutions on the labour market) itself has different forms, from the

version where you vary the size of specific faculties such as engineering to meet precisely defined manpower requirements across a country, to the hit-and-miss mode where you provide higher education to as many people as possible in order to strengthen the general pool of highly educated skills. The second approach coincides with the sort of popular demand for higher education as a form of basic education on an equity basis which appears to have informed Kenyan policy making during recent years.

Equivalence of degrees

The problem of establishing the equivalence of university degrees has been mentioned. The problem, of course, did not exist with the first universities as there was a high degree of concordance after the Renaissance. However, once educational systems were confined in political boundaries in the 19th century, difficulties arose. In 1966, Unesco produced a report that was reprinted almost 10 years later (Unesco 1973). In the preface to this comparative study of degree-granting systems, it is noted that, during the latter half of the last century, bilateral agreements were more frequent between nations. The problem was left on record, but it was diluted among the principal subjects of the agreements, which, depending on the friendship and good will involved, included trade, navigation, and economic matters (Granados 1991).

Now the problem has increased, because as Harrel-Bond says, "The 20th century can be characterized as the century of the refugee, of the immigrant" (see Dias 1991a), a concern that also appears in Guiton and Charpentier (1984). As a result, Unesco found it impossible to compare diplomas and degrees particularly in scientific subjects, but with agreement between all parties, the training of professionals could be recognized between countries. However, this issue has deeper roots that have been well analyzed in Unesco (1992a):

International agencies and national organizations engaged in international co-operation have an obvious role to play in facilitating cross-national interchange of staff, students and ideas. They can help promote recognition of degrees and diplomas by the countries of a region, which, in turn, will enhance staff and student mobility. They can provide aid in the form of fellowships or scholarships and serve as a forum for the interchange of information and ideas. Academia, at its basic disciplinary level, is an international enterprise that abhors parochial isolation. All great universities are simultaneously national assets and international forums that know no frontiers.

Higher education institutions, however, can hinder the mobility of staff, students and ideas if they adopt overly opportunistic attitudes towards such interchanges. Many of the institutions in the more developed countries of the region, for example, have realized that the recruitment of full-fee paying overseas students is big business. But some of these institutions have done little to either modify their curriculum or student support services in order to better cater for their overseas clientele. This is an area in need of much more research and evaluation and such activities could help orientate higher education institutions to both the diversity of culture and development requirements of the countries of the Asia and Pacific region.

It also should be recognized that much of the staff and student flow is from the less developed to the more developed nations, while the higher education systems in the developed countries retain a monopoly of ideas and technology. To a large extent this is due to differences in level of national economic development, not a product of higher education per se. But wherever possible, institutions should encourage a two-way flow in the traffic of staff, students and ideas. International agencies through various incentive schemes could help facilitate such a flow. Also, various national agencies and service organizations can, and do, assist with promoting mobility of staff, students and ideas.

Some governments expend a proportion of their international aid in the form of overseas fellowships and scholarships. By so doing, of course, they recoup some of the international aid via overseas student financial expenditure at the host institutions. At the same time, governments may impose quite restrictive visa requirements on non-sponsored staff and students. This is not the place to argue the pros and cons of international aid or restrictive immigration laws. However, it may be necessary for all governments in Asia and the Pacific to adopt a regional orientated view and attitude to both aid and immigration. This is another area deserving of much more research and evaluation.

A recent study on equivalence conventions prepared by James Wimberley (1990, p. 11) concludes that

The idea of a huge Domesday Book defining the equivalences of all conceivable diplomas and qualifications is a chimera. It is no accident that the attempts of the European Community to resolve the difficult problems of recognition of professional qualifications by detailed regulations have been replaced by a newer approach which is based precisely on mutual trust in the professional training and accreditation systems of the Community states. There are real problems in running an equivalence system based on trust and confidence, but this remains the only basis possible.

[The] criteria for a model of a recognition system [ought to be based on the fact that they be] comprehensive, meaning that all institutions, whether private or public, should in one way or in another be brought within it. A major weakness in the system, not only of the Council of Europe Conventions but also of the other instruments that complement them, has come to be that they cover only the public, state-funded systems of higher education.

Increasingly, the boundaries between higher and other forms of tertiary education are dissolving, while the balance between initial and continuing education, as well as that between traditional young full-time students and older, part-time, and minority students, continues to shift. The role of the private sector is likely to increase in the Cultural Convention countries both as an opportunity and as a problem. The private sector, which is covered by no international agreements, ranges from institutions of impeccable academic standing, such as branch campuses of leading American universities, to criminal fraudsters. For the diplomas of the private sector to be brought within the recognition system, in a way that is fair as compared to the treatment of the diplomas of traditional institutions, requires the development of a number of common principles in the regulation and accreditation of the private sector, and efficient international co-operation in their application.

Finally, the recognition system should be reliable, in the sense that it should not only give consistent but also sensible results.

Efficiency is not, however, the only value which the Council of Europe fosters. The fair recognition of qualifications is also a part of the right to education. An individual whose qualifications are not given due recognition as a result of discrimination, ignorance, or academic vanity is not simply the subject of a dysfunctioning market, but the victim of an injustice.

The professional profile

If the concept of professional profile is maintained in the university, it should be understood in its full sense of the development of a person's intellectual, volitional, and affective abilities and faculties as well as his or her study habits. The profile also encompasses true mastery of the necessary sciences and disciplines. Both aspects guarantee the effectiveness of the operative part of the profile; it should be creative and versatile enough to adapt to changing situations and demands. *Homo sapiens* is not only work; above all, our species is a person and an intellect (Páez Urdaneta 1991).

Krismanic (1988) presents a similar idea:

> The education of professionally flexible specialists requires a change in educational processes in which a far stronger emphasis should be put on cognitive functions, such as planning, deciding, testing of hypotheses and problem solving skills. In addition to the stimulation of intellectual, emotional and social development, it is necessary to incite the attainment of professional maturity too, by providing adequate opportunities for the development of abilities and interests, values and personality characteristics.

Thus, the university as institution must be mindful of its place as head of the postsecondary system, of the educational system in general, and of the professional training programs that are its responsibility. The university should also be aware that it should be training scientists, rather than merely workers and providing guidance in culture and development. The university should not continue to fall into the snares of professionalism (Ortega y Gasset 1976) and meaningless "title-giving" as has been the case for almost 200 years. Once the university is freed, as far as realistically possible, of pressures to grant degrees, it will be able to concentrate more on attending to its other social missions.

Combes (1991, p. 103) takes into account the continual development of technology, the obsolescence of knowledge, competition between companies, and the gradual disappearance of differences between markets and national and international companies in his description of the "company man." These characteristics are similar to those in the "professional profile" and, like the "company man," can be imparted by the university.

> [He] should be able to take into account the effects of changes in the international context (knowledge of and sensitivity to the world at large which are just as important as technical know-how); he should be able to develop a realistic strategy in relation to existing resources; he should be able to negotiate, in changing and/or new environments, with each type of business partner whether social or economic, private or nationalized; he should be able to deal in terms of human resources with changes (new international horizons, new techniques, mergers).

Consequently, the "company man" should be able to face up to changes and, therefore, be flexible and enterprising, have initiative and be good at human relations, and possess "experience within a company environment." In the university training of the "company man," Combes considers:

> The temptation to increase the workload of students should be avoided, efforts should be made to give less technical subject matter which is becoming more and more rapidly obsolete. More room should be given to subjects which develop the intellect. Would it not be better to give preference to teaching subjects which help develop the intellectual capacity of students which would allow them to deal judiciously with imperfect situations? Would it not be better to make

room for courses directed at giving a better understanding of the world today (history, politics, economic blocks, the comprehension of economic debate...)? This would reinforce awareness and understanding of others, of cultural and geopolitical environments and the ethical and philosophical extensions of management. Students should be trained to work everyday in an international context. Would it not be better to make the teaching of foreign languages and cultures an essential part of higher education? Students should be trained in human relations: it would seem to be essential that our future executives acquire the necessary skills in the management of human resources....

How should undergraduates be trained? The following conditions should be met: universities should accept to select students with a high potential (judgement, intuition, common sense); subjects taught should be less specialized which would make it easier to create links between subjects taught and the mutual benefits which can be gained by cross reflection and which would give them a more forward-looking dimension; it appears essential to alternate periods of in-company experience with periods of study; should not the theoretical training of students be linked with their own personal experiences in the company environment (taking full advantage of the opportunity this gives for mixing different generations) by combining more and more frequently theoretical courses and periods of work experience within companies to strengthen their ability to put to use their knowledge in real situations? This may include creating a system within business schools and universities of continual education allowing graduates to return to their school from time to time for refresher courses throughout their professional career and which would also allow non graduates to progress? Above all a greater permeability must be created between business schools and companies; teacher training within the company (sabbatical year), projects managed within the company; refresher courses for company staff held by teaching institutions and the detachment of company executives on teaching missions in business schools.

Jelinic (1988) expresses similar ideas:

Universities at present, and even more in the future, can not be viewed as independent and autonomous parts of the social structure, but as its integral part. In the framework of that integral part, expert and scientific personnel should be created, and personnel should contribute, thanks to the power of their creativity, to the general development and progress. The work and the results of the work at universities are understood as one of the levers which make progress possible, while progress as such is understood as a "conditio sine qua non" of the survival of a nation.

In order to enable universities to have enough human resources to satisfy the requirements of their role in society, it is important to secure the permanent inflow of new, fresh experts, fully qualified and selected (the best among the best) who had occasions, in their earlier professional life, to solve problems and to get acquainted with the achievements of the modern technical–technological revolution in the world. It is also necessary to create and institutionalize possibilities for the return of scientists from the universities and from other scientific institutions with business organizations, in order to find new ideas, to get acquainted with problems imposed by ordinary life. In that sense, the legal and practical favouring of the permanence of jobs, starting with better salaries for senior workers in a company, should be critically analyzed, for such favouring makes things static, it keeps knowledge and experience in closed circles, etc.

Conclusion

It is important to discuss the close relation between university service to society through the professions and service to culture. Culture can be developed through work, and the university elevates this work to the category of a profession.

However, most of the subjects discussed in this section have concentrated on the relation between the university and the work world, omitting that all-essential ingredient of culture. The concerns have been about the number of professions created to meet demands of work; the "diploma disease" and the "points of tension" between the academic world and work, exacerbated by anxiety about increased unemployment and subemployment of professionals; the reduction of the "professional profile" to its

operational aspect; and the almost unsolvable problem
alence of degrees.

Consequently, it is often felt that economic criteria take
precedence over the cultural development of people and nations.
This reduces professional work to quantitative purposes: the
profession is not conceived of as "the cultural and moral eleva-
tion of people and nations" (García Garrido 1992), but reduced
to what is necessary but not sufficient, that is, tangible output
and per capita income.

UNIVERSITY EXTENSION SERVICES

◆

University extension services vary widely between universities.
Nevertheless, there are three main types separated according to
their goals: nonformal education, university service, or inter-
institutional relations. The first two topics are dealt with in the
following section; the third is left for later.

Life-long education

At the beginning of civilization, education was largely informal
and lacked institutional context. As formal school courses
appeared, obstacles delimited the methods and procedures of
formal and nonformal education. Consequently, formal education has been limited to certain parameters of space and time;
that is, the age of the pupil and the school space in its institutional
sense. For that reason, formal education starts in the first years
of life and in school. In an intentionally radical declaration,
Cropley (1977, 1980) says that "youth studies but cannot act"
and that "the adult must act but has no opportunity to learn." As
Lengrand (1970) expressed it, "up to the 19th century it was
accepted that an individual's life was divided into two large

periods of unequal length. The first included the period from birth to an age fixed arbitrarily by society...to assume his social responsibilities."

However, important educators had earlier insisted that education continues throughout one's life. Plato said, "To educate oneself is what every man must do without fail throughout his life and as far as his strength permits him." John Amos Comenius also said: "In the same way that the entire universe is a school for all of the human race from the beginning to the real end of time, all of life is a school for all men, from birth to the grave.... Every age is destined to learn, nor has man been conceded any other goals for learning than his own life." At the end of the 18th century, Condorcet wrote: "We have observed that instruction should not abandon individuals at the moment they leave school; it should embrace all ages" because "this second instruction is much more necessary than that of infancy, which was enclosed within tight limits."

These comments reinforce the concept that people continue their education and learning throughout their lives as there are facilities available, even though this enhances the distinction between formal education and nonformal education. The former is considered worn-out, scholasticized, and institutionalized; it is confined to the school group and the individual, and it is education for children and youth; it is elitist, selective, pedagogical, and always linked to the immediate action and vigilance of the teacher. In contrast, nonformal education is not restricted by space and time and is permanent, open, descholasticized, and deinstitutionalized; it is massive, democratic, and popular; it uses modern means of social communication, such as radio, television, the press, and teleinstruction, and is thus even "teacher-less" and self-taught (Knowles 1969).

The critically tinged attributes used to describe formal education are the result of the recent antischool movement, due, according to García Garrido's (1992) fair evaluation, "to the scholarly optimism of the last century and the first half of this one." A consequence of this was "an increasing distrust in the school (including the university) as the only or main institutional channel for education," and reactions against the educational systems for being "made up of a more and more complex and inextricable school machine that maintains the fiction of considering itself as an educational system when in reality education — or the absence of education — of citizens is also mainly produced in other ovens."

The antischool and antiuniversity movement has become weaker, but it can still be seen in the concept that formal education should get rid of many of its rigid traditions and "deformalize" itself a little, and that nonformal education nowadays tends to formalize itself, as shown by the many programs and open universities.

Informal education

Between formal and nonformal education, we have the mediating and reconciling concept of informal education. Both formal and nonformal education are based on the concept that all our surroundings should have some educational value: the family and the social environment, the country and the city, sports and relaxation, hospital and health, conversation and silence. This is the idea contained in the expression "city" or "polis" or educational "civitas" (Unesco 1972). It is like a climate, for informal education contrasts with formal education and nonformal education in the same way that spontaneous, uncontrolled respiration does with consciously controlled, deliberately practiced respiration. Dave (1978) states that both formal and nonformal education include all the things people "informally" gather throughout life in different moments and situations.

Lengrand (1970) contends that the 19th century was the beginning of the movement to deformalize education, and of university extension services. In 1850, William Sewell, professor of philosophy at Oxford, published a tract entitled, *Suggestions for the Extension of the Universities*. It was a timely publication, for a Royal Commission insisted that Oxford spread its services to all of England. Sewell (see Gordon and White 1979, p. 101) wrote:

> Though it may be impossible to bring the masses requiring education to the University, may it not be possible to carry the University to them? [Both the ancient universities] would become the great centers and springs of education throughout the country, and would command the sympathy and affection of the nation at large.

Years later, Arthur Acland, a great admirer of the historian Arnold Toynbee, gave conferences on *The Education of the Citizen* in which he said: "I speak to those who feel more assured every day they live, that while the period of instruction may cease before we are 20 years of age, the work of education is the work of our lives, and that education in the true sense ends when our lives end" (see Gordon and White 1979)

A short time later, this concept was expressed as "lifelong education" and Acland would appropriate for himself the objectives and desires of education that Toynbee had already noted: political education, industrial education, and health education, because "if true citizenship were to be achieved, a start could be made with existing voluntary associations of free men which pointed toward the higher life possessing high ideals."

This foresight fell onto fertile ground, for there was social unrest in favour of what today we call nonformal and informal education. The British, Gordon and White (1979) affirm, moving away from the idealist conceptions of the Germans,

> Did not see formal instruction as the sole, or even in some cases as the chief way of educating the nation. Schools, universities and adult classes were all, of course, indispensable; and most of the reformers' effort went into their improvement and extension. But society educates, or mis-educates, also. Churches, factories, families, political and legal systems are also potential educators. In bringing organized religion closer to society, in industrial and economic reform, in extending political democracy, in temperance work, and in the creation of systems of social welfare, one could be furthering educational ends as much as if one were a teacher or educational administrator.

The working class reacted favourably to these expectations, as did the universities. Previous relations between Oxford and the cooperative movement, allied to the new cultural interests of the trade unions, provided Albert Mansbridge with the opportunity in 1899 to fulfil workers' desire for education. This wave of interest condensed into the Association for Higher Education of Working Men, the WEA, in 1906. Mansbridge thought that universities ought to inspire people to want education that included not only intellectual and academic interests but also natural interests in "education for and in what is superior." In 1910, Balliol College, Oxford, at the instigation of A.L. Smith, promoted the first conference of the WEA. He also chaired the Adult Education Committee of the Ministry of Reconstruction, created at the end of World War I. In 1919, A.L. Smith (1979 [1919]) declared:

> It is a truth brought out by the war that there is latent talent in the mass of our people, a capacity far beyond what was recognized, a capacity to rise to the conception of great issues and to face the difficulties of fundamental problems when these are visualized in familiar form. They only require teachers whom they can trust.

Also in 1919, the First World Conference on Education for Adults was held in Elsinor, Denmark. The idea and the goals of nonformal, continuous education were set. In 1933, Alfred North Whitehead stated: if humanity "was trained to adapt itself to fixed conditions" today rapid changes would occur and their "time-span is considerably shorter than that of human life, and accordingly our training must prepare individuals to face a novelty of conditions. But there can be no preparation for the unknown" (Whitehead 1964).

Tardy (1970) adds:

> Nobody will be excluded from continuous education. The benefits of the system will be shared equally by all men. It will be oriented towards the world population, whatever the level of their qualifications and mastery. Schematically, there is an attempt to replace an aristocratic system with a democratic system.

In the same year, Paul Lengrand (1970, p. 16) reaffirmed that "the notion that a man can accomplish his lifespan with a given set of intellectual and technical luggage is fast disappearing," and Gaston Deurinck (1974, p. 17) wrote:

> In a society that is rapidly changing, in order to adapt, an individual must learn; that this process takes place in all one's surroundings (family, society, profession, etc.) and that the problem of modern society is that of valuing the immensity of human experience.

Educational deformalization

Nonformal education can be seen as having three basic characteristics: it is stable and permanent; open, because of its wide range; and it can cover a great distance through the use of modern communication and computers. Educational deformalization is primarily oriented toward the adult population, and has three main objectives: social–demographic and political; functional, professional, and labour; and cultural. Politically speaking, nonformal education tries to make equal educational opportunities a reality and to respond to the changing needs of society. This type of education assumes an autonomous commitment to the individual's integral development (Carton 1983; Smith 1991).

The first social–demographic objective outlined by A.L. Smith after World War I stated that there was a need for adult education. This need persisted throughout the 1930s and grew stronger by the mid-60s when student movements became popular and Philip H. Coombs prepared his study on the "world crisis of education" (1971) for the 1967 conference on that theme in Williamsburg. The conference was called by President Lyndon B. Johnson and organized by James Perkins, at that time President of Cornell University. Coombs rethought his work, which was republished in 1985.

The second objective of a functional, professional, and job-related nature quickly became connected with the first objective. In North America, emphasis on work was related to the Great Depression until the end of World War II. Expressions like nonformal education "on the job," "through one's job," and "through work" arose. It was implied that work is the instrument and the objective of education, whether we are dealing with children, young people, or adults. In *Terminology of Technical and Vocational Education*, Unesco (1978) distinguishes between on-the-job training and off-the-job training where the classroom is set up to be similar to and use the resources of a workshop. The goal sought is job training and retraining for new or modified jobs. Unesco's *World Charter on Education for All* (1990), the frame of reference for action leading to the satisfaction of basic learning needs and continuing education for up-to-date professional practice, deals with this topic. According to Houle (1981), on-the-job training was already well established at the end of the 1940s.

The cultural objective has various meanings and specific goals, starting from the basic ones of literacy training to teaching those who have absolutely no knowledge of how to read or write or those with such limited mastery of these arts that they are functionally illiterate. Teaching literacy is not beyond attempts at political indoctrination, such as that of Paolo Freire in Brazil. Knowing, enjoying, experiencing, and analyzing the universals of historic and present-day culture are taught along with literacy and the culture of leisure, a trend from Europe (Dumazedier 1977). At the 42nd session of the international conference on education, Unesco (1990c) highlighted the role of universities in the face of illiteracy. Speakers from Asia and the Pacific, the Caribbean, North America, the United States, and Africa participated in this discussion.

Continuing education

There are many types of nonformal education programs with these or other planned objectives. All, however, have to deal with the questions about their target population, the instructional elements used, and the means used to distribute the desired message.

Some programs will be used to provide basic literacy or the

first stages of formal education, such as primary and secondary education, for young people, adults, and the elderly. Others will complement formal educational processes for people who have not been able to finish their regular education, unlike the programs that are properly called continuing, recurring, or recycling education. Finally, there are programs for improvement in cultural aspects. These are for people who wish to fill the gaps in their general education.

In all these programs, especially in relation to work, it is customary to refer to alternating work and study or to integrating and creating links between the specific objectives of the educational establishment and those at work. This is the corporate or cooperative education (Bruce 1982) of the United States, or England's "sandwich courses" (Carton 1983), which stimulate the relation between education, research, and production. These systems imply previously agreed-upon activities, a special category of professors and teaching methods developed in the university classroom, laboratories, production establishments, and even in extracurricular activities and "in-the-field" periods of contact and learning.

Many nonformal education programs have until recently been part of formal education; this is typical of continuing education. This occurs most often in universities in highly developed industrial countries. The advance of technology and its applications to all aspects of economic life and the consequent need to maintain scientific and work capacity force many adults to return to university. CERI (1987) states that "although in the past adults were only infrequently accepted as students in higher education, today they are a veritable new group in universities and other institutions of higher education." In countries with a limited young population, the retraining of adults becomes even more necessary (EC 1991).

García Garrido (1992) points out that the formalization of continuing education has to keep its sense of life-long education as a "habit that is freely and voluntarily assumed and enacted by the person" not merely required by the educational system (Pineau 1977).

On the other hand, there should be differences between a research graduate program and continuing education programs and courses. Graduate programs should maintain their research component; continuing education normally provides education or precise, concrete training. The dedication required of the student in the "new style" continuing education cannot and usually is not as strict and absorbing as that of a graduate program, which requires a thesis director. Graduate programs require a research project; continuing education requires a learning experience, training, or retraining to update one's skills.

There are two important ways nonformal education serves society. The first is through the open universities that go beyond the traditional concept of university students; there are also centres or other institutions within the university. These are connected to the general structure or the academic structure (see Unesco 1990b). In general, it is thanks to universities and university professors, in large part, that research and nonformal education are at the service of society (Brunelle 1973; Chevrolet 1977).

University service

University service is a relatively new concept with a virtually universal value in many cases related to student activities. In a 1976 resolution, Unesco understood university service to be the attempt of universities and their students to promote development that combines theory and practice. This concept began in socialist regimes and spread to developed and less-developed countries during the 1960s. The goal was to bring together education and job activity; respond to the demands of research and different technological operations; and help marginal sectors of the population, which provided the opportunity for political indoctrination.

In analyzing the conclusions issued by ministers of education at conferences held in Arab countries (1977), Asia and Oceania (1978), Latin America and the Caribbean region (1979), Europe (1980), and Africa (1982), Topentcharov (1985) attempts to outline the course of the university in the future. He calls university service an innovation in higher education derived from patriotic motives during economic reconstruction and the struggle against illiteracy in recently independent countries. Later, "little by little the initiative changed; it became generalized and formed part of the methods of higher education" with differences in each country. Thus, students in developed countries advocated university service for charitable reasons to help people who had been victims of natural catastrophes. Students from socialist countries were busy with agricultural harvests, housing construction, and other work for the common good. In developing countries, students worked to raise the cultural level of their compatriots and to train qualified manual labour.

Dickson (1981), quoting Robert Browning, justifies university service because "action begets thought"; he follows with ideas from Warren Bryan Martin and Puey Ungphakorn, ex-rector of the University of Thanmasat. The former states: "As long as university establishments help to inspire a positive ideal in students, they are providing an invaluable service to society. Nevertheless, students should experience these values during the time they are at the university and not be satisfied with studying about them. And just as it is not enough to study examples of creativity in order to create, to practice judgement and show proof of generosity it is necessary for the student to have opportunities to put these virtues into practice." From a different slant but with the same objective, Ungphakorn states: "We have been taught that the students' principal duty is to study in order to serve society"; however, "that same service has been reduced to another topic of study par excellence, and consequently, it turns into a vicious circle. Service becomes a curricular subject," but it does not lead to action.

The Unesco resolution characterized university service as training the student for a real job and stimulating the social conscience, not simply a requisite for obtaining a degree. Students involved in university service should be committed physically, intellectually, and voluntarily and it should be beneficial for the communities or social groups, whether teaching literacy, community development and social organization, hygiene and health, or cultural dissemination. It should also encourage cooperation between the university and productive sectors.

Dickson (1981) proposes the following guidelines: achieve balance between the objectives of university service without letting the teaching overshadow the aid. The program should last at least a semester, but a year would be better, especially if it is in out-of-the-way areas. The work should be stimulating to develop the student's self-confidence, and, as far as possible, be very general and not as specialized as study programs. However, service should be obligatory, and it would be better if only one student provides service in a given location so that he or she can become part of the social environment and create contacts with community leaders. The community benefited will take care of the basic needs of the person providing help. It is also advisable to prepare those benefiting from the service, and also the students who will provide it. The evaluation of the work carried out by the student should only be in terms of "satisfactory" or "unsatisfactory" so that subsequent services can be better planned. In addition, the benefit to the student of alternating theory with practice needs to be evaluated.

Any inventory of university extension programs shows their diversity: voluntary or paid, for all students or only some, based on all or some disciplines or professional majors, directly assisted by professors or left in large part to students, financed by the university's regular budget or partially or totally through the government, foundations, enterprises, or the benefitted community. Unesco (1984a) carried out case studies on the experiences of 21 countries on all continents and published a report on experience with adult education in Argentina (Unesco 1990d).

INTERINSTITUTIONAL RELATIONS

◆

Interuniversity relations

Because of institutional similarities, international relations between universities tend to be homogeneous. The UNITWIN project and Unesco's Plan for Professors, which were launched after the 25th meeting of the General Conference of Member States in 1989, seek to strengthen cooperation among universities and academic mobility and focus on agreements leading to the establishment of sister universities and other links among universities in basic disciplines related principally to lasting development. UNITWIN will function in two main sectors: support for higher education networks and Unesco professorships in all academic disciplines. Moreover, there will be activities related to the administration and management of higher education, the training of academic personnel, support for university and scientific libraries, and distance education.

The state and universities

The relations between the state and universities are bilateral because of their uneven nature. Education is a responsibility of the state, and it is also the state's responsibility to create a propitious environment for scientific development and to set guidelines for scientific policies. However, the state is not a master of the knowledge in the university, nor does it have the immediate functions of teaching, researching, or educating. Because of this subtle difference of meaning, the relations between governments and the university are not always easy. Referring to Africa, Auala (1991, p. 6) says:

> The government wants to see results on its investment, while the university on the other hand wants to protect its autonomy. I think that a university torn by power-hungry groups,

outside and inside the university, is in danger of becoming an inefficient instrument for education.

The university and industry

The interinstitutional relations between the university and industrial, commercial, or service enterprises are also bilateral. University–industry technological transfer is one aspect. However, the university and industry differ greatly in their approach to the task of education (Calleja 1990).

The university focuses more on the business administration sciences to develop those aspects of students that awaken the spirit of enterprise. Business, on the other hand, is more interested in work performance. In the university, students acquire the instruments, tools, and abilities; in business, all this is put to the test. The university is a nonprofit enterprise with the goal of intellectual production; business looks for a profitable product.

In any case, the relations between the university and industry are related to the economy (Pitner 1988; Senic 1988) and are expressions of real or apparent inconsistencies between academics and work. These can be overcome with agreements that bring the two sides together and are the basis for students' work–study experiences in various enterprises (Pitner 1988).

Study can also be alternated with work. "In-service training" is the expression for this type of education and can be more integrated when the university and the business agree on theoretical–practical curricula.

The practice of alternating and integrating has a long history. Medical schools instituted practical training for students in hospitals (internships or residencies) in the 17th century, and today students have to follow a residency in a medical specialty. The increase in night shifts and the distinction between students who work and workers who study suggest a new inventiveness that is deformalizing university education and helps university–business relations.

The first industrial parks (Lacave 1991) can be seen in the

origin of England's "civic universities," which were located in thriving industrial cities. These "parks" are where the symbiosis of education in work and for work is carried out. In Israel, the "technological incubators" are arriving at similar goals but with different names like technopolis, technological parks, and techno-cities.

In the United States, the Morrill Land Grant Act of 1862 endowed universities with property on which to locate farms for training and productive work. However, this never went as far as the iconoclastic extremism of Mao Tse-tung, who, a century later, as a result of the Cultural Revolution of 1966, came up with the unjustly arrogant idea that the workshop is the university and the university is the workshop, destroying both education and science.

Theses on the subject of business enterprises, continuing education courses run in conjunction with public or private business, and research contracts (Trajkovski 1988) are other aspects of university–business relations. Research contracts in great part depend on the university's capacities, resources, and opportunities to enter the research market, which is undoubtedly substantial for research universities in the United States.

Far-sighted, provident laws should sanction significant tax exemptions for the businesses that contribute to the university's development. In this way, legislators make it possible for business to pay back its debt to the university, for business benefits from the product made by the university without having contributed to it.

The parallel development of businesses and universities in Latin American countries and the awareness that all aspects of development are the responsibility of all social institutions has served to extend relations between businesses and universities. In addition, other ways have been discussed and commented on in countless forums, courses, roundtable discussions, panel discussions, and conferences promoted by universities, by business associations, or by common agreement between both institutional forms.

International agreements like those of the European Economic Community, the close relations of the countries of eastern Asia, the United States and Canada, and those in other political–geographic areas around the world have shown Latin American countries that they must unite. This interest touches immediately on the relations between universities and companies producing raw materials, and industrial, commercial, and service companies. The Common Agreement of the South, among Argentina, Brazil, Uruguay, and Paraguay is one of the most recent examples and one in which the universities of the four countries are especially involved.

Many students in evening school programs are employees in companies during the day. There are also students in job-training programs in businesses who are still enrolled at the university. Technological parks or institutions and activities with a similar name have thrived in Brazil. EXPOCIENCIA, an annual science exposition in Colombia, and similar ideas in other countries show the increasing, effective consensus on overcoming the distance between universities and businesses, and to making the dialogue that brings them closer together effective.

Dialogue

Relations among people are closer if they become dialogues. Talking is the mutual, sincere opening of attitudes toward life and things. It is the exchange of feelings, opinions, and points of view. It is the honest discussion of ideas and affections that, by subordinating the stubborn and egotistic interests that often convert dialogues into quarrels, elevate them to shared values and aims. Dialogue can make hostile elements agree harmoniously and efficiently.

The dialogue between business and universities is often marked by suspicion. This is due perhaps to the fact that the relations between the university and business are often unilateral. In these cases, there is an urgent need to open a dialogue with a superior motive to unify a desire that goes beyond perhaps

conflicting institutional egotism. Peace and the integral development of nations should be the inducement that always makes the
dialogue between business and the university cordial and effective. This is even more valid when the university's relations
overcome their local surroundings and become intranational,
international, and supranational.

THE UNIVERSITY'S FUTURE
AS AN INSTITUTION

◆

In his third volume on medieval universities, the British historian, Hastings Rashdall (1936), left a good record of which
institutions remained at the end of the 19th century. Rashdall
asserts that the university is heir to traditions that have to be
adjusted to the surrounding social environment and must be
prepared to change if it wishes to guarantee its future.

He predicted the possible shape of things to come for the
university institution, although he could not foresee the effects
of two world wars in the first half of the 20th century. However,
shortly after World War II, there were many national and international fora, congresses, seminars, conferences, and symposia
with their literature on the university in the 1960s, 70s, and 80s.
The goals set in the 1990s, approaching the year 2000, were
similar to those at the close of the first millennium: to replace
scientific poverty with research and ideas.

Today, with an abundance of science and research ventures,
scholars have been anticipating the future for universities. Participants in panel discussions and roundtables, in their desire to
project the university's future developments, have debated the
deductive method, with its desirable, academic, and historic–
social situations, and the inductive, analytic method. In spite of
this methodological dilemma, there is no doubt about the future
of the university as institution: "universities have not doubted

their future," no matter what difficulties or crises they might have to face. "They begin with a confident presupposition which, although it is not held by everyone, obliges them to think that the affaire of the university is the university itself" (Carrier 1984, p. 1).

In 1991, in a forum sponsored by Unesco (1991b) and the University of Pittsburgh, the working groups prepared four suggested agendas that should be put into practice in the future. The recommendations dealt with policy, administration and management, and governance systems; curriculum, teaching methods, educational materials, and technologies; student and faculty development and evaluation; and, finally, implementation strategies.

The first area of research raised questions about the effects of institutions of higher education and their research on national policies, economic development, the physical environment, class structure and its participation in and access to higher education, and influence on the lower levels of education. In the second area, development of higher education, research should be oriented toward overcoming the gaps between policy and practice, and to improving the effectiveness and efficiency of higher education institutions as they fulfill their missions and goals. Concrete themes for research would thus be the mechanism and processes of national and institutional decision-making, planning, and resource allocation; the links between research, applied and theoretical, and policy formulation on both the governmental and institutional levels; training of students at the undergraduate and graduate levels, keeping in mind the union of research and teaching; the relation between development universities (those able to serve the state, society, and their own members, the faculty); and the well-known problem of how to maintain or develop academic freedom and still be accountable to the state and society, the role played by the faculty in the government of an institution and the incentives that stimulate the faculty to participate actively in research, and the relevance of higher education to society, including the indicators of quality used to judge the institutions and their level of excellence.

With regard to the curriculum, teaching methods, and educational materials, the working group suggested analyzing the attitude and behaviour of the groups in relation to teaching techniques. Topics raised were the teaching role of the university in professional education programs; the humanization of the curriculum and its contribution to the development of creativity and the critical analysis of values, information, and assertions; the creation of responsible awareness of social needs; and the relations between class size, teacher education, salaries, and student achievement.

Concerning student and faculty development, the first concern is the conditions under which the work of the faculty, staff, and students is carried out, and how these conditions are related to the goals and outcomes of higher education. This would include systematic studies of the teaching and learning processes, the ways faculty can adapt to student learning styles and culture, and questions concerning student life and faculty qualifications.

Finally, regarding the implementation of strategies, the working groups agreed on the different forms of support that intergovernmental organizations, governments, educational institutions, nongovernmental organizations, individuals, and foundations should give to the studies and research on higher education (Berstecher 1974).

In 1983, Unesco held an international symposium on the probable developments in the goals and social roles of higher education during the coming decades. Topics proposed for discussion were democratization of higher education, interpenetration of higher education and society, professionalization of higher education in relation to the planning and administration of institutions, current functions of higher education, and implementation of new teaching approaches. Other topics dealt with factors capable of influencing or modifying university action during the coming decades in the context of democratization and social change. These included increase in student enrolment;

priorities of the vital sectors of agriculture, industry, transport, and communication and the pressing needs of food, health and shelter; the knowledge explosion and the technological revolution; specialization to cope with the growing intensity of division of labour; value of research and its place in academic programs; life-long education; new alternatives for entry to the educational system and the workplace; equalization of opportunities or democratization of higher education; internal democracy within the structures of educational institutions themselves to allow for student participation in academic decision-making and the representation of younger teachers in university bodies; the training of highly qualified personnel and the absorptive capacity of the economy; relations between the university and the state; the manifold advantages of a multidisciplinary university instead of single-faculty universities; the world peace factor; and the various forms of international cooperation of universities with different institutions and organizations (Unesco 1983). A similar approach to the internal and external factors in the development of higher education in the future was adopted by the Conférence intergouvernementale sur les politiques d'enseignement supérieur dans les annés 80, which was called for by the OECD in Paris in 1981.

Reflecting on the titles of recent works about the university on the verge of the year 2000, Carton (1983) wondered about the danger the university faces if it, rather than other social institutions, plans to be the institution chosen to lead higher education on the current "perspective of social transformation, educational democratization, and continuing education." He sees four predominant trends for the university during the next 20 years: "linking of higher education with production and research; relations with the collective community; participation in national and regional cultural development, and inclusion in the international problem of socio-economic development."

Niblett and Butts (1972) propose the university's future trends in the following terms (Carton 1983): "emphasis on research or emphasis on teaching general preparation or specialized preparation; independence or integration; academic liberty or national interest; quality or quantity; emphasis on the definition of the objectives of preparation or emphasis on student orientation."

A short document from Unesco (1984b), approached the future of the universities by posing "seven issues or critical problems" to their planners: "the evaluation of demand," which could change from the traditional university types to "non-traditional ones (for example, part-time teaching, teaching for short periods or in relation to jobs)"; professional unemployment and underemployment, both visible and invisible, about which there is unsatisfactory statistical data; "the growing shortage of financial resources"; the problem of educational "democratization" with regard to the relatively limited participation of women, "discrimination caused by geographical reasons," and "disparity caused by socio-economic conditions"; the difficulty in applying systems of educational planning and the problem of university management; "international cooperation"; and "socio-cultural aspects" related to the quality of life. Sanyal (1984) refers to similar challenges in light of a "new international order" based on "socio-cultural factors" and not only on "political" and "economic" factors, and he studies the impact of the world economy on the growth of higher education and its relation to employment.

Stanojevic (1988) adopts a procedure similar to Niblett's. He points out the difficulty of transformations, which he calls "aporia," that face the university in the present-day "crisis of the society." The first contradiction consists of the fact that

> The inertia of the university led to the situation in which the creators of the past reforms were mainly people outside the university. The majority of the reforms represented nothing else than demagogic concessions to students and projections of the visions of some politicians to the university. Even if the ideas of reforms are well conceived, they can not succeed if the university feels them as something imposed. The solution should perhaps be sought in the dialogue between the university and the other segments of the society.

[Second,] almost all modern methods assume the intensification of the learning process, and that cannot be achieved at faculties which become bigger because of the explosion of high education. One of the ways to remove this obstacle could be, beside the creation of new universities, the splitting of old universities; of course, the new universities would not necessarily have the same profile as the old ones.

Stanojevic goes on to warn that

The trend to distribute knowledge on an equal basis is hampered by great social differences, which offer better possibilities for learning for some students. A greater percentage of good students comes from well-off families. On the other hand, some families cannot afford to send even their gifted children to universities.

Finally, he presents the fourth problem, the difficulty of overcoming "the traditional concept of learning" that he calls "digestive," or "nutritional" as Sartre would say, and of introducing another concept that "should make our students active subjects in the learning process and not mere containers of crammed data."

Vandal (1988) reflects on "the point of shift from the industrial society to the society of informatics." He says:

The changing nature of our era is also reflected in the university and in its environment. There exist many factors which support the inertia and rigidity of the existing situation and push the universities into the old schemes of traditional school systems. On the other hand, the forces which put the universities, and their production of new knowledge into the focal point of a qualitatively new stage of development, are gaining momentum. Therefore, the modelling of the modern university should take into account three problems: In what way is the university going to educate people, on the basis of scientific and consultative work, for the society of the future, and for the existing society as well? What will be the role of the university in the creation and in the accomplishment of the development strategies of modern societies and in the development of national identities and the conscience of one's own existence and one's environment? What will be the structure and the dialectics of the relations between the participants in the global activities of the university, and what will be its organizational scheme?

Ratkovic (1988) collects previous reflections and, anticipating the "models of universities before the third millenium," observes more vigorous relations among education, science, and technology that "would change the autonomy of the universities and continue to develop the creative and rational criticism of social phenomena, processes and creations"; require the "modernization of pedagogic and scientific work and of radical organizational, didactic, and methodological changes, i.e., the necessity of the so-called internal reform, which is an indispensable pre-requisite for the development of a modern university"; because it takes into account the "human differences in the education of university students...instead of traditional methods," systems of workshops for research, dialogue, and learning will be adapted, while research projects, through methods of discovery, will open new ways for the development of individual capabilities and talents; and, finally, methods and strategies for the implementation of reforms "without administrative correction and political pressures, with the active participation of the society and the universities" will be created.

The Canadian report on university education (Smith 1991, p. 134), after analyzing present-day situations, carefully and precisely lists actions to be taken for the development of higher education: funding, the relations between teaching and learning, curriculum design, the international dimension of universities, continuing and distance education, the necessary research on higher education, the facilities that should be offered to students for accessibility to higher education, annual analysis of attrition rates, transfers, and trends in educational patterns, and the effectiveness of programs undertaken at individual universities, relations between universities and the secondary school system, cooperation within higher education, tenure and the future supply of faculty, and quality control and performance indicators of educational institutions.

Yero (1991), after analyzing the prospects of Latin America and the Caribbean, deduces the resulting educational developments in the region.

Unesco (1992a) states:

> Higher education institutions, by nature, are complex organizations containing both conservative and progressive forces. They can serve immediate needs, but their main orientation is to the future. They are responsible for the future generation of educated, skilled manpower. Changes are difficult in established institutions, but once made, are long-lasting. Many countries in the Asia and Pacific region are going through a period of expansion and dramatic economic shifts as well as social and political readjustments, which results in a substantial strain on a country's pool of knowledge and educated manpower. Countries less economically well-off still are experiencing a rising demand for higher education. While most higher education systems attempted to gear themselves to emerging needs, they have found it difficult to keep pace with the changing demands — falling short both quantitatively and qualitatively. The challenges ahead are indeed great.

Among these challenges is the quantitative expansion that requires agreements between governments and educational entities to plan the most appropriate structure of particular higher education systems in the context of national needs, with the participation of government and private agencies, including business enterprises and industry. There is consideration of the relations between higher education and work-force development; the many responsibilities of higher education to society; the urgent need to stimulate innovation and reform; the planning and management of resources; the mobility of staff, students and ideas; and the fostering of cooperation and collaboration.

An international seminar in Beijing (2–25 June 1988) brought together 34 eminent Chinese scholars on higher education and 13 foreign experts. There was heated discussion on current international trends in higher education development and reform in the future. On many points, opinions diverged noticeably. Although many representatives believed that the

development of higher education would tend to stress improvement in quality rather than quantity (the trend of the 60s), others
thought that both tendencies would coexist.

Some participants proposed a higher education primarily
oriented to meet the practical needs of social and economic
development and give precedence to the disciplines of an applied
nature over the disciplines of an academic nature; others advocated guarding against the tendency to emphasize specialized
education to the neglect of general education. "Institutions
should not only turn out engineers, but also qualified personnel
in human sciences, social sciences, art and culture." Consequently, some point out that in teaching, professors of universities should offer ethical and moral education and institutions
should be responsible for solving economic (the development of
technology) and moral problems (the development of the
society). Scientific research linked to economic development is
important, but basic research and research programs of far-
reaching significance should not be neglected. Universities
should not depend only on the guidance of the economy because,
even in developing countries, they have the double mission of
meeting the needs of the society and maintaining its academic
excellence and these two functions should not be separated;
culture and arts also have social values.

Moreover, the participants at the Beijing seminar agreed that
university education in the future would become a system of
life-long education as a result of the rapid development of society,
economy, science, and technology, which require updating
knowledge and changing professions; that the postsecondary
system would move toward diversification to meet the needs of
society and the diversified composition of student populations;
that the macro-management and control of the government and
the autonomy of institutions would become more balanced; and
that education would be internationalized in terms of experience,
exchanges in human, material, financial, and information
resources, mutual support, and the training of qualified personnel oriented to world development.

In Africa, the prospects for education in general and university education in particular deserve our attention. They are inseparable from the political, social, cultural, and economic situations that affect the different countries. Shortly after the symposium organized by the Organization of African Unity (OAU 1979), the Sommet économique africaine was able to formulate a plan of action for the economic development of Africa for 1980–2000 (Plan d'Action de Lagos). The heads of state and governments issued a declaration after examining different situations: "We have perceived with uneasiness the great dependence of our continent on the exportation of raw materials and minerals. This phenomenon has converted the African economies into tributaries of external developments, followed by the consequential harm to the continent's interior" (OAU 1979).

In 1983, the African Economic Community (AEC) undertook a prospective 35-year study inspired by the Plan d'Action de Lagos; among other declarations, it said (MINDAEF VI 1991):

> To avoid the specter of an increase in poverty, sub-employment, and general instability,...the African countries have to conceive of measures at a national, sub-regional and regional level and set them into operation. In other words, the future that arises from this normative background depends mainly on the "will" of Africa and the will of its people to initiate the change.

As MINEDAF VI asserts, the prospective study proposed actions "in the domains of food production, energy development, industrial development, transportation and communications, trade and finances, and general development policies."

In spite of these valid aims, MINEDAF VI continues by saying that "the situation has quickly degenerated," and for this reason successive meetings in 1984 and 1985 converged in the Programme d'action des Nations Unies pour le redressement économique et le développement de l'Afrique (PANUREDA), which stated: "Africa cannot wait for the external equilibrium of its fiscal balance before it endeavors to improve the condition of its population; it cannot delay its investments in human training that reinforce its institutional, scientific, technical and productive capacity in a balanced environment." The AEC formed the Cadre alternatif aux programmes d'adjustement estructurel pour le redressement et le changement socio-economique (CARPAS), which recognizes that Africa has to adapt to the changes in internal and external economic means, but in such a way that will favour self-sufficiency, self-development, growth, and change. In other words, the adjustment should promote the aims of the Plan d'Action de Lagos. Above all, it should promote and not prejudge the development of people. Hence, like the Lagos plan, CARPAS concludes with the importance of ensuring education and training, and of keeping an eye on the health, welfare, and vitality of its population so that they can fully and effectively participate in the development process.

According to Salifou (1983), the reflection on higher education in Africa "appears to have really begun on September 3–12, 1962, when a conference on the future of this teaching took place in Tananaribo, Madagascar." It was there that "in addition to its traditional function and obligations to teach and to advance knowledge through research," the conference "proposes the following as the goals of higher education in Africa," as they appear in the report of the conference (Taiwo 1991, p. 2):

◆ To maintain adherence and loyalty to world academic standards;

◆ To ensure the unification of Africa;

◆ To encourage appreciation for African culture and heritage and to dispel misconceptions of Africa through research and teaching of African studies;

◆ To develop completely the human resources for meeting manpower needs;

◆ To train the "whole man" for nation building; and

◆ To evolve over the years a truly African pattern of higher learning dedicated to Africa and its people yet promoting a bond of kinship to the larger human society.

The discussion on higher education in Africa continued at the conferences of Ministers of Education that were held in Abidjad in 1964 and in Nairobi in 1968, followed by the Plan d'action de Lagos (1976). In Harare, 28 June to 3 July 1982, MINEDAF V had a similar aim and this was followed by four meetings in Dakar.

"After 20 years," stated Salifou (1983), "the number of studies devoted to the topic of higher education is countless." They are full of recommendations that are more or less pertinent and should have been implemented so that systems of higher education should already have adapted to our realities.

According to MINEDAF VI, achieving educational pertinence in Africa has faced serious challenges: the systems of school education are like foreign bodies inserted into the social environment; endogenous and national languages can be used in technics and technology in educational processes; and as traditional and indigenous knowledge is gradually forgotten, new learning is diluted or deteriorates into illiteracy; finally, there is such a distance between education and the productive sector, that the inevitable result is unemployment. As a result of all that has been said, *Priorites de développement économique et social pour les années 90* concludes (MINDAEF VI 1990):

> The development of human capacities is an important preamble for the changes and socio-economic development of Africa.... The first step to carrying out this objective should place literacy as a primary goal and the increase of basic educational possibilities on the continent; it should consider what is important to lead people to be more receptive to ideas and to development practices, and to raise and prepare people's aptitudes more positively and actively for political, social, economic, and cultural activities.

The Plan d'action de Lagos gathered opinions, impressions, points of view, and recommendations from the documents mentioned above and from others such as Unesco/BREDA (1992) and

Unesco (1990e). The situation of higher education in Africa was analyzed on nine important points: the mission of higher education in African society; access to higher education; women's access to higher education; quality and content of education; harmonization of curricula and mobility of scholars; inter-university cooperation and pooling of resources; higher education as a factor of societal change; status of tertiary level; teachers, research, and funding. The next step was to prepare a program to determine the actions needed to improve higher education on the continent and set up two stages for implementation: 1992–1993, studies, investigations, analyses to be carried out on various aspects of the current situation; and 1993–1997, application of the measures planned (Unesco 1991a).

African nations enthusiastically watched the effective fulfillment of these goals because their universities are now able to maintain and renew the "vigor, optimism and pride which the same institutions displayed 20 or 30 years ago" (Salmi 1991).

CONCLUSION

◆

This section has dealt with moments of the university's history in the gradual formation of its institutionalism, its missions and functions, and its roles and philosophical guidelines. Because the future is already raising questions for university scholars, this book tries to explain the two implicit meanings of the word "administrate" so that the university understands that it should improve its internal organization and convert itself into the best source of first-rate external services.

The main concern of this book is the university's future. The general and specific themes developed will affect university life, and with time-worn language or with liberated forms of expression, I have discussed the missions, functions, and roles or distinctive manifestations of the university. Deep down, the concern is always the nature and philosophy of the university, its being and acting, and its fate.

Discrepancies are explainable because of the variety and diversity of traditions, situations, and cultural, political, and economic contexts. However, there continue to be themes that treat the structures and organization with an analytical, critical, and projective spirit, and the conditions of a qualified, efficient, and fair corporate action. What and how a student's education and development ought to be like — education for what is superior and in what is superior — is a more or less implicit theme. The questions raised concern research and teaching: whether they should be separate or united, interdisciplinary or individual subjects; whether the emphasis should be on learning what is taught or on criticism and creativity. There are questions about technology and what it should be taught for, and about the complexities that it awakens and creates regarding culture.

Universities have to decide whether their task is to instill in their students a fundamental and creative sense and to ask themselves about the development and usefulness of science and the diverse ways of fulfilling its mission of service. Although service to society is judged important because of its service to culture, it seems that there is more concern for the professional than for the person, for extension than for development, and for relations of all kinds — particularly with the productive sector and economic development — than for how much is said about the total quality of individual and social life.

The documents concerning the university's future raise common themes and questions. They show a desire and yearning and, most important, register actions that have been or are being put into practice by universities that are, therefore, already following the course of action pointed out. Even more, planning and the "recently developed field" (Dockrell 1990) of university institutional evaluation are following these plans and paths.

PART IV

◆

EPILOGUE ON PLANNING
AND SELF-EVALUATION

Planning, execution, evaluation: the natural actions of responsible persons and institutions. They make up the three important stages that complete the cycle of the administrative process. In logical order, planning precedes execution and evaluation, but all planning has to start with evaluation.

PLANNING

◆

Planning, in its obvious sense of constructing plans and projects, adopting the means, and carrying out actions leading to a desired goal, is carried out by high levels of government to develop policies: social, political, economical, cultural, and even ideological.

At lower levels, especially in the business world, the exercise of planning fits into the nature and objectives of each enterprise, and sometimes of associations of enterprises. In the case of the university, planning should be according to its roles, functions, and missions, but it was quickly reduced to a professional relation with work and governed by economic criteria.

Opinions about planning

Carton (1983) points out six broad stages in planning the relations between education and the work environment. In the 1960s, he says, attention was on the theory of "human capital" revived by Schultz in 1960 (Carrier 1990). This theory stated that stability in the employment structure should determine what was taught at the university. In the 1970s, there was more insistence on examining the job market's capacity for absorption, which was done with a certain level of autonomy for educational systems, taking into account the evident flexibility of employment. This approach led to the third stage, the perception that many people who were being trained could be replaced, in identical jobs, by others from a different profession. The fourth stage is, therefore, characterized by the strategies of the utilization of qualifications and, by the end of the 1970s, there was greater interest in specific technological training programs. Once again, the role of higher education systems was examined and the difference between traditional or professional universities and universities providing a technological orientation was discussed.

The opinion of the International Institute of Education Policies (IIPE 1988) is critical:

> Since the end of the 1950s and the beginning of the 1960s, educational planning has experienced rapid development. Already practiced in the centrally planned economies, it was gradually introduced into Western industrialized countries and the developing world. This infatuation can be partly explained by the very important role accorded by the different social and economic theories developed at the time to education as a motor of development and an instrument of social change....

> Educational planning developed in the 1960s in the context of unprecedented economic expansion was then seen as having the task of orchestrating a great expansion of educational systems within the dual perspective of democratizing education and of furnishing the economy with the qualified manpower which it needed. In most countries, one or more planning units were created. Great hopes were placed on planning which was expected to serve as a framework for setting objectives and priorities, give direction to educational policies and optimize the use of resources.

> [In the same decade, educational planning] was based essentially on the techno-rational model. This model, inspired by systems analysis, supposes that individuals and governments behave rationally, seeking optimal solutions to problems both in terms of results and resource utilization. The first stage, then, consists of defining the objectives sought as precisely as possible. Thereafter, the various means of achieving these objectives are studied, particularly in terms of their costs and advantages. Having selected what seems to be the best solution, a plan of action is drawn up, its steps carefully identified as well as the means necessary for the completion of each stage of the process.

Looked at this way, the process of planning appeared to be mainly technical; in the sense that there was supposed to be consensus over the objectives, the problem was essentially one of identifying the best way of reaching them. Several techniques to help in decision-making were developed, in particular: cost–benefit analysis, optimization techniques based upon operational research, simulation models and sensitivity analysis. It was optimistically assumed that a viable and coherent plan could be implemented without difficulty.

[However,] 30 years later it has to be admitted that educational planning has lost much of its prestige. It has been accused of being sometimes too influential and sometimes not influential enough. That the context in which it operates has changed a great deal is undeniable.

In the first place, economic expansion has given way to crisis or to severe instability, limiting the resources available for education. Secondly, the great myths of education as a motor for development and as a great leveller in society have waned. After 30 years of expansion of educational systems, serious problems have emerged: graduate unemployment, technological backwardness, bureaucratization of the administration; while other problems, such as lack of equality both in education and in the society, persist. Far from improving, educational conditions in the poorest countries have deteriorated. Finally, the State seems less and less able to confront the educational demands made upon it; private education is developing, and everywhere new forms of education outside the traditional school system are coming to the fore.

[Moreover, the decades of the 1970s and 80s] were marked by disillusionment about the role of education. Most of the theories then developed called into question the relationship between education, productivity and income levels. Attention seems to have been shifted away from the characteristics of the manpower supply towards the characteristics of demand.

At the end of the 1980s, in an atmosphere of crisis and public spending cuts, rate of return and cost–benefit analyses are coming back into vogue, inspiring a number of educational strategies (privatization of education, cutting expenditure on higher education, etc.). On the other side, faced with the technological challenge, many governments of industrialized countries are again talking — in the absence of any viable alternatives — about massive investment in education. The idea of intellectual investment, including not only training but also research and development, marketing, etc., is now on the agenda.

As a consequence of the previous historical analysis, the IIPE concludes that, "in practice, things have not been so simple and the process of planning was shown to be much more complex." Therefore, economic theories of education planning continue to conflict with social theories, and there is an awareness that

> The scope of planning has widened aspects of the development of education, aspects which are much harder to plan and put into operation, [and] planners have had to pay much more attention to the degree of acceptability of decisions and their likelihood of being implemented.

> Rarely involved in preparing decisions, planning structures have above all been used to implement them, and even sometimes to justify them after the fact. Planning has, therefore, more often been operational than strategic.

Obviously, there are also those who, avoiding the debate, "rejected planning as useless and prefer to allow educational systems to develop freely, relying on social (or rather private) demand as stimulus." In response to this attitude, the IIPE (1988) says that education "plays too important a role in society, the stakes are too political to allow its development to take place this way," and therefore,

> There is a continuing need for planning to guide the development of the educational system, contribute to a greater economy of resources, encourage equality of opportunity and to allow actors to examine initiatives in detail before implementing them.

However, it also becomes necessary to take into account that official, higher educational planning "is perhaps out-of-step with a world characterized by complexity, uncertainty, and rapid change."

[The] recognition of this complexity implies in turn recognition of the difficulty of imposing minutely detailed global reforms and recognizing that the effects of an individual decision are never entirely predictable, hence the need for feedback to allow modification or refinement of the original decision.

[Moreover,] complexity accentuates the imperative in planning of links with intermediate levels closest to the problems and realities being confronted.... [In turn,] planners must be adaptable to changing situations and be able to draw up alternative plans which could be used if and when necessary. Uncertainty and change also require a suppleness and speed which are rarely suited to large bureaucracies like education administrations.

The practice of planning must evolve if it is to help countries cope with the challenges which they and their educational systems face. It has become urgent to rethink its structures, functions and processes; in particular, the role of the intermediate — specifically the institutional — levels, and the means by which the State or the central authority intervenes in the process. Perhaps it is necessary to establish other, contractual modes of intervention which would allow greater freedom from the existing system, support innovative projects, encourage promising experiments at the expense of blind alleys, instead of direct intervention through control of the curricula, the allocation of resources and the distribution of teaching equipment.

Taking account of the scarcity and unpredictability of resources and of the participation of an increased number of actors external to the ministries, planning must change its nature. It can no longer function in a linear fashion based on relatively constant inputs.

From now on, it is a question of being able to adapt rapidly. Thus, perhaps paradoxically, this type of behavior requires that principal objectives be identified on the basis of which strategic monitoring will replace traditional linear planning.

Planning must, then, widen its area of activity. It must begin with a look into the future to identify possible and desirable paths to development. In the short term, planning should become part of the decision-making process: identifying occasions when decisions need to be made; looking for foreseeable and workable solutions, and, once the decision has been made supervising its implementation while taking account of the various actors and levels of resolution.

In order to do this, planning could make use of new techniques, especially in information technology which will modify the nature, form and the volume of communication between the educational reality (establishments), the authority structures (intermediate or central) and the normative decision centres (central structures). A better understanding of the reality of decision-making could rely on the application of more modern and sophisticated information, management and forecasting systems, in particular expert systems.

Universities and planning

The methods and procedures for business management taught in the classrooms should be applied to the university for their own planning, execution, and institutional and academic evaluation. Of course, universities are aware that because they deal with people and have their special roles, missions, and functions, they are not comparable to business organizations.

Since "strategic planning" (Ohmae Kenichi 1975; Keller 1983; Arguin 1986), "administration by objectives" (Reyes Ponce 1975), and systems of "total quality" are frequently discussed, it is natural to adopt these means of planning, which are as old as humanity even though they were not formalized until the end of the 18th century (Peters 1982). Some experts place greater emphasis on the act of planning, some on the course of action needed to achieve goals, and, finally, some are concerned mainly with results.

However, these emphases are not mutually exclusive. In addition, the rational task of planning the course of action for business and university supposes the development of a particular culture and the common consent of people.

In the case of planning in higher education, difficulties arise especially in lesser developed countries and when it is being done

term. Some of the problems include the "inapplica-
estern models, lack of trained personnel, lack of
⌐⌐⌐⌐⌐⌐⌐ of the value of long-term planning, instability or
discontinuity of political leadership that will see plans to completion, and inadequacy of valid and reliable information that
serves as the basis for planning" (Unesco 1988a). We can add the
dilemma already mentioned by the IIPE (1988) between the
narrow definition of planning proposed by economists "strictly
in terms of forecast of demand for skilled personnel and of
student places in higher educational institutions, and in terms of
the efficient use of scarce resources," contrasted with the "social
and broad definition." García Guadilla (1991) makes a similar
statement when she refers to "naive traditional theories: human
resources and human capital," and P. Demo (1991), in a similar
vein, judges those theories that "instrumentalize society in terms
of growth and market" as being "very out-of date." Kamba (in
Unesco 1991c) synthesizes the situation well when he states:

> One feature of the questioning may be discontent with "an age
> of pragmatism" — a period in which too many decisions of
> consequence have been made with mainly short-term objec-
> tives in view…. There may be a need for structural changes to
> accommodate social pressures for efficiency, while retaining
> traditional academic freedom, detachment and opportunities
> for contemplation.

EVALUATION

Evaluation should logically follow from planning, but it awakens
doubts at the level of official policies. In the preface to its report
(OECD 1990), the Institutional Management in Higher Education (IMHE) study group says:

> In the last 20 years, evaluation has become a critical issue for
> academicians, administrators and politicians. This is due in
> large part to the great expansion of higher education systems,
> the increasing financial constraints in the public sector and

the corresponding demand for accountability, and to the general tendency towards decentralization over the past two decades. The relative importance of any of these factors varies between countries. However, in combination they highlight the importance of evaluation in higher education in all countries.

A primary problem is to determine to what extent evaluation should serve as an information basis for resource allocation by governments, other funding agencies and boards of governors. In addition, we must consider to what extent evaluation can be used as a constructive means of improving teaching and research within universities and colleges. Further, is there an inherent conflict between these two basic aims or can they be complementary, and under what kinds of conditions?

Other problems originate from the very nature of higher education, which is rooted in national cultures and subject to changing situations and conditions. Besides alluding to the changing situation of professions in relation to the organization of work, and taking into account that "the whole structure of education itself is changing with lifelong learning," the IMHE report points out that private industry has taken on the task of training and retraining its professionals and that performance indicators are very unreliable measures of work performance. It also supports official deregulation and self-regulation of universities as a means to gain greater accountability. Underlying this debate, like the one concerning planning, is the dilemma of economic theories versus social theories of education.

In the case of the university, permanent evaluation is the logical consequence of planning to act and a fair justification for autonomy. Although the right of the highest institution of knowledge to dictate its own norms is inherent, it must demonstrate this to itself before it can be demonstrated to society and the state. It can then rightly demand that its autonomy be recognized and not granted out of complacency. The university's self-evaluation inspires confidence and authority.

The term evaluation is used to mean assigning values of quality to something. This meaning is preferred to avoid confusion with concepts used in many works that deal with how to evaluate institutions and enterprises other than the university. It is also preferred because just as planning is the right and duty of the university to maintain its autonomy, so is the concept of the university and the determination to examine its actions.

With this understanding of evaluation, the following questions should be posed: Who is the agent evaluating? What is the object of university institutional evaluation? How is the evaluation practiced? Once these questions are answered, there are some considerations that lead us to think of the ultimate goals of institutional evaluation.

Agents of evaluation

The process of assigning values of quality can have two agents: the institution itself (self-evaluating) and an external person who accredits or judges the university's conditions from outside. This is hetero-evaluation, which in some cases is verified by the state or social institutions (Cruz Cardona 1991).

In external evaluation, the procedures used in the United States, where accreditation had two initial goals, are well known (Rudolph 1965). One was to establish the system that would determine the quality of the student coming from high school. This goal began to gain momentum in the last decade of the 19th century because of the debate between President Eliot at Harvard and President Warfield at Lafayette College. Eliot's idea of looking for a common consensus among institutions for guidelines to determine the abilities of candidates prevailed. As a result, in June 1902, the first college board was established. It was an interinstitutional organization in charge of promoting standards and measures of competence for college entrance. In 1910, 25 institutions in the northeast had joined the system, which was copied by other regions of the United States with modifications. However, the Carnegie Foundation had meanwhile become interested in the matter. In 1908, it sponsored a conference on entrance requirements. The so-called Carnegie Unit was the result: a more or less accepted unit of measurement to evaluate a candidate's qualifications.

Years later, the university associations created after 1887 met in Williamstown, Massachusetts, and in 1906 agreed on the second great effort at accreditation of colleges and universities and on interinstitutional hetero-evaluation to obtain the best academic level possible in the associated institutions through the exchange of ideas and mutual evaluations.

Today, after grouping higher education institutions into various categories, the Carnegie Foundation for the Advancement of Teaching reports the results of the external evaluation that the Foundation periodically carries out on the institutions examined. In 1967, the foundation instituted the Carnegie Commission of Higher Education in the United States as we approach the year 2000 (Carnegie Foundation for the Advancement of Teaching 1974). US News has been using methods similar to the Foundation's to report the results of its investigations in the annual *America's Best Colleges*.

Hetero-evaluation and self-evaluation could easily combine when a university requests another similar institution to make an evaluation and also when both agree to evaluate each other. Concerning the university's hetero-evaluation, Carton (1983, p. 29) states:

> Universities must take into account the opinions of different social, national and international participants. These pressures will be contradictory and will create conflicts in the bosom of the university because they will have to do with the value of university knowledge, and, hence, with those who control it.

Later, Starapoli (1990) clearly noted that there are various factors: the state, or more concretely the government and ministries, especially if there is a ministry of education. Considering the differences in each country, different factors work on the educational system in different ways. Another factor in hetero-evaluation is the market, represented by the employers of graduates, companies having contacts with universities, and other participants who are potential users, such as students and families deciding which university to attend. Funding bodies, funding institutions, and private donors make up another group of hetero-evaluators, in some cases attracted by the cost–benefit criterion or by philanthropy. Finally, public opinion plays a role because of social interest.

Those involved in self-evaluation are all part of the university community: directors, faculty, students, and support personnel. In short, the university's human resources make their point of view about the institution's progress known through their opinions and attitudes, formally or informally, and to different extents and from the different jobs and specific functions they perform.

The object of university evaluation

The object of university evaluation is obviously the university itself, some of whose actions can be quantified, whereas others can only be valued. The effects of the latter type of actions, such as educational or cultural, cannot be expressed numerically. In addition, the university's philosophy inspires it and directs its life. For this reason, it constitutes the principles that form the basis for the judgement about the institution's performance. The university's statutory charter, although it is stable and directly arises from the university's philosophy and principles, can be changed because of self-evaluation. It is clear that the university's philosophy and principles are not the subject of hetero-evaluation in the way that organization and the effects produced by the university could be.

Carrying out the evaluation

Much has been written on evaluating, but two procedures can be highlighted here. In both (Tables 3 and 4), it is fitting to adopt the "themes" or "criteria" proposed for evaluation. For the first procedure, these are the institution's physiognomy, its functions, its relations, and its planning. In the second procedure, they are organizational resources, human resources, academic, teaching

Table 3. First procedure for university evaluation.

Theme	Determiners and subdeterminers of themes	Aspects of immediate evaluation
Physiognomy	Principles	Structures
	Statutes	Simple
	Regulation	Sufficient
	General structure (administrative	Flexible
	areas and levels)	Intelligent
	Academic area (structure)	Efficient
	Divisions	Human resources
	Faculties	Directors
	Departments	Professors
	Programs	Students
	Institutes	Support personnel
	Centres	Materials
	Administrative and financial area	Physical
	Area responsible for university	Technical
	and student welfare	Economic
	Programs	Equitable distribution
	Activities	Characteristics of action
	Services	Participation
		Decision-making
		Clear understanding of
		decisions
		Solidarity
		Fast, flowing action
		Efficiency
Functions	Research function (science policy)	Structures
	Technology	Simple
	Lines of research	Sufficient
	Teaching and educational function	Flexible
	Cultural	Intelligent
	Scientific	Efficient
	Professional (degrees)	Human resources
	Technological	Directors
	Entrepreneurial	Professors
	Education for what is superior	Students
	Interdisciplinary	Support personnel
	Computer sciences	Materials
	Pedagogical types	Physical
	Open and distance	Technical
	Continuous education	Equitable distribution
	Service function and extension services	Characteristics of action
	To social culture	Participation
	To nationality	Decision-making
	To the critical function	Clear understanding of
	To development	decisions
	Library and information	Solidarity
		Fast, flowing action
		Efficiency

(continued)

Table 3 concluded.

Theme	Determiners and subdeterminers of themes	Aspects of immediate evaluation
Relations	Internal Interinstitutional Domestic International	
Planning	General Specific	

and research resources, physical material resources, and economic and financial resources. Other themes could be proposed, such as the university's service to culture, to economic and social development, to educational democratization, and to relations with business (Unesco 1981).

It is also necessary to delimit the "determiners and subdeterminers" of the proposed theme. Finally, in the third procedure, the "aspects," items, or performance indicators used to evaluate are specified. These indicators can be surveys or questionnaires set up for each of the items (Unesco 1981).

It is worth noting the correspondence between the first two procedures, which collect performance indicators and have been used in evaluation systems in Denmark, Finland, Norway, and Sweden (Chinapah 1992) and Alain Bienaymé's (1984) proposal (Figure 5), which interrelates what we have called determiners and subdeterminers with "performance indicators." Documents presented in the IMHE report are useful to evaluate the university's contribution to society (Shattock 1990), to evaluate research (Staropoli 1990), and to evaluate teaching.

In the Delphi study coordinated by McDaniel (1990), participants were asked to judge the possibilities and potential for European higher education policy using a number of performance indicators related to quality assessment. Ranked in order of support given, the following performance indicators were distinguished:

Academic reputation of the academic staff, external peer review on the contents of the curriculum, completion rates,

Table 4. Second procedure for university evaluation.

Theme	Determiners and subdeterminers of themes	Aspects of immediate evaluation

Resources of institutional organization	Principles
	Statutes
	Regulations
	General structure (administrative
	    areas and levels)
	Academic area (structures)
	    Divisions
	    Faculties (schools and colleges)
	    Departments
	    Programs
	    Institutes
	    Centres
	    Centres, departments, and offices for
	        administrative support
	Relations
	Planning
		Structures
		    Simple
		    Sufficient
		    Flexible
		    Intelligible
		    Efficient
		Characteristics of action
		    Participation
		    Decision-making
		    Clear understanding of
		        decisions
		    Solidarity
		    Fast,flowing actions
		    Efficiency

Human resources	Directors
	Professors
	Researchers
	Students
	Support personnel
		Selection
		Orientation
		Preparation
		Participation
		Relations
		Welfare
		    Programs
		    Activities
		    Services

Teaching and research academic resources	Teachers
	    Cultural
	    Scientific and technological
	    Professional (degrees)
	    Entrepreneurial
	    Technological
	    Educational for superiority
	    Creative
	    Participatory
	    Services
		Teaching methods
		    Seminars
		    Lectures
		    Informational media
		    Continuing education
		Research
		    Research environment
		    Contracts
		Extension services to:
		    Culture
		    Nationality
		    Critical function
		    Development

Physical material resources	Technical resources
	    Library
	    Centres
	    Physical plant resources
		Libraries
		Laboratories
		Increase modernization
		Increase maintenance

Economic and financial resources		

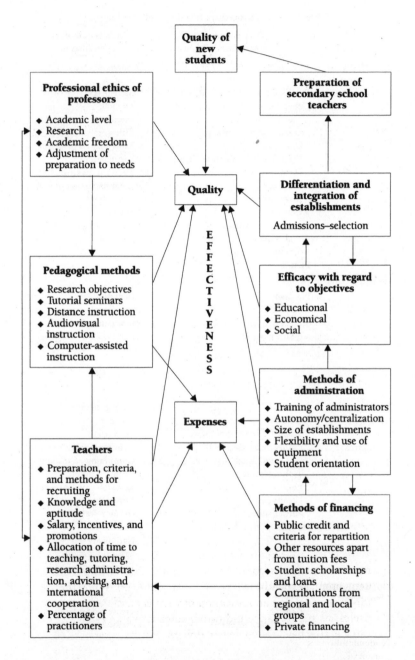

Figure 5. Variables determining the efficacy of higher education
(source: Bienaymé 1984).

external peer review on the teaching process, average duration
of student's stay, student evaluation of staff teaching motivation, entrance qualification of students, formal qualification of
staff, number of PhDs, percentage of staff members with a PhD.

Askling (1990) gives a paradigm that graphically juxtaposes
the policies or planning statements adopted in a coordinated and
decentralized system with an evaluation of the results obtained
(Figure 6). A concrete criterion of the paradigm is the relation
between academe and work.

Questionnaires to obtain internal and external opinions
about institutional evaluation are not always well received, and
there are objections to the value of quantitative indices and the
bureaucratic role that questionnaires play. On this point, the
Canadian report on higher education (Smith 1991, p. 123) refers
to quality control and performance indicators:

> When the AUCC conceived of this Commission, it was at least
> in part because of a desire to determine how Canadian univer-
> sities were performing in comparison with those of other
> countries, particularly after so many years of increased finan-
> cial pressure. One of the first tasks of the Commission was to
> become familiar with the work which has been done in Europe
> and North America on the subject of performance indicators.
>
> It is widely agreed that university research can be compared
> (up to a point) on the basis of major international awards,
> publications in respected refereed journals, citation of articles,
> patents granted, and the ability to attract postdoctoral fellows.
> In addition, countries frequently organize international peer
> review assessments of their national performance in a given
> area of research.
>
> With respect to administration, there are many aggregated
> measures such as student to faculty ratio, floor area per stu-
> dent, annual expenditures per student, and so on. While these
> measures may give an indication of what is possible, they are
> useless as performance indicators since no value judgement
> can be attached. Using fewer dollars, faculty members, or
> square metres per student may be a sign of an impoverished
> system or a highly productive one, depending upon the view-
> point being taken. In other words, these are input measures,

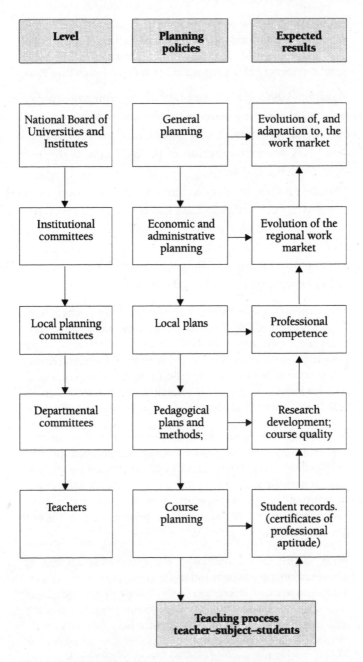

Figure 6. Policies and expected results at various levels in Sweden's system of higher education (source: Askling 1990).

not indicators of the quality of output. Such figures are still worth gathering, so as to allow Canadians to be aware of trends and to keep reasonable pace with their colleagues elsewhere.

In the crucial area of the quality of teaching and learning, however, the Commission has concluded that there are no performance indicators that would be useful for purposes of international comparison and very few that would permit valid inter-institutional comparisons within Canada. The Commission is persuaded that the ongoing hunt for international performance indicators is futile.

This is not the same as saying that national populations cannot be compared with one another on some commonly accepted measure, such as literacy, numeracy or basic scientific knowledge. A random sample of 25-year-olds from the population of several different countries could be compared on such measures and conclusions could be drawn about the relative merits of the entire educational system of the countries involved, as well as about implications for future competitiveness. Such tests of course, would not compare university graduates but entire populations.

The difficulty with respect to comparing just university graduates is that the university system in each country is unique. The role of the university in a country like Germany or the United Kingdom, where the participation rate is low or where there are other prestigious post-secondary institutions, is entirely different from the role of the university in Canada. The closest possible comparison for Canada would be the United States, which also has high participation rates and broad mandates for its universities. Even there, however, the system is one of such great, deliberate diversity that inter-institutional and inter-system comparisons are difficult. The real need, as far as the Commission is concerned, is for measures which indicate how well the university system is meeting the reasonable expectations of its own society and how well a given university is fulfilling its own declared missions. Such measures would permit accountability within the society which is funding the university system, and within each individual university community.

The search for accountability measures is what has driven the hunt for performance indicators. While the Commission recommends against performance indicators, it has no objection to the concept of accountability.

The problem is that various governments, particularly in England, Australia and some US states, have seen fit to impose rigid requirements and/or budgetary formulas in the name of accountability. The Commission believes that Canada would be ill-served by adopting a heavy-handed bureaucratic approach to this matter. For example, Canada should avoid the elaborate, bureaucratic and time-consuming questionnaires and site visits which the British universities have adopted as a way of heading off even more draconian measures by the government itself. Apart from normal financial auditing, what Canadian universities need to demonstrate is that they are genuinely accessible to those with the appropriate abilities, are equitable in their admission practices, and are producing an appropriate number of graduates who are satisfied with the education they have received and whose work is satisfactory to their employers. That is what people expect and that can be measured.

A similar debate was posed by Gellert (1991) when he referred to the use of evaluating "the place of [institutional] elites" through quantitative performance indicators, in which "the unit of analysis is usually the individual researcher, since only this output can be measured." Gellert (p. 10) says:

> The objections to such attempts are well-known, and can be summarized as follows: (1) The number of publications is misleading; quantity does not necessarily reflect quality. (2) The emphasis of the debate is too narrowly on research. Teaching is usually left out. And the service function, extra-curricular activities, etc., hardly play a role at all. (3) Citation indices, leading roles in professional associations, editorial boards, etc., are sometimes mostly reflections of power structures or of friendship networks in scientific communities. (4) Finally, external funding depends on the prestige of the academic institutions.

At the basis of these and other objections lies the reductionist tendency to look at the research aspect, ignoring the everyday relation between research and teaching, the very personal nature of the means used to evaluate quality, and the omission of so many other aspects that also have to do with comprehensive institutional evaluation and that can only be appreciated and not quantitatively measured.

Retrospective considerations

Divide and conquer

To conclude this difficult matter of university institutional evaluation, it should be noted that no matter what procedure is adopted, the principle of divide and conquer should be kept in mind. This can be understood in at least three ways. The first is that not everything in the university is subject to continuous evaluation; the statutes and general and academic structures are not, whereas the curricula, pedagogical systems, finances, and budget, for example, are, in addition to other performance indicators. The second is that once a theme for evaluation is proposed, it can be reduced to one or two of its determiners and subdeterminers, and it is worthwhile to do so. Finally, evaluation can be limited at specific moments to one or several of the university's schools or colleges and the programs they offer.

Self-evaluation and the roles, missions, and functions of universities

Another retrospective consideration can be that whatever evaluation methods or procedures adopted, the university that puts them into practice is examining the way it understands its roles of scientific, universal, and autonomous corporation, its missions regarding science and society, and its functions of teaching, doing research, and providing service.

Institutional goals of evaluation

In addition, institutional evaluation should achieve at least two goals. Once the required data have been collected through surveys, questionnaires, or polls, the first is to arrive at an appraisal using, for example, value scales such as sufficient–good–excellent and fair–deficient–poor. The second, more important goal is to make certain that institutional quality in the university's intellectual and educational missions and its mission of social service are beneficial and effective, without external pressures deflecting the university from what it considers most suitable for social needs. Federico Mayor (1991) gives the following qualifying terms:

> It is impossible to guarantee the quality of education without having the aim of excellence resting on the domain of research, teaching, preparation, and learning.... The search for excellence reaffirms its pertinence and closely links it to quality.

Hutchings and Marchese (1990) point out that although quality has been made to depend on the available resources and processes, this would result in "the greater the resources (financial resources, which are so important; the more brilliant the students, the better; the wealth of the library; demanding academic programs,...), the better the quality." However, they add that today it is thought that without excluding resources and processes, the "results obtained count for a lot" and, therefore, "the highest-quality establishment is the one that most supports the students' learning processes, whatever their level, in order to make them progress. It is the model of aggregate value."

Effectiveness is measured in terms of what has been achieved. However, the pertinence of university work goes beyond the immediate usefulness of knowledge and the sciences which, although necessary to improve living conditions, have a deep commitment to society and cultures. If this were not so, they could also be used for humanity's destruction.

Terms like quality, excellence, effectiveness, and pertinence lead us to accountability. "In the strictly technical sense, accountability means rendering accounts not only in the bookkeeping sense of the term, but also with reference to the relationships between the objectives and the means, in conformity with the needs of society" (Albornoz 1991, p. 211).

Regarding the university, accountability, "is a relatively new concept in the modern academic world" (Albornoz 1991), as are performance indicators, efficiency and effectiveness, and competition, also taken from economic jargon. These terms arose in the 1980s when this "appealing concept...also caught the interest of the public in general as well as of the state administrators and politicians who have to decide upon the allocation of public resources on higher education as part of public spending" (Hüffner 1991).

Moreover, the concept of accountability "is bound up with that of autonomy" (Albornoz 1991). Indeed, if by accountability we understand the relation between ends and means, in university terms they are the relations that ought to exist between the missions and functions. If these are well conceived and well achieved, the university strengthens its institutional autonomy and deserves to be recognized. In turn, the clear distinction that K.P. Mortimer (see Albornoz 1991) makes between external and internal accountability is the same as the two senses of the verb administrate, which constitute the organization of this document: the university organizes itself internally to provide external service to society.

In synthesis, if the concept of accountability is accepted as part of the academic lexicon, it is equivalent to the capacity that the university has for accounting for its roles, missions, and functions to itself, and for accounting to society how they are translated into efficient service.

Federico Mayor (1992) wrote:

> The accountability of the university is ultimately no different from that of any other social actor; it must demonstrate the relevance of its role to social needs and the effectiveness with which it performs that role. Its function in this context is not something determined once and for all. It has a heredity, rooted in the freedom of inquiry, but this heredity must be expressed in interaction with an ever-changing social environment. Its autonomy is, in fact, an existential one; it exists and is defined through the exercise of the freedom that is essentially the freedom to act.

Altbach (1991) relates accountability to the felt need of university administration as a specific field of academic study and of training for what many understand as university governance. This ought to include the interdisciplinary interweaving of themes in this book.

It is evident that the levels of excellence and quality obtained are relative to the context in which each university operates, which varies from country to country, and are apreciable according to conventional parameters that can with difficulty be subjected to quantification. For this reason, even though the formal

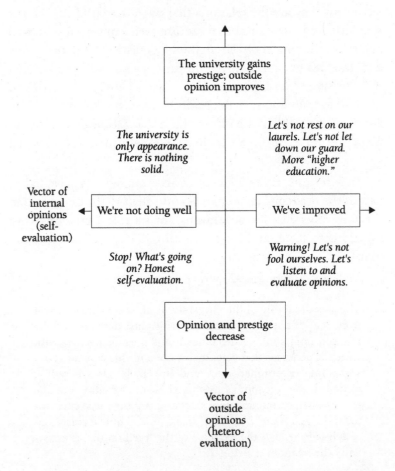

Figure 7. Comparison of the results of self-evaluation and hetero-evaluation.

effort of institutional evaluation might be necessary and advantageous, it is more important that the university wish to achieve quality, excellence, and relevance to such an extent that all its members are anxious to keep raising these values. The strong desire to raise the standards the university sets for itself is the best indicator of institutional strength. All will perceive and appreciate it, although no one can measure it.

Self-evaluation and hetero-evaluation

Finally, returning to the difference between self-evaluation and hetero-evaluation, it is advantageous to compare the results of both so that the university is engaged in reflection. From the positive or negative outcomes of performance indicators or items proposed for self- or hetero-evaluation (as indicated in the horizontal and vertical crossing arrows in Figure 7), the university will be able to reflect on its performance, similar to the reflections in the four quadrants of Figure 7.

This is a helpful process if the university is to think and act for the benefit of its institutional quality, accountability, and relevance.

BIBLIOGRAPHY

◆

Adams, R.S.; Battersby, D. 1987. Pedagogical staff development in higher education. Unesco Principal Regional Office for Asia and the Pacific, Bangkok, Thailand.

Aigrain, R. 1935. Les universités catholiques. Éditions Auguste Picard, Paris, France.

_____ 1949. Histoire des universités. Presses Universitaires de France, Paris, France.

Albornoz, O. 1991. Autonomy and accountability in higher education. Prospects 21(2).

Alfonso X the Wise. 1843. Las siete partidas del Rey Alfonso El Sabio: cotejadas con varios códices antiguos por la real academia de la historia, y glosadas por el licenciado Gregorio López, del Consejo Real de Indias de S.M. (5 vols.). Lacointe & Lasserre, Paris, France.

Altbach, P.G. 1980. University reform: an international perspective. American Association for Higher Education, Washington, DC, USA. AAHE-ERIC Higher Education Report No. 10.

_____ 1991. Patterns in higher education development: towards the year 2000. Prospects, 21(2).

Alvarez, B. 1991. Conocimiento y poder: nuevas relaciones entre la universidad y la empresa. In Reunión internacional de reflexión sobre los nuevos roles de la educación superior a nivel mundial: el caso de América Latina y del Caribe, futuro y escenarios deseables (vol. 4). Unesco/CRESALC, Caracas, Venezuela.

Anonymous. 1984. Encyclopedia of careers and vocatinal guidance. J.F. Ferguson, Chicago, IL, USA.

Archer, M.S., ed. 1982. The sociology of educational expansion: take off, growth and inflation in educational systems. Sage Publications, London, UK. Studies in International Sociology, 27.

_____ 1984. Social origins of educational systems. Sage Publications, London, UK.

Arguin, G. 1986. La planeación estratégica en la universidad. Presses de l'Université de Québec, Québec, QC, Canada.

Arheim, E.M.; Brungs, R. 1992. The Vinegard, scientists in the church. Institute for Theological Encounter with Science and Technology, St Louis, MO, USA.

Ashby, E.; Anderson, M. 1972. Ecología de la universidad. Editorial Científico-Médica, Barcelona, Spain.

Ashmore, H.L. 1979. The College President: pressures and challenges. American Association of Colleges and Universities, Washington, DC, USA.

Askling, B. 1990. Les influences extérieurs qui s'exercent sur les programmes de l'enseignement supérieur en Suéde. Gestion de l'Enseignement Supérieur, 2(1).

Auala, R.K. 1991. Current main trends and issues facing higher education in Africa. Paper presented at the Consultation of Experts on Future Trends and Challenges in Higher Education in Africa, 28 February–1 March 1991, Dakar, Senegal. Unesco, Paris, France.

Barzum, J. 1969. The American university: how it runs, where it is going. Oxford University Press, Oxford, UK.

Beckmeier, C.; Neusel, A. 1990. Les mécanismes de la prise de décision dans les universités françaises et allemandes. Gestion de l'Enseignement Supérieur, 2(1).

Ben-David, J.; Zloczower, A.; Halsey, A.H.; Raymond, A.; Trow, H.; Dahrendorf, R. 1977. La universidad en transformación. Biblioteca Breve, Editorial Seix Barral, Barcelona, Spain.

Bereday, G.Z. 1973. Universities for all. Jossey-Bass, San Francisco, CA, USA.

Berger, G.; Katz Thevenin, T.; Coulon, A. 1985. Évaluation des experiences novatrices sur la démocratisation dans l'enseignement supérieur. Unesco, Paris, France. Cahiers sur l'enseignement supérieur, 10.

Beridze, D. 1990. University teachers training. Paper presented at the International Colloquium, the University Pedagogy, October 1990, Barcelona, Spain. Unesco, Paris, France.

Berstecher, D.; Drèze, J.; Fragnière, G.; Guyot, Y.; Hamby, C.; Hecquet, I.; Jadot, J.; Lodrièr, J.; Rouge, N. 1974. L'université de demain. Elsevier Séquoia, Paris, France.

Bienaymé, A. 1984. Efficience et qualité dans l'enseignement supérieur. UER Sciences des Organizations, Université Paris Dauphine, Paris, France. Cahier 131.

Biljanovic, P. 1988. High technology and education. In University today, 33rd session, 28–31 August 1988: models of modern universities (abstracts). Union of Universities of Yugoslavia, Dubrovnik, Croatia, Yugoslavia.

Bocheński, J.M. 1979. Qué es la autoridad? Biblioteca Filosófica Herder, Barcelona, Spain.

Bodelle, J.; Nicolaon, G. 1988. Les universités américaines. Technique & Documentation-Lavoisier, Paris, France.

Boisot, M. 1970. Discipline and interdisciplinarity. Paper presented at the Conference on Interdisplinarity: Problems of Teaching and

Research in Universities, 7–12 September 1970, University of Nice, Nice, France. Ministry of Education, Paris, France.

Boumard, P.; Hess, R.; de Lapassade, G. 1987. L'université en transe. Éditions Syros, Paris, France.

Boutros-Ghali, B. 1992. The agenda for peace. United Nations, New York, NY, USA.

Brauer, V.; Pieck, W. 1988. Teaching and studying modern science. In University today, 33rd session, 28–31 August 1988: models of modern universities (abstracts). Union of Universities of Yugoslavia, Dubrovnik, Croatia, Yugoslavia.

Brown, W.R. 1982. Academic politics. University of Alabama Press, Tuscaloosa, AL, USA.

Bruce, J.D. 1982. Lifelong cooperative education. Report of the Centennial Study Committee (October 2, 1982). Massachusetts Institute of Technology, Cambridge, MA, USA.

Brunelle, L. 1973. L'éducation continue. Éditions ESF, Collection science de l'éducation, Paris, France.

Brunner, J.J. 1990. Educación superior, investigación científica y transformaciones culturales en America Latina. In Vinculación universidad sector productivo. BID-SECAB-CINDA, Santiago, Chile.

_____ 1991. Investing in knowledge. Strengthening the foundation for research in Latin America. International Development Research Centre, Ottawa, ON, Canada. IDRC-281e.

Brunsko, Z. 1988. Pedagogic process in the contemporary era. In University today, 33rd session, 28–31 August 1988: models of modern universities (abstracts). Union of Universities of Yugoslavia, Dubrovnik, Croatia, Yugoslavia.

Calleja, T. 1990. La universidad como empresa: una revolución pendiente. Ediciones RIALP, Madrid, Spain.

Cameron, J.M. 1979. On the idea of a university. University of Toronto Press, Toronto, ON, Canada.

Canovic, S. 1988. Student's subjectiveness — an essential characteristic as a modern organization of studies. In University today, 33rd session, 28–31 August 1988: models of modern universities (abstracts). Union of Universities of Yugoslavia, Dubrovnik, Croatia, Yugoslavia.

Cantor, N.F. 1991. Inventing the middle ages: the lives, works and ideas of the great medievalists of the 20th century. Morrow, New York, NY, USA.

Carnegie Foundation for the Advancement of Teaching. 1974. A digest of reports. Carnegie Foundation for the Advancement of Teaching, Princeton, NJ, USA.

Carrier, D. 1990. La réglamentation publique et l'innovation en matiére de Programmes d'Études. Gestión de l'Enseignement Supérieur, 2(1).

Carrier, H. 1984. L'avenir de l'université, son affaire. Paper presented at Assemblée général de la CRE, 10 September 1984, Athens, Greece. Conférence permanente des recteurs des Universités européens.

———— 1985. Culture: notre avenir. Presses de l'Université Grégorienne, Rome, Italy.

Carter, C. 1980. Higher education for the future. Blackwell, Oxford, UK.

Carton, M. 1983. Tendances et perspectives de développement de l'enseignement supérieur dans la région Europe. Unesco, Paris, France. Cahiers sur l'enseignement supérieur, 2.

Casebeer, A.L. 1991. Multicultural dialogue and student development in American University. In The role of higher education in society: quality and pertinence. The 2nd Unesco–Nongovernmental Organizations Collective Consultation on Higher Education, 8–11 April 1991. Unesco, Paris, France. New Papers on Higher Education, 1.

Castro, G. 1991. Educación superior y ciencias sociales en América Latina y el Caribe: el perfil de los nuevos retos para entrar al nuevo siglo. In Reunión internacional de reflexión sobre los nuevos roles de la educación superior a nivel mundial: el caso de América Latina y del Caribe, futuro y escenarios deseables (vol. 2). Unesco/CRESALC, Caracas, Venezuela.

CEPES (European Centre for Higher Education). 1990. Higher education in the European Community: the challenges of 1992. Higher Education in Europe, 15(2).

CERI (Center for Educational Research and Innovation). 1987. Adults in higher education. Organisation for Economic Co-operation and Development, Paris, France.

———— 1970. Interdisciplinarity: problems of teaching and research in universities, 7–12 September 1970, University of Nice, France. CERI and Ministry of Education, Paris, France.

Cerych, L. 1975. Access and structure of post-secondary education: from a global to a diffused system. European Cultural Foundation, Paris, France. Occasional Papers, 1.

Chevrolet, D. 1977. L'université et la formation continue : signe et sens d'une situation de l'éducation. Casterman, Paris, France.

Chinapah, V., ed. 1990. Evaluation of higher education in a changing Europe. Report from a seminar organized by the Institute of International Education, Stockholm University, and Unesco Educational Management and Policies Unit, May 1990, Stockholm, Sweden. Unesco, Paris, France.

Clark, B.R. 1983. The higher education system: academic organization on cross-national perspective. University of California Press, Berkeley, CA, USA.

Cobban, A.B. 1971. The medieval universities: their development and organization. Methuen & Co., London, UK.

Colombo, H. 1985. Science, technology and development. Paper presented at the Conference on South–North Cooperation in Sciences, 5–10 July 1985, Trieste, Italy. Third World Academy of Science.

Combes, J.E. 1991. Education and training tomorrow: higher education seen from the point of view of the company. In The role of higher education in society: quality and pertinence. The 2nd Unesco–Nongovernmental Organizations Collective Consultation on Higher Education, 8–11 April 1991. Unesco, Paris, France. New Papers on Higher Education, 1.

Coombs, P. 1971. La crisis mundial de la éducation. Ediciones Península, Barcelona, Spain.

———— 1985. La crisis mundial en la educación. Perspectivas actuales. Aula 21, Madrid, Spain.

Corson, J.J. 1968. Governance of colleges and universities. McGraw-Hill, London, UK.

Costa, M. 1991. Alternativas de financiamiento de la enseñanza superior. In Reunión internacional de reflexión sobre los nuevos roles de la educación superior a nivel mundial: el caso de América Latina y del Caribe, futuro y escenarios deseables (vol. 5). Unesco/CRESALC, Caracas, Venezuela.

Council of Europe. 1989. The mission and means of the university: issues and prospects for the financing of the European university system. European Colloquy, 4–6 September 1989, Barcelona, Spain. Council of Europe, Strasbourg, France.

Cropley, A.J. 1977. Lifelong education: a psycological analysis. Pergamon Press, Oxford, UK.

———— ed. 1980. Towards a system of lifelong education. Pergamon Press, Oxford, UK.

Cruz Cardona, V.E. 1991. Calidad de la formación avanzada en Latinoamérica. In Reunión internacional de reflexión sobre los nuevos roles de la educación superior a nivel mundial: el caso de

América Latina y del Caribe, futuro y escenarios deseables (vol. 3). Unesco/CRESALC, Caracas, Venezuela.

Dave, R.H. 1978. Foundations of lifelong education. Pergamon Press, Oxford, UK.

Davidson, B. 1964. The African past: chronicles from antiquity to modern times. Penguin Books, Harmondsworth, Middlesex, UK.

de Lagarde, P. 1959a [1878]. Sobre la ley de enseñanza. *In* Idea de la universidad en Alemania. Editorial Sudamericana, Buenos Aires, Argentina.

_____ 1959b [1881]. Otra vez sobre la ley de la enseñanza. *In* Idea de la universidad en Alemania. Editorial Sudamericana, Buenos Aires, Argentina.

Delich, F. 1991. Las asignaturas pendientes de la reforma universitaria. *In* Reunión internacional de reflexión sobre los nuevos roles de la educación superior a nivel mundial: el caso de América Latina y del Caribe, futuro y escenarios deseables (vol. 1). Unesco/CRESALC, Caracas, Venezuela.

Demo, P. 1991. Educación superior y desarrollo. *In* Reunión internacional de reflexión sobre los nuevos roles de la educación superior a nivel mundial: el caso de América Latina y del Caribe, futuro y escenarios deseables (vol. 1). Unesco/CRESALC, Caracas, Venezuela.

Deurinck, G. 1974. Preface. *In* Berstecher, D., L'université de demain. Elsevier Séquoia, Paris, France.

Dias, M.A.R. 1991a. Tendencias y Retos en la Educación Superior: un enfoque global. *In* Reunión internacional de reflexión sobre los nuevos roles de la educación superior a nivel mundial: el caso de América Latina y del Caribe, futuro y escenarios deseables (vol. 1). Unesco/CRESALC, Caracas, Venezuela.

_____ 1991b. Trends and challenges in higher education: a global approach. *In* The role of higher education in society: quality and pertinence. The 2nd Unesco–Nongovernmental Organizations Collective Consultation on Higher Education, 8–11 April 1991. Unesco, Paris, France. New Papers on Higher Education, 1.

Dickson, A. 1981. Service universitaire: problems and possibilities. Unesco, Paris, France.

Didon, O.P. 1884. Los alemanes y la francia: estado actual de estas dos grandes naciones. Translation by C. Frontaura and C. de Ochoa. Carlos Bailly-Bailliere, Madrid, Spain.

d'Irsay, S. 1933. Histoire des universités françaises et étrangères des origins à nos jours (vols. I and II). Éditions Auguste Picard, Paris, France.

Dockrell, W.B. 1990. Evaluation procedures used to measure the efficiency of higher education systems and institutions. In The role of higher education in society: quality and pertinence. The 2nd Unesco–Nongovernmental Organizations Collective Consultation on Higher Education, 8–11 April 1991. Unesco, Paris, France. New Papers on Higher Education, 1.

Dore, R. 1976. The diploma disease: education, qualification and development. George Allen & Unwin, London, UK.

Dressel, P.L.; Mayhew, L.B. 1974. Higher education as a field of study. Jossey-Bass, San Francisco, CA, USA.

Drèze, J.; Debelle, J. 1968. Conceptions de l'université. Éditions Universitaires, Paris, France.

Dumazedier, J. 1977. Loisir-éducation permanente — développement culturelle. In Pineau, G., ed., Éducation ou alienation permanente? Repères mythiques et politiques. Dunod, Sciences et Culture, Montreal, QC, Canada.

EC (European Community). 1991. Memorandum on higher education in the European Community. EC, Brussels, Belgium.

Eicher, J.C.; Chevaillier, T. 1992. Rethinking the financing of post-compulsory education. Higher Education in Europe, 17(1).

Emerson, R.W. 1940. The American scholar. In The writings of Ralph Waldo Emerson. Random House, New York, NY, USA.

Ferrer Pi, P. 1973. La universidad a examen. Ariel, Barcelona, Spain.

Feuer, L.S. 1971. Los movimientos estudiantiles. Paidós, Buenos Aires, Argentina.

Fichte, J.T. 1959 [1807]. Plan razonable para erigir en Berlín un establecimiento de educación superior que esté en conexión adecuada con una academica de ciencias. In Idea de la universidad en Alemania. Editorial Sudamericana, Buenos Aires, Argentina.

Flexner, A. 1930. Universities: American, English, German. Oxford University Press, New York, NY, USA.

Forbis, W.H. 1975. Japan today: people, places, power. Charles E. Tuttle, Rutland, VT, USA.

Fordhan, P. 1970. Adapting a tradition. Extramural policy in Africa. Universities Quarterly, Higher Education and Society, Winter 1970.

Frangnière, G. 1974. Structures du système universitaire et relations avec le pouvoir. *In* Berstecher, D., ed., L'université de demain. Elsevier Séquoia, Paris, France.

Galino, M.A. 1973. Historia de la educación: edades antigua y media. Editorial Gredos, Madrid, Spain.

García Garrido, J.L. 1984. Sistemas educativos de hoy: Alemania, Inglaterra, Francia, USA, URSS, España. Dykinson, Madrid, Spain.

———— 1992. Problemas mundiales de la educación: nuevas perspectivas. Dykinson, Madrid, Spain.

García Guadilla, C. 1991. Mirada al futuro a partir de una visión retrospectiva: el caso de la investigación sobre la educación superior en América Latina. *In* Reunión internacional de reflexión sobre los nuevos roles de la educación superior a nivel mundial: el caso de América Latina y del Caribe, futuro y escenarios deseables (vol. 1). Unesco/CRESALC, Caracas, Venezuela.

Gellert, C. 1991. Higher education: changing tasks and definitions. Higher Education in Europe, 16(3).

Giner de Los Ríos, F. 1916. La universidad española: obras completas de Francisco Giner de Los Ríos (vol. II). University of Madrid, Madrid, Spain.

Goffi, J.Y. 1988. La philosophie de la technique. Presses Universitaires de France, Paris, France.

Gordon, P.; White, J. 1979. Philosophers as educational reformers. Routledge & Kegan Paul, London, UK.

Granados, M. 1991. Retos a los aspectos legales de las ínstituciones de educación superior con especial referencia al convenio regional de convalidación de estudios y diplomas en América Latina y el Caribe. *In* Reunión internacional de reflexión sobre los nuevos roles de la educación superior a nivel mundial: el caso de América Latina y del Caribe, futuro y escenarios deseables (vol. 5). Unesco/CRESALC, Caracas, Venezuela.

Guiton, J.; Charpentier, J. 1984. Recognition of studies and competence. Unesco, Paris, France. Educational Studies and Documents, 44.

Gusdorf, G. 1963. Pour une recherche interdisciplinaire. Diogène, 42 (April–July).

———— 1964. L'université en question. Payot, Paris, France.

———— 1977. Past, present and future in interdisciplinary research. International Social Science Journal, 29(4).

Harris, G. 1992. A Canadian perspective on current developments in university finance and administration. Unesco/IDRC Meeting on Higher Education, 6–10 July 1992, University of British Columbia, Vancouver, BC, Canada.

Heckhausen, H. 1970. Discipline and interdisciplinarity. Paper presented at the Conference on Interdisciplinarity: Problems of Teaching and Research in Universities, 7–12 September 1970, University of Nice, Nice, France. Ministry of Education, Paris, France.

Heer, F. 1962. The medieval world. New American Library, New York, NY, USA.

Hetland, A. 1984. International student mobility. In Hetland, A., ed., Universities and national development. Almquist & Wiksell, Stockholm, Sweden.

Houle, C.O. 1981. Continuing learning in the professions. Jossey-Bass Publishers, San Francisco, CA, USA.

Hüffner, K. 1991. Accountability for more efficiency and effectiveness in higher education. In Planning and management for excellence and efficiency of higher education. Unesco/CRESALC, Caracas, Venezuela.

Hull, C.J. 1991. Transfernecia de tecnología entre la educación superior y la industria en Europa: obstáculos que impiden su desarrollo y propuestas para ayudar a superarlos. In Reunión internacional de reflexión sobre los nuevos roles de la educación superior a nivel mundial: el caso de América Latina y del Caribe, futuro y escenarios deseables (vol. 4). Unesco/CRESALC, Caracas, Venezuela.

Husén, T. 1987. Higher education and social stratification: an international comparative study. International Institute of Education Policies, Unesco, Paris, France.

_____ 1991. The idea of a university: changing roles, current crisis and future challenges. In The role of higher education in society: quality and pertinence. The 2nd Unesco–Nongovernmental Organizations Collective Consultation on Higher Education, 8–11 April 1991. Unesco, Paris, France. New Papers on Higher Education, 1.

Hutchings, P.A.; Marchese, T. 1990. Évaluation des résultats de programmes d'étude : l'experinece des États-Unis. Organization for Economic Cooperation and Development, Paris, France. Gestion d'Enseignement Supérieur, 2(1).

IAU (International Association of Universities). 1967. The administration of universities. IAU, Paris, France.

IIPE (International Institute of Education Policies). 1988. Extracts from the orientation note of the Workshop on the future of strategic educational planning. IIPE Newsletter, 6(3).

Ikenberry, S.O.; Friedman, R.C. 1972. Beyond academic departments. Jossey-Bass, San Francisco, CA, USA.

Iredale, R. 1991. The year of the university. Paper presented at the Conference on Higher Education and Development, 6–8 January 1991. University of Bristol, Bristol, UK.

Ishumi, A.G.M. 1990. Harmonization of higher education progammes: trends in the mobility of students, teachers and researchers. Unesco Regional Office in Africa, Dakar, Senegal.

Jaeger, W. 1957. Paideia. Fondo de Cultura Económica, Mexico, Mexico.

_____ 1974. Cristianismo primitivo y paideaia griega. Fondo de Cultura Económica, Mexico, Mexico.

Jaspers, K. 1970. Le renouveau de l'université. *In* Essais philosophiques. Petit Bibliothèque Payot, Paris, France.

Jelinic, S. 1988. Personnel mobility from and to the universities as a form of links between science and economy. *In* University today, 33rd session, 28–31 August 1988: models of modern universities (abstracts). Union of Universities of Yugoslavia, Dubrovnik, Croatia, Yugoslavia.

Kant, E. 1963 [1798]. El conflicto de las facutades. Editorial Losada, Buenos Aires, Argentina.

Kazem, M.I. 1991. Higher education in Arab states. Paper presented at the Conference on Higher Education and Development: Problems and Future Prospects, 6–8 January 1991. University of Bristol, Bristol, UK.

Keller, G. 1983. Academic strategy: the management revolution in American higher education. Johns Hopkins University Press, Baltimore, MD, USA.

Keller, P. 1982. Getting at the core: curriculum reform at Harvard. Harvard University Press, Boston, MA, USA.

Kerr, C. 1963. The uses of the university. The Godkin Lecture. Harvard University, Boston, MA, USA.

Kerstesz, S.D. 1975. La tarea de las universidades en un mundo que cambio: el problema universitario contemporáneo (tratado por 32 especialistas de diferentes países). Editorial Americana, Buenos Aires, Argentina.

Ki-Zerbo, J. 1991. Quelques idées pour contribuer à la consultation d'experts sur l'enseignement supérieur en Afrique. Paper presented at the Consultation of Experts on Future Trends and Challenges in Higher Education in Africa, 28 February–1 March 1991, Dakar, Senegal. Unesco, Paris, France.

Knowles, M.S. 1969. Andragogy: an emerging technology for adult learning. Follett Books, Chicago, IL, USA.

_____ 1985. Andragogy in action: applying modern principles of adult learning. Jossey-Bass, San Francisco, CA, USA.

Krismanic, M. 1988. Informative and consulting service at the university and its influence on the student's psychological adaptation and efficacy of studying. In University today, 33rd session, 28–31 August 1988: models of modern universities (abstracts). Union of Universities of Yugoslavia, Dubrovnik, Croatia, Yugoslavia.

Kuhn, T.S. 1962. La estructura de las revoluciones científicas. Fondo de Cultura Económica, Mexico, Mexico.

Lacave, M. 1991. Parques científicos y universidades: condiciones, su contribución al desarrollo económico. In Reunión internacional de reflexión sobre los nuevos roles de la educación superior a nivel mundial: el caso de América Latina y del Caribe, futuro y escenarios deseables (vol. 3). Unesco/CRESALC, Caracas, Venezuela.

Latorre, E. 1980. Sobre educación superior. Instituto Tecnológico de Santo Domingo, Santo Domingo, Dominican Republic.

Lengrand, P. 1970. An introduction to lifelong education. Unesco, Paris, France.

Lewis, R. 1983. Meeting learners' needs through telecommunications. Center for Learning and Telecommunications, Washington, DC, USA.

Lipset, S.M. 1971. Rebellion in the universities. Unversity of Chicago Press, Chicago, IL, USA.

Luyten, N.A. 1970. L'université et l'integration du savoir. Éditions Universitaires, Fribourg, Switzerland.

MacGregor S.J., F. 1991. La universidad-IDEA y las responsabilidades sociales de la educación superior. In Reunión internacional de reflexión sobre los nuevos roles de la educación superior a nivel mundial: el caso de América Latina y del Caribe, futuro y escenarios deseables (vol. 1). Unesco/CRESALC, Caracas, Venezuela.

Magna Charta delle Università Europea. 1988. Bologna 18 settembre. Con motivo del Noveno Centenario de la Universidad de Bolonia.

Mallinson, V. 1981. The western European idea in education. Pergamon Press, Oxford, UK.

Mayor, F. 1987. Universidad, todavía? En educación. Noticias de Educación, Ciencia y Cultura Iberoamericana, 4 (supplement) (July–October).

_____ 1991. Closing Address to the Second Collective Consultation of NGOs on Higher Education, 11 April 1991, Paris, France. Unesco, Paris, France.

_____ 1992. Address to the International Conference on Academic Freedom and University Autonomy, 5 May 1992, Sinaia, Romania. Unesco, Paris, France.

McDaniel, O.C. 1990. Towards a European higher education policy? possibilities and potentialities. Paper presented at the 6th EARDHE Conference: Cross-Cultural Dialogue and Development in Higher Education, 1–5 October 1990, Berlin, Germany. European Association for Research and Development of Higher Education, Berlin, Germany.

Mesnard, P. 1956. La pédagogie des Jésuits 1548–1762. In Chateau, J., ed., Les grands pédagoges. Presses Universitaires de France, Paris, France.

Mialaret, G.; Vial, J. 1981. Histoire mondiale de l'éducation. Presses Universitaires de France, Paris, France.

MINDAEF VI. 1991. Sixième Conférence des Ministres de l'éducation d'Afrique, 8–11 July 1991, Dakar, Senegal. Unesco, Paris, France.

Mitrovic, L. 1988. University models and social development. In University today, 33rd session, 28–31 August 1988: models of modern universities (abstracts). Union of Universities of Yugoslavia, Dubrovnik, Croatia, Yugoslavia.

Moncada, A. 1971. Administración universitaria: introducción sistemática a la educación superior. ICE de la Universidad Complutense, Instituto de Pedagogía (CSIC), Fundación Monaca-Cayón, Madrid, Spain.

_____ 1983. Más allá de la educación. Editorial Tecnos, Madrid, Spain.

Morin, E. 1982. Science avec conscience. Fayard, Paris, France.

Murray, A. 1982. Razón y sociedad en la Edad Media. Taurus, Madrid, Spain.

Nagai, M. 1971. Higher education in Japan: its take-off and crash. University of Tokyo Press, Tokyo, Japan.

_____ 1981. Higher education in a changing world. Proceedings of the 7th International Conference on University Teaching, 15–18 July 1981, Japan.

Neave, G. 1992. The financing of higher education. Higher Education in Europe, 17(1).

Newman, J.H. 1959 [1852]. The idea of a university. Doubleday, Dublin, Ireland.

Niblett, W.R.; Freeman Butts, R., ed. 1972. Universities facing the future. Jossey-Bass, San Francisco, CA, USA.

Novakovic, B.; Rajkoviv, J. 1988. The triad of the contemporary university. In University today, 33rd session, 28–31 August 1988: models of modern universities (abstracts). Union of Universities of Yugoslavia, Dubrovnik, Croatia, Yugoslavia.

OAU (Organization of African Unity). 1979. Quelle Afrique à l'horizon 2000? OAU, Addis Ababa, Ethiopia.

OECD (Organisation for Economic Co-operation and Development). 1971. Vers des nouvelles structures de l'enseignement post-secondaire. OECD, Paris, France.

_____ 1987. Rôles et functions de l'université aujourd'hui. Organisation for Economic Co-operation and Development, Paris, France.

_____ 1990. Report of the Institutional Management in Higher Education study group on evaluation in higher education. Organisation for Economic Co-operation and Development, Paris, France.

Ohmae Kenichi. 1975. The corporate strategist. Penguin Books, New York, NY, USA.

Ortega y Gasset, J. 1965. Meditación de la técnica. Austral, Madrid, Spain.

_____ 1976. Misión de la universidad. El Arquero, Madrid, Spain.

Osman, O.M. 1983. Perspectives of the development of the university in the Arab region from the present to the year 2000. Unesco, Paris, France. Papers on Higher Education, 4.

Ostar, A.W. 1990. The interactive university: a model for the 21st century. Paper presented to 18th Assembly of the 21st Federation of Mexican Institutions of Higher Education (FIMPES), 30 August 1990. FIMPES, Mexico, Mexico.

Ouchi, W. 1982. Teoria Z: cómo pueden las empresas hacer frente al desafío japonés. Editorial Norma, Bogotá, Colombia.

Oyen, O. 1988. On the non-hierarchical models of communication across disciplines. In University today, 33rd session, 28–31 August 1988: models of modern universities (abstracts). Union of Universities of Yugoslavia, Dubrovnik, Croatia, Yugoslavia.

Páez Urdaneta, I. 1991. Calidad de la educación y calidad de la docencia: posibilidades teóricas e institucionales de una integración. *In* Reunión internacional de reflexión sobre los nuevos roles de la educación superior a nivel mundial: el caso de América Latina y del Caribe, futuro y escenarios deseables (vol. 5). Unesco/CRESALC, Caracas, Venezuela.

Pajin, D. 1988. Modern university: a culture mediator. *In* University today, 33rd session, 28–31 August 1988: models of modern universities (abstracts). Union of Universities of Yugoslavia, Dubrovnik, Croatia, Yugoslavia.

Paulsen, F. 1906. The German university and university study. Charles Scribner, New York, NY, USA.

———— 1986. German education, past and present. T.E. Unwin, London, UK.

Pérez, C. 1991. Nuevo patrón tecnológico y educación superior: una aproximación desde la empresa. *In* Reunión internacional de reflexión sobre los nuevos roles de la educación superior a nivel mundial: el caso de América Latina y del Caribe, futuro y escenarios deseables (vol. 3). Unesco/CRESALC, Caracas, Venezuela.

Perkins, A.J. 1967. The university in transition. Princeton University Press, Princeton, NJ, USA.

Peters, T.J. 1982. In search of excellence. Harper & Row, New York, NY, USA.

Pierson, G.W. 1950. American universities in the nineteenth century: the formative period. *In* Clapp, M., ed., The modern university. Archon Books, Hamden, CT, USA.

Pineau, G. 1977. Éducation ou alienation permanente? Repéres mythiques et politiques. Dunod, Sciences et Culture, Montreal, QC, Canada.

Pitner, G. 1988. Models of cooperation between university and the economy. *In* University today, 33rd session, 28–31 August 1988: models of modern universities (abstracts). Union of Universities of Yugoslavia, Dubrovnik, Croatia, Yugoslavia.

Ploman, E. 1991. Higher education and development: evolution and prospects (introductory overview). *In* The role of higher education in society: quality and pertinence. The 2nd Unesco–Nongovernmental Organizations Collective Consultation on Higher Education, 8–11 April 1991. Unesco, Paris, France. New Papers on Higher Education, 1.

Popovic, B. 1988. The changes in the existing model of the content of teaching at the university today. *In* University today, 33rd session, 28–31 August 1988: models of modern universities (abstracts). Union of Universities of Yugoslavia, Dubrovnik, Croatia, Yugoslavia.

Quiles S.J., I. 1984. Filosofía de la educación personalizada. Ediciones Depalma, Buenos Aires, Argentina.

Rashdall, H. 1936. The universities of Europe in the Middle Ages (vols I, II, and III). Oxford University Press, Oxford, UK.

Ratkovic, M. 1988. New models of universities before the third millenium. *In* University today, 33rd session, 28–31 August 1988: models of modern universities (abstracts). Union of Universities of Yugoslavia, Dubrovnik, Croatia, Yugoslavia.

Reyes Ponce, A. 1975. Administración por objetivos. Editorial Limusa, Mexico, Mexico.

Rodek, S. 1988. Didactical aspects of new information technology in university instruction. *In* University today, 33rd session, 28–31 August 1988: models of modern universities (abstracts). Union of Universities of Yugoslavia, Dubrovnik, Croatia, Yugoslavia.

Rodin, D. 1988. The social and political limits of the development of science and its institutions. *In* University today, 33rd session, 28–31 August 1988: models of modern universities (abstracts). Union of Universities of Yugoslavia, Dubrovnik, Croatia, Yugoslavia.

Rodríguez Cruz, O.P., A.M. 1975. Historia de las universidades hispano-americanas. Instituto Caro y Cuervo, Bogotá, Colombia.

Rudolph, F. 1965. The American college and university. Vintage Books, New York, NY, USA.

Salifou, A. 1983. Perspectives du développment de l'enseignement supérieur en Afrique dans les prochaines décenes. Unesco, Paris, France. Cahiers sur l'enseignement supérieur, 1.

Salmi, J. 1991. The higher education crisis in developing countries. World Bank, Washington, DC, USA. Background Paper Series No. PHREE/91/37.

Sansom, G.B. 1985. Japan: a short cultural history. Charles E. Tuttle, Rutland, VT, USA.

Sanyal, B.C. 1984. Higher education in a changing world: recent trends and future outlook. International Institute of Education Policies, Paris, France.

Sasaki, N. 1981. Management and industrial structure in Japan. Pergamon Press, Oxford, UK.

Scheler, M. 1959 [1921]. Universidad y universidad popular. *In* Idea de la universidad Alemania. Editorial Sudamericana, Buenos Aires, Argentina.

———— 1972. El saber y la cultura. Editorial La Pléyade, Buenos Aires, Argentina.

Schleiermacher, F. 1959 [1808]. Pensamientos ocasionales sobre universidades en sentido alemán, con un apéndice sobre la erección de una nueva. *In* Idea de la universidad Alemania. Editorial Sudamericana, Buenos Aires, Argentina.

Schlemper, B.R., Jr. 1991. El futuro de la investigación sobre la educación superior. *In* Reunión internacional de reflexión sobre los nuevos roles de la educación superior a nivel mundial: el caso de América Latina y del Caribe, futuro y escenarios deseables (vol. 1). Unesco/CRESALC, Caracas, Venezuela.

Schumacher, E.F. 1989. Small is beautiful: economics as if people mattered. Harper & Row, New York, NY, USA.

Schütze, H.G.; Ndunda, M.; Yang Chen. 1992. Higher education at the threshold of the third millenium: research and policy agendas for future developments. Paper presented at the Unesco/International Development Research Centre Meeting on Higher Education, 6–10 July 1992, University of British Columbia, Vancouver, BC, Canada. Unesco, Paris, France.

Searle, J.R. 1967. *In* Gorovitz, S., Freedom and order in the university. The Press of Case Western University, Cleveland, OH, USA.

Seidel, H. 1991. The social significance of higher education. *In* The role of higher education in society: quality and pertinence. The 2nd Unesco–Nongovernmental Organizations Collective Consultation on Higher Education, 8–11 April 1991. Unesco, Paris, France. New Papers on Higher Education, 1.

Senic, K. 1988. Collaboration between universities and the economy. *In* University today, 33rd session, 28–31 August 1988: models of modern universities (abstracts). Union of Universities of Yugoslavia, Dubrovnik, Croatia, Yugoslavia.

Shattock, M. 1990. The evaluation of universities' contribution to society. Report of the committee on Institutional Management in Higher Education. Organization for Economic Cooperation and Development, Paris, France.

Smith, A.L. 1979 [1919]. *In* Gordon, P.; White, J., Philosophers as educational reformers. Routledge & Kegan Paul, London, UK.

Smith, S.L. 1991. Report of the Commission of Inquiry on Canadian University Education. Government of Canada, Ottawa, ON, Canada.

Stanojevic, O. 1988. The reform of the university as an aporia. *In* University today, 33rd session, 28–31 August 1988: models of modern universities (abstracts). Union of Universities of Yugoslavia, Dubrovnik, Croatia, Yugoslavia.

Starapoli, A. 1990. The evaluation of research. Report of the committee on Institutional Management in Higher Education. Organization for Economic Cooperation and Development, Paris, France.

Stubbs, W.H. 1990. Funding and steering in higher education. Paper presented at the 10th General Conference of Member Institutions, 5–7 September 1990, Paris, France. Institutional Management in Higher Education, Paris, France.

Sulton, F.X. 1969. Las universidades africanas y el proceso de transformación en Africa Central. In Kertesz, S.D., La tarea de las universidades en un mundo que cambia. Editorial Americana, Buenos Aires, Argentina.

Taiwo, A.A. 1991. Innovations and reforms in higher education in Africa: an overview. Paper presented at the Consultation of Experts on Future Trends and Challenges in Higher Education in Africa, 28 February–1 March 1991, Dakar, Senegal. Unesco, Paris, France.

Tardy, M. 1977. Le champ sémantique de l'expression "education permanente." In Pineau, G., ed., Éducation ou alienation permanente? Repéres mythiques et politiques. Dunod, Sciences et Culture, Montreal, QC, Canada.

Thomas, J.E. 1985. Learning democracy in Japan: the social education of Japanese adults. Sage Publications, London, UK.

Thorens, J. 1992. Libertés académiques et autonomie universitaire. Paper presented at the International Conference on Academic Freedom and University Autonomy, 5–7 May 1992, Sinaia, Romania. Centre européen pour l'éducation supérieure, Paris, France.

Tibawi, A.L. 1979. Islamic education: its traditions and modernization into the Arab national systems. Luzac, London, UK.

Timina, S.I. 1988. Humanisation of university education as an important factor of education and upbringing. In University today, 33rd session, 28–31 August 1988: models of modern universities (abstracts). Union of Universities of Yugoslavia, Dubrovnik, Croatia, Yugoslavia.

Todd Pérez, L.E. 1991. reflexiones sobre el papel de la universidad en el contexto de los tratados de globalización económica. América Latina: drama y vitalidad. In Reunión internacional de reflexión sobre los nuevos roles de la educación superior a nivel mundial: el caso de América Latina y del Caribe, futuro y escenarios deseables (vol. 1). Unesco/CRESALC, Caracas, Venezuela.

Topentcharov, V.V. 1985. L'évolution probable des finalités et des rôles sociaux de l'enseignement supérieur au cours des prochaînes decens. Unesco, Paris, France.

Tot, L. 1988. Important factors for footholds for the improvement of the teaching process and of scientific research work at universities. *In* University today, 33rd session, 28–31 August 1988: models of modern universities (abstracts). Union of Universities of Yugoslavia, Dubrovnik, Croatia, Yugoslavia.

Trajkovski, B. 1988. Some aspects of comparative work in science and research between Yugoslav universities and industrial corporation through free exchange of labour. *In* University today, 33rd session, 28–31 August 1988: models of modern universities (abstracts). Union of Universities of Yugoslavia, Dubrovnik, Croatia, Yugoslavia.

Tunnermann, C. 1979. 60 años de la reforma universitaria de Córdoba. Fondo editorial para el desarrollo de la Educación superior, Caracas, Venezuela.

Turner Venable, P. 1985. Campus: an American planning tradition. The Architectual History Foundation, MIT Press, New York, NY, USA.

Unesco (United Nations Educational, Scientific and Cultural Organisation). 1972. Learning to be. Unesco, Paris, France.

_____ 1973. Les études supérieurs. Unesco, Paris, France.

_____ 1978. Terminology of technical and vocational education. Unesco, Paris, France.

_____ 1981. Combination of education, research and production in higher education. Unesco, Paris, France. ED-81/WS99.

_____ 1982. Declaración de Mexico, 26 July–6 August 1982. Unesco, Paris, France.

_____ 1983. International symposium on the probable development in the goals and social roles of higher education during the coming decades, 5–9 December 1983, Sofia, Bulgaria. Unesco, Paris, France.

_____ 1984a. Le service universitaire: un instrument d'innovation dans l'enseignement supérieur. Unesco, Paris, France. Cahiers sur l'enseignement supérieur, 6.

_____ 1984b. Nouvelles tendances dans l'enseignement supérieur. Unesco, Paris, France.

_____ 1988a. Long-term planning in higher education. Regional Cooperative Program in Higher Education for Development in Asia and the Pacific, Unesco, Bangkok, Thailand.

_____ 1988b. Higher education and national development in four countries: India, Bangladesh, Thailand, and the Philippines. Unesco Principal Regional Office for Asia and the Pacific, Bangkok, Thailand.

_____ 1989a. Enseignement supérieur scientifique et technique : nouvelles technologies de l'information et de la communication. Roundtable sponsored by Unesco and Association des universités partiellment ou entierment de langue française. Unesco, Paris, France. Cahiers sur l'enseignement supérieur.

_____ 1989b. Education and informatics: strengthening international co-operation. Final Report from the International Congress, 12–21 April 1989. Unesco, Paris, France.

_____ 1989c. Project Copernicus: cooperation program in Europe for research on nature and industry through coordinated university study. Unesco, Paris, France. Papers on Higher Education, 32.

_____ 1989d. Academic staff development units in universities. Report of the Regional Workshop held at Tribhuvan University, Kathmandu, Nepal, 31 October–4 November 1988. Unesco Principal Regional Office for Asia and the Pacific, Bangkok, Thailand.

_____ 1990a. La ciencia y la tecnología para el futuro de América Latina. Final Report of Colloquium, 3–6 December, 1990, Acapulco, Mexico. Unesco, Paris, France.

_____ 1990b. Handbook on the organization and management of distance education study centers. Unesco Regional Office for Asia and the Pacific, Bangkok, Thailand.

_____ 1990c. Literacy and the role of the unversity. Debate at an International Roundtable, 42nd Session of the International Conference on Education, 7 September 1990, Geneva, Switzerland. Unesco, Paris, France.

_____ 1990d. Study service on adult education: analysis of an experience. Faculty of Education, University of Lujan, Lujan, Argentina. New Papers on Higher Education, 2.

_____ 1990e. Priority Africa: management of higher education. Unesco, Paris, France.

_____ 1990f. The university pedagogy: a challenge in higher education. International colloquium, October 1990, Barcelona, Spain. Unesco, Paris, France.

_____ 1990g. World Charter on Education for All. Unesco, Paris, France.

_____ 1991a. Consultation of Experts on Future Trends and Challenges in Higher Education in Africa, 28 February–1 March 1991, Dakar, Senegal. Unesco, Paris, France.

_____ 1991b. Research on higher education in developing countries: suggested agendas and implementation. University of Pittsburg–Unesco Forum of experts on trends in research on higher education, 17–19 March 1991. Unesco, Paris, France.

_____ 1991c. A European platform to develop a mechanism for co-operation in the field of information technologies in education. Final Report and Proceedings of a Conference held 17–21 June 1991, Moscow, Russia. Unesco, Paris, France.

_____ 1991d. The role of higher education in society: quality and pertinence. The 2nd Unesco–Nongovernmental Organizations Collective Consultation on Higher Education, 8–11 April 1991. Unesco, Paris, France. New Papers on Higher Education, 1.

_____ 1992a. Trends and issues facing higher education in Asia and the Pacific. Regional Cooperative Program in Higher Education for Development in Asia and the Pacific, Unesco, Bangkok, Thailand.

_____ 1992b. Experts Meeting on the Integration of International Education into Higher Education, Tunis, 21-25 September 1992. Final Report. New Papers on Higher Education, Meeting Documents, 3.

Unesco/BREDA. 1992. Future directions for higher education in Africa. Unesco Regional Office in Africa (BREDA), Dakar, Senegal.

Unesco/CEPES (European Centre for Higher Education). 1985. University teaching and the training of teachers. In Proceedings of the European Regional Seminar, 25–29 November 1985, Prague, Czechoslovakia. Unesco, Paris, France.

Unesco/CRESALC. 1991. Reunión internacional de reflexión sobre los nuevos roles de la educación superior a nivel mundial: el caso de América Latina y del Caribe, futuro y escenarios deseables (5 vols.). Unesco/CRESALC, Caracas, Venezuela.

Unesco/REDESLAC. 1989. Cooperación regional sobre la formación y perfeccionamiento pedagógico de docentes de educación superior en América Latina y el Caribe: 3rd interregional workshop, Havana, Cuba. Unesco/REDESLAC, Paris, France.

Vandal, K. 1988. Modern university — unity or differences. In University today, 33rd session, 28–31 August 1988: models of modern universities (abstracts). Union of Universities of Yugoslavia, Dubrovnik, Croatia, Yugoslavia.

Verger, J. 1973. Les universités au moyen age. Press Universitaires de France, Paris, France.

Vessuri, H.M.C. 1991. El futuro de la investigación científica y tecnológica en las universidades. In Reunión internacional de reflexión sobre los nuevos roles de la educación superior a nivel mundial: el caso de América Latina y del Caribe, futuro y escenarios deseables (vol. 1). Unesco/CRESALC, Caracas, Venezuela.

von Humboldt, W. 1959 [1810]. Sobre la organización interna y externa de los establecimientos científicos superiores de Berlín. *In* Idea de la universidad en Alemania. Editorial Sudamericana, Buenos Aires, Argentina.

Weber, M. 1959 [1919]. La ciencia como profesión vocacional. *In* Idea de la universidad en Alemania. Editorial Sudamericana, Buenos Aires, Argentina.

———— 1967. El político y el científico. Alianza, Madrid, Spain.

Weiler, H.N. 1991. La política internacional de la producción del conocimiento y el futuro de la educación superior. *In* Reunión internacional de reflexión sobre los nuevos roles de la educación superior a nivel mundial: el caso de América Latina y del Caribe, futuro y escenarios deseables (vol. 1). Unesco/CRESALC, Caracas, Venezuela.

Weymouth, L. 1973. Thomas Jefferson: the man... his world... his influence. Putnam, New York, NY, USA.

Whitehead, A.N. 1964. The aims of education. New American Library, New York, NY, USA.

Wierzbowski, M. 1988. Role of students at the modern university. *In* University today, 33rd session, 28–31 August 1988: models of modern universities (abstracts). Union of Universities of Yugoslavia, Dubrovnik, Croatia, Yugoslavia.

Wimberley, J. 1990. Report on the Council of Europe Equivalence Conventions. Higher Education in Europe, 15(2).

Yero, L. 1991. Tendencias que señalan los resultados de los estudios prospectivos en la región: Latinoamericana y Caribeña. *In* Reunión internacional de reflexión sobre los nuevos roles de la educación superior a nivel mundial: el caso de América Latina y del Caribe, futuro y escenarios deseables (vol. 1). Unesco/CRESALC, Caracas, Venezuela.

Yusufu, J.M. 1973. Creating the African university: emerging issues of the 1970s. Oxford University Press, Oxford, UK.

Zagefka, P. 1989. L'enseignement supérieur entre démographie et sociologie: diversifications institutionnelles et variations sociales. Unesco, Paris, France. Cahiers sur l'enseignement supérieur, 35.